A BENCHMARK SERIES BOOK

The Poodle

An Owner's Survival Guide

Diane Morgan

Published by Doral Publishing, Sun City, Arizona
Printed in the United States of America.

Edited by MaryEllen Smith
Interior Design by The Printed Page
Cover Design by 1106 Design
Cover photos from the collection of Lesley Sims

Library of Congress Card Number: 2002103419
ISBN: 0-944875-78-5

For Bette Beal Pierson—
and in memory of the inimitable Prince Charlemagne (Charlie)

Contents

Introduction

"I have never known, or even heard of, a bad poodle.
Theirs is the most charming of species, including the
human, and they happily lack Man's aggression,
irritability, quick temper, and wild aim."
— James Thurber, *Christabel: Part One*

I came to Poodles by means of the Iditarod. Although it seemed odd at the time, it now seems almost inevitable. I was writing a book about Siberian Huskies then, and in the course of my research came across the strange tale of John Suter, whose team of Standard Poodles pulled his sled in that most famous of North American races. Yes, Poodles. Like many people, I thought of Poodles only as show dogs and friendly pets. I knew they were good in agility and obedience; I had heard that they could even hunt and track. But the Iditarod? Was there nothing beyond the uncanny abilities of this breed? As it turns out, no. Coifed, elegant, sedate, stretched out royally on a pouf; plunging through the marsh to retrieve felled ducks; guide to the disabled, companion to the infirm, child's delight, solace of old age—all of these are included in the personality and capability of the Poodle.

Like so many others, I soon fell under their magic spell, and I want to share with you the glory of Poodles.

Poodles are truly the premier pet. Most people are used to seeing Poodles in one way—as pampered, spoiled rotten little things with polished-pink toenails who are trotted all about town on narrow rhinestone leashes, or carried about like invalids to be cooed at. This unfortunate stereotype has deprived many a deserving person of the joys of Poodle ownership. Poodles of all sizes

1

are hardy, active animals who put up with humans because of their inherent good nature and extreme tolerance for our foibles.

Nearly every other breed has a fatal flaw—they chase cats or are aggressive; they are stubborn or smell funny or shed; they are too large or small; they are chewers or barkers or can't be trusted off lead; they drool. The Poodle exhibits none of these disconcerting habits. He is simply perfect. Here are just a few reasons why a Poodle is a great choice for a prospective dog owner.

Variety

Poodles come in more packages that any other breed of dog. There are three sizes and a abundance of colors from pure white to jet black—and almost everything in between. When you add the plethora of clips that are possible with Poodles, it's fair to say that your choice is nearly infinite!

Looks

A Poodle is a handsome, well-put-together dog. He is athletic, graceful, elegant, and energetic. Large Poodles are great partakers of country life, while smaller ones make perfect companions for apartment dwellers and the elderly.

Intelligence and Trainability

The Poodle's superior intelligence and eagerness to please propel him well beyond the "pet" category and into that of "companion." Poodles excel at dog games like obedience, agility, and flyball. They make perfect partners for blind and disabled people. They keep secrets well, too.

Longevity

Not only are Poodles the Einsteins of the dog world, but they also live for a long time—in fact, they are one of the longest-lived of all breeds. It is not unusual for a Poodle to reach his mid or late teens. Of the three varieties, the middle-sized Miniature lives the longest, with the Toy and Standard following close behind.

Incidentally, Poodles are so long-lived that it makes sense to arrange for your pet's welfare in case something should happen to you first.

Prairillon Orion Rising ("Hunter"), owned by Kristi Murdock
Photo courtesy of Kristi Murdock

Sociability

"They make wonderful companions, confidants, and house
guests, and are amenable to argument and persuasion."
—James Thurber, *Christabel: Part One*

Poodles get along well with other pets—and with people, too!
Standard Poodles in particular make excellent companions for
children, since they lack the clumsiness of many other large,
sturdy breeds. They have the patience to be around toddlers, and,
for older children, there is nothing nicer than a romp with one of
these active dogs. Smaller Poodles also have agreeable tempera-
ments, and most of them love kids.

We are speaking, of course, of kind, caring children. No dog,
however tolerant, enjoys being abused by brats. If your kids are
responsible and loving, a Poodle would be an excellent addition
to your family. By responsible, I do not mean that the children
should be solely charged with feeding and grooming chores;
even the most well-meaning and thoughtful child may sometimes forget to feed and brush the dog—and a parent should
always supervise such activities, anyway. I simply mean that a
responsible child is one who will always treat the pet kindly and
take care that he doesn't escape from the backyard. That's enough.

An Answer to Allergies

Poodles are hypoallergenic pets since they shed much less than most other breeds. Although no breed of dog is completely shed-proof, the long life of each Poodle hair keeps it on the dog rather than on your floor. Many people who cannot tolerate other breeds due to allergies have no such problems with Poodles.

Do remember, however, that the Poodle's ever-growing coat needs a great deal of regular—and probably professional—care to keep it at its stunning best. You must be willing to learn to clip your Poodle yourself or pay to have it done by a groomer. This is not a low-maintenance pet.

The Versatile Breed

The Poodle can do almost anything. He is an athlete, a show-man, a flushing and retrieving dog, a protector, a guide dog, an agility dog, an obedience dog, and best of all, a beautiful, loyal, and loving companion. Few breeds do any of these things as well as a Poodle, and none combines them all so well. Furthermore, Poodles seem to understand exactly what you want of them and do their best to please. What more could one ask? The Poodle is truly a versatile breed. By the way, Poodles also have a sense of humor. They must.

Why People Prefer Poodles

An informal survey of Poodle owners revealed the following reasons why Poodles are special.

▼ They are the all-around dog. My two can be consummate farm dogs one day, get a bath and go to a therapy dog session, or compete in agility or obedience without the blink of an eye. If I am sad they are there to cuddle and comfort. If I am happy they dance with me.
    —Linda Hargett

▼ Trying to explain why I prefer Poodles is like trying to explain why I like sunshine or fresh air. They seek out the companionship of people and physically show their joy in being alive. Their grace and fluid movements are unsurpassed. They are my devoted companions, playful clowns, comforting friends, and have completely stolen my heart.
    —Kathryn Bennett

Clint

Courtesy of Barbara Burdick

▼ Poodles are like velcro: everything sticks to them and they stick to you.   —Karen Welsh

▼ Their history is so ancient and so continuous: they provide a window on a fabulously rich and detailed past.
                    —Anon

▼ I prefer big hairy dogs! As a past owner of breeds like St. Bernards, German Shepherds, and Old English Sheepdogs, Standard Poodles fulfill that fondness without all that shedding and drooling! In addition, other breeds pale in comparison to that wonderful, vivacious poodle personality!   —Michelle Mace

▼ I prefer Poodles because they don't smell when they are wet.   —Wendy Newton

▼ They are more like human beings than any other breed of dog—thus they are the most complex and interesting companions.   —Laurel Hood

▼ I prefer Poodles because I enjoy the constant mental challenge their intelligence provides.
                    —Caroline Hair

▼ I love Poodles because of their unbelievable joy of life, intelligence, and magnificent fur.
                    —Maxine Levinson

▼ A poodle can read your mind. Poodles can make you laugh when you require a chuckle or can snuggle in and give kisses if you are sad.   —Pamela Vaughan

▼ My own little Hanna has my heart neatly wrapped around hers.   —Jeanne Lucas

▼ My Poodles are an extension of myself—my love, warmth, and laughter, my artistic self, are all shaped into their personalities, and theirs in mine.
                              —Vickie Haywood Wagram

▼ Poodles are not a pet but a soulmate.
                              —Linda Karr

▼ Poodles are the delight of perfection.
                              —Lindsay Gold

▼ To watch my Poodle run is a heartstoppingly beautiful sight.   —Carol Lee Daniel.

▼ Poodles have a sense of humor which can even occasionally be mistaken for irony.   —Susan Fleisher

▼ Wicket and I are out there doing tracking and hunting and swimming together. I believe the Standard Poodle is the best all purpose sporting and performance dog of all.
                              —Tom Reese

▼ To me the answer is simple. I have two daughters that hate to have me do their hair, and my Poodles never complain when I do theirs.   —Tracy Nichols

▼ Because they just sparkle!   —Mary Anntillian

Poodles, however, are not for everyone. The heavy-handed, the insensitive, and the stupid need not apply. Poodles do not respond to harsh training methods, and they do not make good yard-dogs. Many are more intelligent than their owners. Some, in fact, are a whole lot smarter, which can lead to problems. If you have any doubt about your ability to outsmart your Poodle, consider another breed.

Otherwise, use your *noodle*—get a *poodle*!

Chapter 1
Poodles Past and Present

Are Poodles Dogs?

Well, yes and no. They are dogs without the dogginess, so to speak, of other dogs. Many people who simply can't stand other dogs adore Poodles. Poodles are more intelligent, more dignified, and more sensitive than almost any other breed.

The History of Poodles

The Prehistoric Poodle

Long ago, in the dim dark past, the world was Poodleless. Oh, there were wolves, and dingoes, and even domestic dogs of a sort, but they weren't Poodles. They were just dogs. And as you'll quickly learn (if you haven't already) there's a world of difference between dogs and Poodles.

Nonetheless, let's go back into prehistory and learn how wolves turned into dogs, and how, eventually, some dogs (with a little help from selective breeding) managed to evolve into the higher life form known as a Poodle.

All dogs are descended from wolves. All belong to the biologic family *Canidae*, the genus *Canis*, and the species *lupus*. Dogs and wolves can interbreed successfully and have fertile offspring. There are, however, enough important differences between them

7

for geneticists to put wolves and dogs into separate subspecies. For instance, wolves generally come into heat once a year, and dogs twice. Their lifestyles differ enough to prevent their making frequent contact, and dogs are more likely to be killed by wolves than to breed with them. So dogs now have as their own designation *Canis lupes familiaris*—the familiar wolf.

All breeds of dog have generic dog DNA. A geneticist given a sample of unknown DNA could easily identify it as dog DNA (as opposed to wolf, bat, or human), but could not identify the particular breed from which the sample was taken. It used to be thought that dogs separated from wolves about 12,000 years ago, but new evidence suggests that the dog-wolf split occurred much earlier—perhaps as much as 100,000 years ago. It's unclear whether the first dogs were the domesticated kind or a wild species like the Australian dingo.

It is fair to say, however, that whatever happened so long ago doesn't make much difference to us now. The important question for this book is not, where did dogs come from, but rather, where did that very special breed, the Poodle, originate?

French (?) Poodles

By their very nature, Poodles bring to mind phrases like savoir-faire, joie de vivre, and insouciance—that is, everything French. In light of this, it seems almost too bad that Poodles are probably of German origin.

The earliest mention of Poodles in writing dates back to 1555 and can be found in the works of one Conrad Gesner, a Swiss naturalist. This seems most appropriate, as Switzerland lies between France and Germany—as least partly.

"But they seem so French." Well, yes, they do. In fact, the French have adopted the Poodle as a national dog of sorts. However, we're pretty sure that the modern Poodle originated in Germany. The English word *Poodle* is derived from the German *pudel* (short for *Pudelhund*), which comes from the verb *pudeln*, meaning to splash around. The word *Poodle* thus means splasher. This etymology strengthens the theory that the earliest Poodles were water retrievers.

So we get the impression of a dog splashing around in the marshes, rather than in rivers or deep water, to retrieve game. This is correct, since the Poodle's heavy coat soaks up water and is a hindrance to serious swimming. But as splashers they have no equal. In fact, the Poodle's characteristic clip was probably devised as an aid to retrieving—early hunters were looking for the perfect combination of protection and lightness that would enable the Poodle to dash through both brush and water with ease.

Poodle Parlance

In France today, the word for Poodle is *Caniche*. This term may somehow be derived from *chien canard*, or duck dog, which provides further evidence of the Poodle's history as a water retriever. Certainly Poodles look nothing like ducks. Some of the earliest Poodles in France were called *barbets*, which means bearded. These were apparently small companion Poodles that were not noted for their splashing ability.

From the very earliest times, the French seemed to prefer smaller Poodles—if one can judge by contemporary artwork. The French developed several kinds of small Poodle-like dogs like the *Caniche Nain*, as well as a big white Poodle, named appropriately Mouton, meaning wooly. Corded varieties were called Moufflin.

Mardi Gras Poodles at dress rehearsal backstage for the Disney Magic Kingdom Easter Parade
Courtesy of Jeanne Kennedy

Poodle Relations

Poodles have a great many relatives and ancestors: the Maltese, the Spaniel, the Irish Water Dog, and the now extinct English Rough-Haired Water dog have all been given credit for being related (however distantly) to Poodles. (The Rough-Haired Water Dogs, by the way, were especially popular with poachers living in the northeast of England.)

Some historians of the breed believe that the toy spaniel and the Maltese were ancestors to the smaller Barbet Poodle, while the big duck-retrieving Poodles owe their size to larger spaniels. Certainly Poodles and Irish Water Spaniels look a lot alike, even today.

Poodle Potpourri

Some say the Rough-Haired Water Dog of England is the ancestor of the Poodle; other people, who are equally certain of their stance allege that the two breeds merged. As the argument alarmingly resembles the question of what happened when Cro-Magnon man met the Neanderthal, I prefer to leave depths of the question unplumbed. 🐾

Some fanciers insist the breed was developed in Russia, while the Scandinavian breed standard continues to give credit to France. Spain can make a fair claim as well. Even today there is a Spanish *Cao d'Agua*, which is a water dog similar to and possibly ancestral to the Rough-Haired Water dog and thus, perhaps, to the Poodle.

Roman Poodles

Even though Poodles were not noted in literature until the sixteenth century, it seems certain that they were around long before that date. There are Poodles depicted on several monuments to Augustus Caesar (circa A.D. 30). Some Greek and Roman coins portray a Poodle-like creature sporting the traditional lion clip (a long mane and clipped body). Carvings with images resembling Poodles have been found on Roman tombs, but the connection between Poodles and death is not made clear—at least to me.

French Poodles–Again

Louis XIV, the Sun King, owned a little Poodle named Filou, who turned up in all kinds of art and novels produced by syco- phants who thought they could worm their way into the Sun King's good graces by including his dog in their art. It usually worked. King Louis XVI had a Poodle, too, but that's about the best thing one can say about him. (I didn't mean to leave out Louis the XV, by the way. He also had Poodles.)

The last king of France, Louis Phillipe, also owned a Poodle. Sadly, it did him no good. There exists a print of Louis Phillipe dashing through the snow in an attempt to escape a rabid mob of Republicans—accompanied by his wife and Poodle.

Poodles Everywhere

Eventually the Poodle's fame spread across Europe into Eng- land, Italy, and Scandinavia. There were Poodles in Belgium and the Netherlands as well, where they were hitched up to carts and hauled vegetables around. Luckily, this sort of thing didn't last.

Belgian Poodles were supposedly also used to smuggle lace; the animals were shaved, wrapped in lace, and then covered with false hair. I suppose anything is possible with Poodles.

The Dutch and Belgian dog was not called a Poodle, however, or even a *Pudel*. It was known as a *Poedel*. Greek Poodles are something else again, namely *Thasytrichons*. I just thought you might like to know.

The Poodle Club of England was founded in 1886. Most Poo- dles were Standard and corded until the First World War, but Miniatures gradually became more popular.

Hunting Poodles

Early Poodles, both French and English, were widely used for fowling. In 1621, a certain Gervaise Markham published a train- ing book for fowlers, optimistically entitled *Hunger's Prevention, or the Art of Fowling*. Although Markham seemed to think that a dog's primary function in hunting was to drive a molting duck into a preset trap (an amazing contraption of glue, willow branches, and string), the book does have some historical interest.

In addition to their role as duck-drovers, Poodles were used to retrieve wounded ducks in the marshlands. Nineteenth-century sportsmen were especially fond of night hunting, and "…without a dog gifted with sense, nose, and pluck, it would be perfectly impossible for the shooters, in the dead of night, to collect their game. This the poodle does, with a rapidity and intelligence which are simply unsurpassable" (Lewis Clement, *Dogs of the British Islands* [J.H. Walsh: Stonehenge] ed. 1878). Why Poodlers were hunting in the dead of night in the first place remains a mystery to me, although more than one person has tried to explain it.

(Those who believe that both Poodles and the setting breeds were partly descended from Spaniels point to some old pictures of Poodle-like dogs flushing game from the water. Whether or not they were any good at it is another matter.)

The Poodle Comes to America

The earliest Poodles may have arrived in North America as early as 1600. They were to be used for hunting in marshes and swamps. No one, however, is really sure who these early dogs were, or what they looked like. Everyone was too busy to take pictures.

Recognizable Poodles, both large and small, came to America during the 1880s. The first one entered the American Kennel Club studbook in 1887. The Poodle Club of America, however, was not founded until 1931. The large or Standard size was the most popular at the time (people had more room), and the most popular colors were black, white, and brown.

The first job of a national club is to draw up a standard—a document describing what the ideal dog of a particular breed should look like. Unfortunately, early Poodlers couldn't agree on this issue. Some preferred the German-type Poodle, which seems to have been a bit large (and in the opinion of some, a little coarse), while others leaned more to the English/French variety. The latter won the day, and the Poodle Club of America wrote a very nice letter to the Curly Poodle Club of England asking to adopt their standard. Naturally, the Curly Poodle Club of England was delighted, and the deal was made. The American Club approved the new standard without delay. The only problem was that most of the Poodles in the country at the time really looked nothing like the new standard. In fact, they looked like German Poodles.

The result was a mad rush by rich Poodle fanciers to import English Poodles and get the breed up to standard. This endeavor was tremendously successful, and most experts agree that the American Poodle is really the finest example of the breed in the world today.

Originally, Standard and Toy Poodles were considered separate breeds. They did indeed look quite different in many ways. For instance, the first Toy Poodles were always white; it wasn't until 1943 that other colors were introduced into the breed.

When Miniatures (who are midway between Toys and Standards) appeared, they were lumped in with the Standards for showing purposes. In 1943, however, the Poodle Club of America decided that Poodles were Poodles, just divided into three sizes. The Club oversaw the admixture of Miniature Poodle bloodlines into the Toys. After a brief period, all Poodles were considered by the same standard

Poodle Potpourri

The first Standard Poodle to win at the prestigious Westminster Dog show was Ch. Nunsoe Duc de la Terrasse, a white Poodle, in 1935. By today's standards he looks a little—well, scruffy. The first Miniature won the event in 1943; his name was Ch. Pitter Patter of Piperscroft. And the first Toy Poodle to win a Best in Show at Westminster was Ch. Wilbur White Swan (known as Peanut to his friends) in 1956. 🐾

By 1960, more Poodles (counting all varieties as one) were registered than any other breed in the country, a position they held until 1983. Part of their popularity was a fad, of course, but the Poodle's truly excellent qualities and tremendous versatility made that popularity well deserved.

Notable Poodles of the Napoleonic Wars, and So On

In some ways the Napoleonic Wars can be considered the golden age of Poodles. Well, at least a lot of famous ones made their names during that era.

Boye or Boy

No discussion of Poodles would be complete without a mention of Prince Rupert of the Rhine (1619-1682). Actually, we could get along perfectly well without mentioning Rupert, but we do need to talk about his Poodle. Rupert was a nephew of King Charles I (the one who got his head cut off—and not a minute too soon). Rupert owned a white Poodle named Boy (or Boye, making allowances for archaic spelling) who had magical powers, such as catching bullets in his mouth and making himself invisible.

Rupert was taken prisoner at the Battle of Lemgo in 1638. As he languished (sort of) under house arrest at Lintz, the British ambassador to Vienna, Lord Arundel, gave him the Poodle for company. (Poodles make better company than most people.)

Rupert and Boy hit it off right away. Boy slept in Rupert's bed and, it is said, received more haircuts than the Prince himself. The sycophantic Rupert taught Boye to jump for joy at the very mention of the word *Charles*, and the duly impressed king fed the dog tidbits of roast beef and capon. Rupert never did inherit the English throne, although it is rumored that Boy actually got to sit there from time to time—which is more than Rupert ever did.

Poor Boy met a sad end in 1643. During the battle of Marston Moor, somebody forgot to tie him up and the dog was shot by a soldier. Boy's bullet catching abilities had apparently failed him that day.

"Here Lies the Brave Moustache"

A tale of valor stirs behind these perfect iambics. It would be inexcusable to write a book about Poodles without mentioning the brave Moustache. This famous black Poodle was born in Normandy in 1799, and fought for Napoleon in the Battles of Marengo and Austerlitz. He even warned his grenadier regiment of the approach of the Austrians. Although this feat doesn't seem all that remarkable in retrospect, it impressed the French enough to award the animal a fancy tricolor collar.

This morale booster urged Moustache on to greater efforts. During one battle, he attempted to rescue a soldier carrying the regimental colors. The soldier was killed, but Moustache came away with the colors and returned them proudly to his regiment. (Some say he actually unwrapped the colors from the dead body of the soldier, but that seems to be stretching it a bit.) Whatever the case, the French put Moustache on the payroll and awarded him a silver medal, of which he was no doubt quite proud.

Moustache was far more than a war Poodle, however. His regimental unit had a lively sense of humor and taught the animal to lift his leg and urinate at the mention of Napoleon's enemies.

Moustache was killed in 1811 at the Battle of Badajoz in Spain. The French buried him with his collar and made him a headstone which read, "*Ci gît le brave Moustache* ("Here lies the brave Moustache.")." This turned out to be a mistake, since it let the Spanish know exactly where their enemy was buried. They ransacked the grave after the war, smashed the headstone, and burned the body of Moustache. They seem to have been rather poor losers.

Barbuche

Barbuche belonged to an orphan boy named Petit Jean (Little John), who became a drummer boy during the Italian campaign. Petit Jean was killed in the course of duty, and Barbuche lost a front leg defending his master. An old sergeant of the company kept the Poodle, and later made quite a living for himself by teaching the dog some clever tricks. Apparently a three-legged performing Poodle was more impressive to the public than the regular four-legged kind.

Sancho

In 1812, at the battle of Salamanca, Lord Worcester found a large white Poodle lying upon the grave of his master, a lieutenant in the French army. Lord Worcester adopted the dog, named him Sancho, and later commissioned a print featuring the loyal animal.

Moffino

Moffino, an army dog, became separated from his master in Russia. This remarkable Poodle followed the retreating army for many thousands of miles, all the way to Milan. His master, an Italian corporal, opened a door only to see Moffino, covered with wounds and a phantom of his former self.

Mohiloff

This Poodle belonged to the Duc d'Enghein, whom Napoleon suspected of treachery and had shot. The faithful dog, however, had to be forcibly removed from his master's grave. It was a wonder he wasn't shot himself; perhaps it was the fact that he had been a gift from the king of Sweden that saved him. At any rate, Mohiloff was adopted by the commander of the fortress, and when the animal finally died, his owner had him stuffed and placed under glass.

Duc

Impossible to omit from the annals of great Poodles is the tale of Duc, a white Standard Poodle who was known professionally as Champion Nunsoe Duc de la Terrasse of Blakeen. In 1935, Duc was the first Poodle to win the Westminster Dog Show—a notable accomplishment at any time. Trophies notwithstanding, this internationally acclaimed dog was banished to the upstairs of his home during an elegant dinner party. None too pleased with his enforced exile, Duc chose an appropriate lull in the conversation to saunter into the dining room carrying aloft an enema bag. No one knew quite what to say. Nor do I. Interestingly enough, Duc's owner and handler, Hayes Blake Hoyt, was the first woman to handle a Best in Show at Westminster. All this, incidentally, happened before the enema bag incident.

Poodle Potpourri

A Toy Poodle is the mascot of Sigma Gamma Rho Sorority, the first African-American sorority founded at Butler, a predominantly white university, in 1929. This Poodle is referred to as a "French Toy." 🐾

Poodles and the Arts

Since the beginning of Poodledom, Poodles have been immortalized in the arts, especially the visual arts and literature. We should not forget the Poodle's immortal contribution to the sartorial arts, however, as evidenced in the Poodle skirt of the 1950's.

Literary Poodles

Most sinister of all literary Poodles is the one in Part 1 of Goethe's *Faust*. In this work, the Poodle is Mephisto himself, who charms Faust into taking him home. Although the identification of Poodles with the devil may only indicate the great poet's sense of humor, the idea was tantalizing enough to be repeated later by the great American-English novelist Henry James.

James created a Poodle character in his early work, *Roderick Hudson*. Stentorello, a large white Poodle, belonged to Christina Light, the fabulously beautiful villainess of the book. Christina "can think of nothing but her poodle," and when the sculptor hero asks to do a bust of Christina, she answers, "I would rather you should make the poodle's." But perhaps this Poodle is not all that he seems. For he may be "a grotesque phantom, like the black dog in *Faust*." Thus the connection between Poodles and Mephisto is drawn.

Honoré de Balzac, the French novelist, also scattered references to Poodles throughout his writings; over thirty such references have noted. Curiously enough, Henry James sighed that he thought Balzac would have done a better job than himself at creating the character of Christina Light—but perhaps he was referring to her Poodle.

James Thurber, the famous essayist and cartoonist, showed Standard Poodles in his day—complaining about it the entire time. He devoted large sections of his writings to his beloved Poodles. For a sampling, read *Thurber's Dogs*.

The following writers have also included Poodles in these works: Louise May Alcott, *Little Women*; Raymond Chandler and Robert Parker, *Poodle Springs*; James Herriot, *The Complete James Herriot*; Maxine Kumin, *Archibald the Traveling Poodle*, Ouida, *Moufflou and other Stories*; John Steinbeck, *Travels with Charley*; and Jacqueline Susann, *Every Night Josephine*.

Of course, a lot of other people have written about Poodles, but no one ever heard of most of them, even if the books are very good indeed. In *Poodle Springs*, contemporary mystery writer Robert Parker has attempted to complete Chandler's last work. In the town of Poodle Springs, everyone is rich and, hence, owns a Poodle. Of course we know that anyone who owns a Poodle is automatically rich, at least in spiritual gifts.

The best-known current writer of Poodle mystery fiction is the award-winning Laurien Berenson, author of the Melanie Travis Mystery series. Berenson is a breeder/exhibitor of both Standard and Miniature Poodles. Among her 18 books are *A Pedigree to Die For*, *Underdog*, *Dog Eat Dog*, and *The Hair of the Dog*.

Pictorial Poodles

The Poodle has been depicted in art almost as long as art has existed. Although no cave paintings of Poodles have been found (yet), they do appear, as mentioned earlier, in Roman art. Bas-reliefs of Poodle-like dogs have been found along the Mediterranean, some of them decorating tombs.

Early artistic renditions of the Poodle can be found in various sixteenth-century illuminated manuscripts. One of the most famous belonged to Margaret of York, the third wife of Charles the Bold of Burgundy.

There's a famous tapestry in Cluny, France, that is part of a series called *The Lady with the Unicorn*. Dating from about 1510, the tapestry features what is, unmistakably, a small Poodle, complete with the lion-like haircut.

Albrecht Durer drew Poodles in the 15th and 16th centuries; Francisco de Goya painted them in the nineteenth. Martin de Vos (1541-1603) painted a picture called *Tobit and his Dog*. The dog certainly looks like a poodle, and is shaved in at least some of the appropriate places.

Sir Edwin Landseer (1802-73) painted the Poodle as *Wisdom Laying Down the Law*. Poodles are fond of doing this in their own homes today.

George Rankin painted a picture of a curly-coated Poodle in the late 1800s. It wore a yellow bow, and had bracelets around his knees, as well as tufts of hair here and there. The entire ribcage was bare.

Okay! Okay! Sometimes I can be a frou-frou dog!

Photo courtesy of Kathie Kryla

Poodles of the Rich and Famous

Poodles being the aristocrats that they are, it seems only natural that as soon as a person becomes famous, that person wants a Poodle. And why not?

Poodle Potpourri

Winston Churchill's Miniature Brown Poodle, Rufus, was run over and killed. Some people tried to give Churchill a Bulldog to replace him, but Churchill, perhaps suspecting something insincere or snide in the offer, gravely replied that if he got another dog it would be a Poodle. 🐾

Famous Poodle owners (and their dogs) include Winston Churchill (Rufus); Mignon Eberhart (Ginger); Helen Hayes (Turvy and Chiquita); Victor Hugo (Baron); Empress Josephine (Fortune); Thomas Mann (Niko); Alexander Pope (Marquis); Gertrude Stein (Basket); John Steinbeck (Charley); Booth Tarkington (Figaro); James Thurber (Medve and Christabel); Richard Wagner (Peps); Jane Alexander (Martini); Lucille Ball (Tinkerbell); Tallulah Bankhead (Daisy); Ingmar Bergman (Teddy); Erma Bombeck (Pockets); Omar Bradley (Beau); Carol Burnett (Beau Jangles);

Walt Disney (Duchess); Katharine Hepburn (Button); Mary Higgins Clark (Porgy); Sammy Davis Jr. (Bo Jangles); Barbara Eden (Annie); Cary Grant (Suzette); Jack Lemmon (Chloe); Vivian Leigh (Sebastian); Marilyn Monroe (Maf); Dorothy Parker (Misty); Bob Hope (Mike); Liberace (Coco); Andrew Wyeth (Eloise); and Vincent Price (Pablo). Most of the kings of France, who were all named Henri or Louis, had Poodles too.

Poodle Potpourri

The Empress Josephine's Poodle, Fortune, carried messages to her from her children while she was in Robespierre's prison. 🐾

Is it a Jumbo Beanie Baby®? No, it's Am./Can. Ch. My Deer Whisperwind Music Man shortly after the show coat was cut off.

Photo courtesy of Marlene Ann Heacock

Chapter 2
Poodle Perfection: The Breed Standard

Varieties

Although the Poodle comes in three delicious varieties—Standard (large), Miniature (medium), and Toy (small)—it is one breed, with one breed standard. All are beautiful, lively, and quick to learn.

Poodles are so desirable as pets that even peculiar poodle mixes are advertised with pride: cockapoos, pudelpointers, labradoodles, and peekapoos. With Poodles, anything is possible.

Scholars have found Poodle relatives in many modern breeds, including the following: American Water Spaniel, Bergamasco, Bichon Frisé, Curly-Coated Retriever, Epagneul Pont-Audemer, Havanese, Irish Water Spaniel, Komondor, Lowchen, Portuguese Water Dog, Puli, Spanish Water Dog, and Wetterhund. Not all of these breeds are officially recognized by the American Kennel Club (AKC), but they are out there.

Standard

BIS Ch. Mardi Gras Alynlee Brass Ring

Courtesy of Jeanne Kennedy

A Standard Poodle in full glory
Courtesy of Leslie Sims

Miniature

Show type Miniature Poodle

Courtesy of Leslie Sims

Miniature Poodle Goldpin's Simon Sez ("Karly")

Courtesy of Mona Kurth

Toy

Toy Poodle Mindy May (notice the undocked tail)
Courtesy of Steven and Moselle Domingue

Toy Poodle

Courtesy of Leslie Sims

The Breed Standard

The current Poodle breed standard was approved August 14, 1984, and reformatted March 27, 1990, by the Poodle Club of America. Again, except for height, the standard is the same for all 3 varieties. You can find the full breed standard in *The Complete Dog Book*, the official publication of the AKC.

The breed standard refers to the ideal dog. No dog is ideal, however, and many dogs excluded from the show ring for minor faults make excellent pets.

Size

Here lies the only difference of note among the three varieties. The Standard Poodle is over 15 inches at the highest point of the shoulders and weighs 45 to 65 pounds. The Miniature Poodle is 15 inches or under at the highest point of the shoulders, with a minimum height in excess of 10 inches. He weighs 14 to 18 pounds, and is the most popular of the Poodle varieties today. The Toy Poodle is ten inches or under at the highest point of the shoulders. He weighs between 6 and 12 pounds. (European standards are somewhat different, dividing the breed into four size categories: Standard, Miniature, Dwarf, and Toy.)

The first Toy Poodles were nearly always white, but the other colors were introduced by breeding white Toy males to Miniature females of various colors. Today, Toys come in the same range of colors as Standards and Miniatures.

Poodle Potpourri

The British and Australian breed standards are similar to that of the AKC; however, in those standards, the Toy Poodle's height must be under eleven (rather than ten) inches. 🐾

The breed standard states that "as long as the Toy Poodle is definitely a Toy Poodle, and Miniature Poodle a Miniature Poodle, both in balance and proportion for the variety, diminutiveness shall be the deciding factor when all other points are equal."

The following is part of the standard for Poodles; the numbers following each heading refer to the percentage that feature is accorded in the show ring.

General Appearance (30%)

The standard states that the Poodle is a "very active, intelligent, and elegant-appearing dog, squarely built, well-proportioned, moving soundly and carrying himself proudly. Properly clipped in the traditional fashion and carefully groomed, the Poodle has about him an air of distinction and dignity peculiar to himself." That describes the Poodle most accurately indeed.

At first, the English and American breed standards were identical. Both the English and the American Kennel Clubs recognized Standard and Miniature Poodles; both recognized all colors. Today, minor differences exist between the two. In America, the Toy Poodle must be under 10 inches; it is shown in the Toy Group, while the other two sizes are shown in the Non-Sporting Group. The English Toy Poodle is another inch higher, and all varieties of Poodle are shown in the Utility group.

Poodle Potpourri

The first English Standard Poodle champion was named Achilles. He was 23 inches tall and wore his coat corded, with the cords measuring 30 inches! Nowadays, we know that any Poodle's coat will cord naturally, but in those days the corded Poodle was considered a separate type. (To get the cords to grow, they were rolled with paraffin and soaked with petroleum jelly.) 🐾

The general appearance of the Poodle is square, meaning that "the length of body measured from the breastbone to the point of the rump approximates the height from the highest point of the shoulders to the ground."

Head and Expression (20%)

The proper Poodle has almond-shaped eyes which are "very dark" and "oval in shape." He should have "an alert intelligent expression." It is considered a major fault if the eyes are "round, protruding, large, or very light." The ears should hang "close to the head, set at or slightly below eye level."

The skull should be "moderately rounded, with a slight but definite stop." (The stop is where the muzzle meets the upper part of the skull.) The muzzle should be "long, straight, and fine with slight chiseling under the eyes." The ideal length is clearly defined; it should be the same as the "length from occiput [the back part of the skull] to stop." A muzzle that is too long is called "snipey" and is considered a fault.

The Poodle should have a scissors bite, in which the top teeth just overlap the lower teeth. This is the standard for most breeds, because it is the anatomically correct. An undershot, overshot, or wry mouth (cross bite) is considered a major fault.

Neck, Topline, and Body (20%)

The ideal Poodle has a neck that is "well-proportioned, strong and long enough to permit the head to be carried high and with dignity."

The topline is "level...with the exception of a slight hollow just behind the shoulder."

Poodle Parlance

The topline is the dog's outline from just behind the withers to the tail set. (The withers are the tops of the shoulders.) 🐾

The shoulders should be strong and "smoothly muscled," with the shoulder blade "well laid back and approximately the same length as the upper foreleg." (Well-laid-back means about 45 degrees.) The forelegs should be straight and parallel when viewed from the front. When seen from the side, the elbow should be "directly below the highest point of the shoulder."

The feet are "rather small, oval in shape with toes well arched and cushioned on thick firm pads." They should not turn in or out.

The angulation of the hindquarters balances that of the fore-quarters. The hind legs should be "straight and parallel" when viewed from the rear.

The chest should be "deep and moderately wide with well-sprung ribs." The loin is short, broad, and muscular. The tail is docked, "set on high and carried up." A tail that is set low, curled, or carried over the back is a major fault.

Gait (20%)

The show ring gait (movement) of a Poodle should be "a straightforward trot with light springy action, and strong hind-quarters drive." (They never ask dogs to run in the conformation ring. I would enjoy seeing them do so; it would be fun to watch the handler try to keep up.)

Coat (10%)

The coat can be "Curly: of naturally harsh texture, dense throughout," or "Corded: hanging in tight even cords of varying length, longer on mane or body coat, head, and ears; shorter on puffs, bracelets, and pompons."

For showing, a Poodle must appear in one of the following traditional clips: a puppy clip, (for dogs under 12 months of age); the English saddle clip; the continental clip; or the sporting clip (for non-competitive classes like veterans or for stud classes). I'll discuss clips in Chapter 8.

Poodle Potpourri

For some reason, Poodles are almost never seen in their more natural corded coats. Few people apparently find such a coat appealing, although I must confess a personal liking for it. The upkeep of corded coats is more difficult than the traditionally clipped and brushed out Poodle. These clips are mandatory only in the United States and Canada, however; other countries seem more enlightened. The corded coat can be combined with the regulation clip, even in this country, but you never see it. Or hardly ever. 🐾

Colors

Poodles may be of any solid color: apricot, black, blue, brown, café au lait, cream, gray, silver, or white, with black and white being the most common. Whatever the color, however, it must be solid. Any parti-colored dog, for instance a black dog with white paws or chest, is disqualified from the show ring—although they make charming pets.

Poodle Potpourri

Even the blackest of black Poodles will very likely have a few white hairs sprinkled among the black. Some pure-black dogs seen in the show ring have, in fact, been dyed. This is against the rules, of course, and clever judges examine dogs using such innovative dye-detectors as polarized sunglasses and baby wipes. In a naturally black dog, the ears and topknot are generally the darkest part, the tail and rump the lightest. Dogs dyed black have a deadly uniformity of color that betrays them immediately to the observant eye. 🐾

Poodle breeders must be very careful if they mix colors—the wrong gene for color could result in parti-colored puppies. White and brown Poodles, for instance, make a dangerous couple. There is nothing genetically wrong with parti-colored puppies, by the way; it just so happens that they cannot be shown. It is only a matter of preference for those who wrote the breed standard.

Poodle Parlance

A "parti-colored" Poodle's coat is made up of two different colors. It is a show disqualification in America; the German Poodle Club, however, allows black and white partis, which are called "Harlequin" Poodles. 🐾

As mentioned, black Poodles are a pure rich black. Another color, blue (sometimes called gray), looks black, but when you compare such a dog to a truly black dog, you can easily see the difference. A young blue puppy has a silver face and perhaps some silver hairs between his pawpads; as the dog matures, his whole body will become that shade. This is called "clearing." Additionally, the clipped parts look bluer than the unclipped parts. A puppy who will become silver will have mostly silver hairs between his pawpads. A perfectly, purely, extra-white Poodle is called an "ice-white," and is quite unusual.

In Poodledom, a dog outsiders might call gray is referred to as silver. A silver Poodle will always have a silver face, although the rest of the body might take a while to catch up. A variation of silver is called "silver beige."

Poodle coloring can be confusing. When the standard talks about a solid color, it means a solid color at the skin. Some shading is common in puppies, but the skin is always a solid color. Shading, incidentally, almost always clears to a pure color at maturity. When purchasing a Poodle puppy, be aware that the color you see may not be the color you'll eventually get. Some Poodles are born black, then later fade to silver.

Brown and Café au Lait Poodles have liver colored noses, eye-rims, and lips, dark toenails, and dark amber eyes. (I have never thought that liver goes all that well with café au lait—or anything else, for that matter—but I suppose the Poodle Club of America knows best.) Poodles of other colors (except apricot) are expected to have black noses, eye-rims and lips, black or self-colored toenails, and very dark eyes. Black is the preferred nose, eye-rim, lip, etc. color for apricot Poodles, but liver colored noses, eye-rims, and lips are permitted, as are amber eyes.

Poodle Parlance

Some Poodles are marked black and tan like Doberman pinschers, which disqualifies them from the show ring. In an interesting variation of this phenomenon, some Poodles begin their lives marked black and tan, but the color fades to silver and cream. This is sometimes called a "Phantom" Poodle. 🐾

Poodles may be disqualified from the show-ring for being over- or undersized, appearing in the wrong clip, or being parti-color.

The Standard Poodle

The Standard Poodle is the oldest of the three varieties, and matures the most slowly. A Standard will not reach maturity until 18 or even 20 months of age. (They grow very fast during their first few months.) A mature Standard Poodle may weigh about 60 pounds. It can be as tall as 28 inches; most of the Poodles you see today tend to be much taller than the standard's 15 inches.

Poodle Parlance

Sometimes you will see a breeder advertise "Royal" Standard Poodles. This is a marketing trick that refers to very large dogs. The AKC does not recognize any such size. 🐾

Standard Poodles require a lot of exercise (1 or 2 hours a day) and a lot of attention. If they get it, they are calm and sensible around the house. For many, the Standard Poodle is *the* Poodle; remember, however, that a Standard will be a little more expensive to feed and a lot more expensive to groom than the smaller varieties.

The Miniature Poodle

The Miniature Poodle was probably the product of the concerted breeding of small Standard Poodles over a period of time. For many it is an ideal dog—not needing as much exercise as the Standard, but sturdy enough to get on with small children. For their owners, the Miniature is a not a compromise between the Standard and the Toy, but the perfect dog for their needs.

The Toy Poodle

Although tiny dogs have been around for hundreds of years (including a dog suspiciously resembling the Toy Poodle), only comparatively recently have breeders developed a "true-to-type" Toy Poodle, one who will faithfully pass on his desirable characteristics from generation to generation. In America, Toy Poodles were treated as a separate breed until 1943. At that time, the AKC gave in and agreed they were just like the other Poodles, only smaller.

Toy Poodles are excellent pets for apartments and for elderly people, since they require little exercise. A mature Toy Poodle will weigh between 6 and 12 pounds, and will get along perfectly well with half an hour of outdoor exercise a day. Of course, they may race around the apartment like mad.

Toy Poodles are easy to pick up and carry from one place to another, and as long as they are trained properly, they are as compliant as the other sizes. Small children, however, must be constantly supervised around a Toy, as they might inadvertently hurt him. In such cases, a more substantial Poodle variety is a better choice.

Poodle Precautions

Sometimes you will see a breeder advertise a "Teacup" or "Tiny Toy" Poodle. The AKC does not recognize these as regulation sizes. These terms are just a sales pitch and refer to very, very small Poodles that are often unhealthy. Reputable breeders will not advertise Teacup Poodles. 🐾

Goldpins Simon Sez ("Karly) Black Miniature Poodle
Courtesy of Mona Kurth

Chapter 3
Poodle Procurement

You've made the big decision—you know you love Poodles and you want one for your own. Now you need to ask yourself the inevitable hard questions.

▼ Can you afford a Poodle? Not including the purchase price (after all, you may get one for nothing), you can expect to spend up to $1,000 a year on food, supplies, and vet bills. Professional grooming can raise the price even more.

▼ Are you willing and able to spend time and energy playing with your Poodle, walking him, and just hanging out together around the house? A dog abandoned in even the most luxurious surroundings is not a happy dog.

If your answers are "yes," you are still not finished. You still need to decide on the right Poodle for you. What qualities are most important to you—size, playfulness, health, age, temperament, looks? Do you want a dog to show, or just a loyal companion? Will you expect your Poodle to be a watchdog? Do tricks? Entertain the children? Sleep in till noon? In this chapter, I'll assume that you are in the market for a well-bred puppy; later on, I'll describe some of the joys of Poodle rescue.

Source

The most important element in choosing the right Poodle is finding a reliable source. This is a matter that requires the utmost care. A Poodle—or any animal—should not be an impulse buy. Do your research; a little extra time and thought now will save you months of heartache down the road. If you are looking for a puppy, seek out a responsible breeder. This is not always a simple task; few of them advertise in the newspaper, and none will be listed in the yellow pages. Since it is almost impossible to make a living by breeding dogs carefully and responsibly, most good breeders are enjoying an expensive hobby. The price of the puppies they sell barely covers their expenses. Yet, because good breeders usually breed from their homes and profit is not their main motive, the price you will pay for a good dog is usually no more than from a commercial establishment, and you'll almost always get a better quality dog.

To find such a breeder, you need to ask around. Ask your veterinarian, groomer, or knowledgeable friends. Check with your local All-Breed Kennel Club or Poodle Club. If you don't know how to find a breeder locally, go to the American Kennel Club's (AKC's) website (www.akc.org) for more information. Go a nearby dog show and check the program to see if anyone showing Poodles lives near you (you can get a schedule online from the AKC). Take a look at their Poodles and see if this is the general type of dog you would like. Ignore the clip, if possible, and look for substance and style.

If you do see a dog you like, pick a quiet time (usually after the judging) to ask questions of the exhibitors. If they are hurried, ask for a business card and make arrangements to call or visit later on.

Poodle Pundit

Every once in a while you'll run into someone who is truly rude to spectators. Pity these people for not comprehending that they are exhibiting at a dog show and not a private viewing for their friends (if they have any). Seek out a more courteous person who is willing to be an ambassador for the breed. 🐾

Although you may get lucky and happen upon a likely litter at just the right time, you will almost certainly have to wait to get your puppy—maybe for as long as several months. If you insist upon a particular sex or color, your wait may be even longer.

Please note—carefully—that going to a show breeder does not mean that you will be getting a show dog. A person interested in showing dogs will most likely take the time and care to have the necessary genetic testing done to prove that the dogs available are healthy and sound. Therefore, you will get a well-bred, healthy animal who has been tested, evaluated, and brought up in a home environment. Don't rely only on the pedigree—it is merely a history of the dog's ancestry, not a guarantee of quality or health.

Mardi Gras Poodles   *Courtesy of Jeanne Kennedy*

Pet Quality

If you're not planning on showing, explain to the breeder that you are looking for a "pet-quality" Poodle. This doesn't mean there will be anything wrong with the puppy; it means that, in the breeder's opinion, the puppy will not achieve a championship in the show ring. Eyes that are too light, a nose of the wrong color, or ears hung too high or low are just a few of the non-important factors which may limit a dog's show-worthiness—but make him just right for your home.

The word *pet* means something different to a breeder than it does to you. For a breeder, *pet* means "non-show quality." To you, it probably means a dog you are going to take home and love. If you are thinking about showing your Poodle as a hobby, tell the breeder you are looking for a "show-quality" dog. Don't use the word *pet*—even though he will be one. And who knows? A show-quality pup may strike your fancy. The breeder may offer to "co-own" him with you, which usually means that the breeder makes the arrangements to show him, while you get to keep him as a pet most of the time.

Whether you're buying a Poodle for a pet or for show, a responsible breeder will ask you many questions about your home situation and may even want to speak with your veterinarian. Although these questions can seem intrusive, a good breeder is looking out for the welfare of her dogs. Ask a lot of questions yourself, even if you think they are silly.

The breeder may use terminology like "inbreeding," "line-breeding," and "out-crossing." If you're not familiar with such terms, ask what they mean. Your questions show the breeder that you care about what you're doing and want to learn.

Poodle Parlance

"Inbreeding" refers to mating between two very close relatives, like sibling to sibling or father to daughter. Although it sounds awful, when it is done between two genetically sound animals the breeder gets a desired uniformity of type. "Line-breeding" refers to the breeding of more distant relatives, and is very common. In "outcrossing," the breeder mates two animals who are unrelated or very distantly related. This is sometimes done to bring fresh blood into a breeding program. 🐾

Asking the Right Questions

When you have found a good breeder with an available litter, make an appointment to see the puppies. Don't go empty handed. Bring a "buyer's worksheet" with you. At the top of the worksheet, write the breeder's name, address, and phone number. Then write down the questions you want answered, including the age, sex, color, and prices of various puppies. The most important questions concern health. You'll need proof that the puppies' parents have been tested for hereditary eye diseases, hip dysplasia (especially for larger Poodles), sebaceous adenitis (for Standard Poodles), and von Willebrand's disease. Ask about the incidence of bloat, epilepsy, Addison's disease, diabetes, thyroid problems, thrombocytopenia, and other diseases that may run in families. Ask what specific ailments or conditions the puppy's parents have had.

Ask for references from people who have purchased dogs from this breeder. Call them and ask specifically about each dog's health and temperament.

The Contract

A good breeder will offer you a contract that clearly outlines the responsibility of both seller and purchaser. Read it carefully.

If you prefer an older dog, many are available from breeders and from organizations like your local Poodle Rescue and the Humane Society or SPCA. Rescue groups and shelters are a wonderful way to acquire a pet, since you are not only filling a void in your own life, but also helping out a homeless dog by giving him the love he craves.

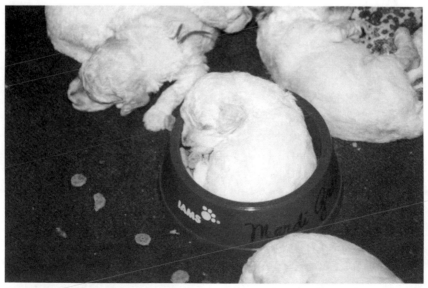

Mardi Gras Poodles   *Courtesy of Jeanne Kennedy*

Size

Personal preference aside, the main consideration in choosing which variety of Poodle you'd prefer is size. Many people admire the substance of a Standard Poodle, but keep in mind that these are large dogs requiring a great deal of exercise every day. They are best suited to country living, although a very dedicated suburban or even urban dweller can satisfy the Standard's exercise needs. Enrolling an urban Standard Poodle in agility classes is an enjoyable way to bond with your dog and work off some of his energy. You should also plan to take up jogging or bicycling.

For those whose space or time is limited, a Miniature or Toy Poodle is preferable. Miniature Poodles, although very active, are happy in a fenced yard, and Toy Poodles are eminently suited for apartment dwelling. An occasional short walk is enough outdoor exercise for these smallest of Poodles.

Poodle Precautions

Too many books state that since a small Poodle eats less than a larger one, a Toy Poodle is more economical choice. Such statements give the reader a distinctly false impression. A major expense of owning any dog is the veterinary bills, which will be about the same (and can be considerable) no matter what the size of the dog. 🐾

All ages and sizes of Poodles need your constant love and guidance. Some people make the mistake of assuming that a smaller dog will be less trouble than a larger one. This may be true, but it's not true enough to make a real difference. They may further believe that little or no training is necessary for a small dog. This way of thinking does a serious disservice to your friends, your neighbors, your dog, and yourself.

Smaller Poodles (and many other small breeds) have earned an unfortunate reputation as yippy little terrors. This can occur, but it is usually the fault of the owner, who has underestimated the intelligence and energy of their pet. Miniature and Toy Poodles need just as much training as their larger relatives, and when they get it, they behave just as well. When they do not, they become household tyrants—because no one has bothered to teach them otherwise.

Ch. Carlyn's Private Label with her brown and black puppies and helping out with a litter of white puppies while their box was being cleaned.

Courtesy of Jeanne Kennedy

Color

Some people have a preference for a particular color. Well-bred Poodles are usually not color-crossed, so all puppies in the litter will be the same solid color as their parents. Experienced breeders can mix certain color combinations safely, but if not done carefully, with a knowledge of the genetic background of each parent, the result could be parti-colored pups—which are not accepted within the breed standard, although they make perfectly charming pets.

White Poodles, for instance, should be mated only to other white or to cream Poodles. The same is usually true of apricots and silvers. Black and brown Poodles may be safely mated without fear of parti-colored pups, but to be sure of an all-brown litter, brown must be bred to brown. When a black Poodle is mated to another black Poodle, the puppies will all be black unless both parents carry a recessive gene for brown. In that case, some of the puppies may be brown.

Any solid color is acceptable according to the breed standard, and, as far as the show ring goes, the richer and purer the better. It does seem to be true that certain colors (notably black or white) are preferred to some others, at least as far as judging goes. This inclination, however, is personal, since the breed standard clearly states that any color, if pure and solid, is acceptable. A "dilute" coat of any color is not preferred.

For a pet Poodle, color makes no difference, so select as you desire. One thing to take into consideration is that a white Poodle takes more washing to keep him at his dazzling best.

Poodles of some colors (like apricot) fade as they mature; others, like Silver, are actually born black. It's important, therefore, to take a good look at the dam (mother dog). Her color will probably be that of your puppy when he grows up. The father (sire) may or may not be on the premises. Do not be concerned if he is not. Many breeders will send their females to another state to be mated with just the right male dog.

Sex

This, again, is an individual preference. A female (or "bitch") is probably easier to housetrain, and may be more trainable all around—but only maybe. The difference between individual dogs is much greater than between sexes. If you are getting a pet as opposed to a show dog, you will undoubtedly wish to have your Poodle neutered or spayed. This operation is usually less expensive for a male than for a female—otherwise costs will be the same.

Of course, there is no reason not to have your pet Poodle neutered. Done early in life, it will keep him healthier and happier. His personality will not change. An unneutered dog or unspayed bitch is not only at increased risk for a variety of cancers, but a bitch in season is a real nuisance for both the owner and the neighborhood. Unneutered males tend to stray if they are let loose.

Female dogs are less likely to roam than males, but since you will keep your Poodle in a fenced yard or on a leash, that's a fairly moot point. Males have more aggressive tendencies than do females, but a well-trained dog of either sex is never aggressive.

Choosing that Special Poodle Puppy

Now that you've selected the size, color, sex, and breeder you want, you get to choose your puppy—sometimes. Some of the puppies in the litter may have already been spoken for, and your choice may be limited. Whatever the case, choose a puppy who seems active, inquisitive, and friendly. A shy or retiring puppy may be ill or too reserved to make a good family pet. A more reserved puppy may be the right choice for a quiet single person, as your personalities may match perfectly. Choosing the right puppy depends ultimately more on intuition than on logic. I always feel that when you see the right puppy, you'll just know it.

While looking at the litter of puppies, take some time to examine the dam (and sire if present) also. These animals are the surest indication of what your puppy will look like when he reaches maturity. Looks aren't all that's important, but temperament is largely inherited, so make sure the dam exhibits the qualities you want in your own puppy. Shyness and aggression are especially heritable.

Let's Play! *Courtesy of Jeanne Kennedy*

Poodle Pundit

Sometimes a breeder may offer you an older puppy or young adult dog who may not have worked out in the show ring. Don't overlook this opportunity for getting a very nice dog at a low cost. Poodles will bond to your entire family very quickly, even if they are older when you acquire them. The same is true, of course, of a rescue dog. 🐾

The eyes and ears of the puppy should be clear and free of discharge, and the coat should look clean and healthy. The gums should be a healthy pink color, not pale or red. Your prospect should exude that delicious puppy scent. Puppies with swollen tummies may have a severe roundworm (toxocara canis) infestation. Nearly all puppies are born with roundworms, but the problem should be resolved by the time you are ready to make your choice. In male puppies, both testicles should be descended into the scrotum. Dogs with only one descended testicle should be avoided. If you can't tell, ask your vet to check for you. Make arrangements for the puppy to see your own veterinarian immediately for a general checkup to make sure that everything is in good order.

Do a little sociability test with your prospective puppy. He should follow you happily with his tail up. When you kneel down and call him, he should run to you eagerly and not fear eye contact. If you are interested in hunting or doing obedience work with your puppy, you might want to test his prey drive by gently throwing a small toy to see if he runs and retrieves it. If a puppy seems unduly frightened of a not terribly loud noise (pills shaken in a bottle or jangling change), he may not be secure.

Spend plenty of time with the litter. You may even want to return in a day or two to look again. A good breeder will not hurry you or pressure you into buying a certain puppy. On the other hand, it's possible that the puppy you have your eye on will be sold out from under you unless you put down a deposit or make special arrangements with the breeder.

Stacking Lessons: Breeders constantly evaluate the potential of each puppy in a litter, but at 5 weeks of age, it's hard to say just what Emma will look like as an adult.

Courtesy of Kristi Murdock

What If I Want Two Puppies?

This is probably not a good idea. Not only will you be looking at double the veterinarian bills and a lot more trouble, but you may also find that two puppies bond much more strongly to each other than to you. The biggest disadvantage, however, is that while you'll have two cute puppies now, later on you'll have two very old Poodles. Caroline Hair, breeder of Cara Hai Poodles, told me, "Losing one dog is sad enough without having two go at the same time . . . I usually encourage people to wait until the first dog is four or five years old, then get a puppy. The older dog can make training easier by showing the puppy the ropes. When the first dog is geriatric, the second is still relatively young."

Pre-Owned Poodles

Okay, I just spent a lot of time talking about how to get the very finest Poodle puppy for your home. I talked about finding a good breeder, investigating genetic diseases, and a host of other things that will help you obtain the best Poodle for your money. Now I am going to change tactics and suggest that you consider another source for your Poodle: your local animal shelter or rescue group. Why? You won't be able to show such an animal; it may have phobias, a medical problem, or bad habits. (Of course this can be true of even the best-bred dog.) It may be a much older dog than you planned on having. And although it will certainly come cheaper than a dog from a reputable breeder, you'll end up spending just as much money on him in short order—or even more if you decide to take in a dog with special medical needs. So why would you possibly entertain such an idea in the first place?

Making a Difference

Adopting a dog from a shelter or rescue makes a tangible difference in more lives than you can imagine. First of all, every shelter, pound, and rescue group in the country is full to capacity. Every day, thousands of dogs are put to sleep—not because they are ill or vicious, but because there is no room for them. Few dogs who go to shelters find homes, and every 6.7 seconds a dog is euthanized. Rescue groups have better success, but most are too small to take in large numbers of dogs. When you accept a shelter or rescue dog into your home, you'll save two lives by making room for another dog who may now have a chance at life.

The difference you'll make in your new dog's life is immeasurable. You may be providing his first toy, first bed, and first love; you may be taking him for his first walk, his first romp, or his first visit. You may be giving him the first kind words he's ever heard.

But the biggest difference will be in your own life. The feeling of having saved a life will enhance and enrich your own. The love you get from a previously unloved and unwanted dog easily matches puppy devotion. Because Poodles combine the qualities of loyalty and adaptability, your new dog will not pine for his former owners, who probably neglected him, but will transfer his abiding affection to you. Besides, you will be absolutely assured of going to heaven.

What Is Poodle Rescue?

If I've sold you on the idea of rescuing a needy dog, your best bet is to contact your local Poodle rescue. Such organizations are maintained by heroic people who know and love Poodles and can usually provide all kinds of extra support and help to adopters. In addition, many animal shelters work with breed rescues directly. The Poodle Club of America or your local Poodle club can provide information about the rescue nearest you.

You can also check out the World Wide Web. Many Poodle rescue groups have photos of available dogs, and some take applications right over the Internet.

Where Do Rescue Groups Get their Poodles?

Sometimes animal shelters turn over purebred dogs to local breed rescues. Sometimes a dog's former owner has died. Sometimes the dog was found as stray, or collected because of owner abuse. Sometimes people decide they no longer want a dog. I have seen dogs given up for the following reasons:

▼ We're moving.
▼ He pees on the floor.
▼ We're getting a divorce and neither of us wants him.
▼ He's too big/small.
▼ He's too active/lazy.
▼ He chases the cat.
▼ He barks too much when chained outside.
▼ The other dog doesn't like him.
▼ He chews the furniture.
▼ The kids want a different kind of dog.
▼ My husband keeps kicking him; I'm afraid he'll kill him.
▼ He costs too much to feed and groom.
▼ He's too old. We're going to replace him with a puppy.
▼ We're tired of him.

Does This Mean I'd Get a Free Poodle?

Probably not. Rescue groups depend on donations and fundraisers. Many of the dogs they receive require extensive medical care, usually due to mistreatment or neglect; it's not unusual for them to spend $1,000 to treat one dog. Your cost to adopt, however, will be considerably less—usually in the $100–$200 range. Some rescues charge less for older dogs and mixed-breed poodles.

Will My Poodle Be Guaranteed Healthy?

Most Rescue Poodles are healthy when they are adopted out. They will also be spayed or neutered. In any case, a good rescue organization will provide a full health disclosure.

Will There Be An Application and a Contract?

A reliable rescue organization will provide an application. The Poodle Rescue Service for Versatility in Poodles, for instance, has a 5-page, 61 question application. This assures us that the rescue is interested in finding the best possible homes for its charges.

A reliable rescue issues a contract the same way a good breeder does. Nearly all rescue groups stipulate that you will return the dog to the rescue, not resell or give him away, if he does not work out. Most rescues also require a home visit and vet check before adopting out a dog. The dogs they deal with have already been severely traumatized; rescue groups want to make sure that their new home will be the last one.

But I Want a Puppy

You'd be surprised at how many purebred puppies are available from rescue groups, although you should be prepared to wait. Many people buy a puppy for Christmas or on impulse, and after a few weeks (or days, in some cases) realize they have made a mistake. The breeder or pet store may refuse to take the dog back, and owners often drive it to a shelter or hand it over to a rescue.

Since entire litters are sometimes left at shelters, you may have an opportunity to select one puppy from several. Go through the same temperament testing that you would if choosing a puppy from a breeder, and be careful to select a happy, outgoing dog that is not shy or aggressive. Be aware, however, that most of these dogs have had a rough start in life and may have medical problems you should be willing to treat.

Older Dogs

Some people recognize the great value of an older animal. Puppies are cute, but unformed—and un-housetrained. An older dog is usually calmer, housetrained, and past the destructive chewing stage. They are also exceedingly grateful for a loving home of their own.

Even elderly dogs make excellent pets and usually give their owners remarkably little trouble. Most of them are happy to live out their last few years in peace, sunning themselves on the porch and going for walks around the block. An elderly friend who recently adopted an older female dog said, "We can be old ladies together."

What Can I Expect from A Rescue Dog?

Just what you'd expect from any dog: lots of love and quite a few problems. With a rescue dog, many difficulties revolve around trust issues. He has been abandoned at least once before, and may be slow to give his heart for fear of breaking it again.

Rescue dogs often come with serious psychological baggage, which is no surprise. Even a well-cared-for dog who has been loved but ends up in rescue may be terribly unhappy and disoriented. He misses his old home and doesn't understand death or moving or divorce. In fact, dogs who have been most abused often make the best pets, because they are so happy to have a good home at last.

Common problems can include dominance issues, shyness, chewing, obsessive-compulsive behavior, barking, poor health, and most frequently, separation anxiety. These concerns will not magically disappear. The dog does not know he's in his permanent home; as far as he's concerned, it's just another way station. Rescue dogs require particular compassion and understanding.

Introducing a New Dog

Many people choose a rescue dog for their second dog. If you are one of these folks, be sure you introduce your new dog to the family in the right way.

Even though it is usually recommended that strange dogs meet on a leash, leashes can actually trigger aggression. I always introduce the new dog in a large fenced area—off lead. If you think the new dog may be the aggressor, have them meet in your old dog's area. If the reverse, remove the old dog from the area and have the new dog there before you bring the old one back. Allow both dogs off lead immediately in the large fenced area. (I keep a heavy-duty water cannon on hand just in case.)

Squabbles may occur, but they are usually self-limiting, and non-damaging. This is normal behavior—just a dog's way to find where he stands in the canine hierarchy. Obviously, you don't want blood drawn, but a little barking, snarling and chasing around is common. A large area reduces territoriality, and, more important, gives the submissive dog a place to run to.

If you do use the leash method, don't have the Poodles simply stand and stare at each other. If possible, enlist the help of a friend and start your dogs off for a walk together, each dog led by one person. If you notice any untoward behavior, distract them by turning them away from each other. Use a treat to divert their attention, if necessary.

If sibling rivalry develops among your dogs, take note of which is the dominant dog and favor him. I know this sounds unjust, but dogs play by their own rules. If you misguidedly attempt to impose democracy on Poodles, they will reward you with ceaseless squabbling. Pay homage to their aristocratic heritage and let the top dog be top dog. This means the dominant dog eats first, is greeted first, gets petted first, and goes in and out of doors first. You'll be surprised to see how well everything works out.

Rescue Dog's Plea

I know I'm not your dream dog. Maybe I'm the wrong color. Maybe I'm too big or too small. Maybe you think I'm too old. Or too sick. Or I bark too much, and get scared when no one is home and chew things. I know I am too thin, and sometimes I have accidents in the house, even though I don't mean to. But please look deeply into my sad eyes and see the dog I really am. I can love so much. My heart is as big as all outdoors. Is yours? Can you find room in your heart to match the love in mine? 🐾

Chapter 4
Your Poodle Puppy

The period between 6 weeks and 6 months of age is the most important developmental period for your puppy. Nearly all major behavior patterns are learned then, and many of them are learned from you. Although mistakes are inevitable, it's better to do as many things right as possible.

Your Poodle Comes Home

The big day has arrived; your new Poodle puppy is coming home with you. In many ways, it's like bringing home a baby—except that, in the case of the Poodle, it is truly forever. You must plan to keep your Poodle for all of his life. He will never grow up, go to college, get a paying job, or get married. You are together for keeps.

Remember that although this is a thrilling day for you, your new puppy may not be so happy about the experience. He's being taken from the only home he's ever known, put in a car where he may get sick, and brought to a new, strange-smelling place with people—and possibly other pets—he's never seen before. Don't blame him if he's not as overjoyed as you'd like him to be. On the other hand, Poodles are good-natured and adaptable. Given the opportunity, your puppy will quickly bond to his new family.

Puppies of all breeds are likely to make trouble—for you and for themselves. To avoid a bad accident, you need to Poodle-proof your home before your Poodle arrives. See Chapter 6 for more details.

Basic Poodle Paraphernalia

Make a checklist of everything you'll need before your pup comes home. Be sure to include the following: crate, bowls, collar and lead, toys, brush and comb, and a first aid kit.

The Crate

The best early investment you can make for your new puppy is a crate. Think of it as his Poodle pad. The crate will be his bed, refuge, and traveling house. It should be a sturdy one made of wire or heavy duty plastic, and big enough for your dog to stand up and turn around in. If it's too big, however, it won't work as well for housetraining purposes, since he may be encouraged to use part of it as a bathroom. You could get a large, grown-up crate with dividers, or you could borrow a small crate from a friend during your Poodle's puppyhood.

Crates resemble a dog's natural den. Dogs go into them willingly and retire there during times of stress. While some dogs seem to prefer the ventilation and clear view afforded by a wire cage, others crave the darkness and security of the fiberglass type. Many owners have and use both.

Some people don't like the word *crate*, convinced that it sounds too much like *cage*. That's all right—don't call it a crate. Call it an indoor kennel or anything else you want, but make sure you have one. It is an indispensable item. Not only is it the ideal puppy housetraining device, but it will come in handy later on when you travel with your dog, or when he must remained confined to quarters, such as during illness or recuperation. A dog that is already crate-trained will travel with ease and accept necessary confinement with grace.

As long as you don't use the crate as a babysitter or keep your puppy confined in it too long, he'll regard the crate as a refuge. He can sleep in the crate all night if you like, but during the day he needs to be active. Puppies suffer developmental problems if kept cooped up for more than a couple of hours at a time.

Collar and Lead

Poodles usually do best in a round collar, which is least likely to rub the fur on the neck. I don't like chain collars for everyday use for any breed; on Poodles they can be especially troublesome because of the Poodle's prolific hair. Be sure you get a collar that fits your puppy now; don't be cheap and get one he'll grow into. This is a dangerous practice, because your Poodle could slip or strangle on a loose collar. The collar should be snug but not tight. You should be able to slide two or three fingers between the collar and his neck comfortably.

Both the collar and lead should be made of fairly lightweight material. Never use a chain lead; they are heavy and noisy, and can snap without warning. Nylon, cotton, or leather are all reasonable options, and the choice depends on your preference. Obviously, the smaller the puppy, the lighter the lead should be. I keep several leashes around the house, and one in the car too. You never know when you'll need one.

Identification Tag

This is one of the most critical pieces of Poodle paraphernalia. If your Poodle becomes lost, it's important that you get him back as quickly as possible. You can buy a metal or plastic tag to attach to his collar, or you can get a collar with your phone number embroidered on it. No matter what other kinds of identification your dog carries, his vital information should be readily visible on his collar. It is a fact that most dogs with visible I.D. tags are returned to their owners. Most dogs without them are not.

Many people are now going the microchip or tattoo route as well. Microchips can be implanted in puppies as young as 8 weeks of age, and your dog does not need to be put to sleep to have the procedure done. Using a large-gauge needle, the vet inserts the chip between your dog's shoulder blades. All methods of identifying your dog are good, and it's not a bad idea to double or triple up on identification. The more kinds of I.D. your pet carries, the greater the likelihood of his getting home to you again.

Always keep a few recent, clear photos of your Poodle handy. If he disappears, you'll want to plaster the neighborhood with fliers—and the sooner the better.

Toys

Your Poodle puppy will enjoy playing with toys, just like a child. Be sure they are safe; toys meant for dogs are usually best. Look for tough, washable items that won't break or splinter. It's best to get toys the puppy will easily be able to identify as his. The toughness of the toy is critical; toys that are too fragile can break and lodge in your dog's esophagus or intestine. Toys that are too hard can break his teeth. Any object that is harder than enamel is dangerous for your Poodle to chew.

Ferrous, 9 weeks, Red/Apricot Standard   *Courtesy of Vikki Kauffman*

The knotted dental ropes and hard (but not rocklike) rubber toys found in your pet supply store are a good choice. Be careful of balls—small ones can become stuck in your puppy's throat. It's best to pick up the ball and put it safely away when the game is over.

Poodle Peril

Beware of battery-powered toys. Batteries can kill your Poodle if ingested. If you must use such a toy, supervise your dog constantly. Even then, I don't think it's such a good idea. 🐾

Grooming Stuff

Puppyhood is the time to get your Poodle used to the never-ending grooming process; hopefully the breeder has started him on the right path at about 6 weeks of age. His face and feet may have been clipped even earlier. If he gets used to the idea early, even though you're not doing much to him yet, he'll be a much happier Poodle later on—and more pleasant to deal with as well. Puppy hair is indeed soft, but don't be fooled; it will grow coarse as the puppy matures.

For basic grooming, you'll need a stainless steel comb, a bristle brush, and a slicker brush. A slicker brush has curved metal teeth. The best Poodle combs have widely-spaced, rounded teeth, which won't irritate his skin.

Brush your puppy every day with the bristle brush. Make sure you get right down to the skin, where mats may form, but try not to irritate the skin itself. See Chapter 8 for particulars.

Bowls

Your Poodle will also need two stainless steel bowls; one for food and one for water. I prefer stainless steel because it doesn't crack and allow bacteria to flourish. It's easy to clean and keeps water colder longer than plastic does. They're also impervious to the inevitable puppy chewing. Stoneware bowls are acceptable, but even these can crack. Wash the bowls in hot soapy water after every meal, just as you do your own plates.

Keep a plastic doggy mat under the bowl to keep mess to a minimum. Even the elegant Poodle is not always a delicate eater.

Complete Pet First Aid Kit

Be prepared for any emergency—keep a first aid kit for your pet on hand. You can keep your supplies in a lightweight tackle or tool box. This list provides you with a pretty comprehensive list of what you need to stock it well. On the inside of the box, write down the correct dosage of each medication for your Poodle, and for each of your other pets as well. That way, you won't have to try to remember what's what in case of emergency. If you have Poodles (or other dogs) of more than one size, figure out the correct dosages in advance for each dog. Keep your first aid medications up to date—check the expiration dates periodically.

▼ Ace or CoFlex bandage

▼ Activated charcoal (4 tbsp. per dose)

▼ Adhesive tape and gauze

▼ Alcohol prep pads

▼ Antibiotic ointment

▼ Benadryl (antihistamine—1–2mg. per pound every 8 hrs.)

▼ Betadine solution (**not** surgical scrub or skin cleanser) or Novalsan (veterinary product) for wound cleansing

▼ Buffered aspirin (5 mg. per pound every 12 hrs.)

▼ Cold pack

▼ Cotton balls

▼ Ear and oral syringes

▼ Epsom salts

▼ Eye wash

▼ Gauze sponges

▼ Hydrogen peroxide (emetic—1-3 tsp. every 10 mins. until dog vomits)

- ▼ Imodium (1 mg. per 15 pounds, once or twice daily—available as liquid or tablet), Kaopectate (1 ml. per 1 pound every 2 hrs.), or Pepto Bismol liquid (1 tsp. per 5 pounds every 6 hrs.) or tablets (1/4 tablet per 20 pounds 3-4 times a day)

- ▼ Magnifying glass

- ▼ Milk of magnesia (as an antacid, give 5–10 ml. per kg. every 4–6 hrs.; as a laxative, give 15–20 ml. per kg. daily until effective.)

- ▼ Mineral oil (laxative—5–30 ml per day)

- ▼ Petroleum jelly

- ▼ Povidone-iodine (Betadine) ointment

- ▼ Rectal thermometer (canine)

- ▼ Rubbing alcohol

- ▼ Safety pins

- ▼ Soft cloth muzzle

- ▼ Scissors (small blunt-end type)

- ▼ Splints

- ▼ Tweezers or hemostat

Extras

- ▼ Here are a few items you may wish to purchase as well:

- ▼ A bed. You may wish to have, in addition to the crate, a bed for your Poodle to snooze in. This is fine, but be sure it is made of some sturdy, non-chewable substance. Be aware that your puppy may gobble the bedding.

Poodle Precautions

A wicker basket is a bad choice for a bed, because it is so attractive to some Poodle puppies that they begin to devour it. Wicker can break off into sharp fragments that can lodge in or pierce your puppy's esophagus, stomach, or intestines. ❧

▼ A pooper-scooper. Several varieties are available. The advantage of a pooper-scooper is that it saves your back and keeps your nose distant from what you're picking up. On the other hand, a pooper-scooper is never around at the right time, and it's silly to carry one on a walk. You can purchase little baggie-type pooper-scoopers at any discount retailer, but a plain old sandwich bag works about as well and is much cheaper.

▼ Carpet deodorizer for pet odors. It never hurts to prepare for the worst.

▼ A grooming table. This is almost a necessity for proper Poodle care. Even if your Poodle will be going to a professional groomer, you'll need to brush him thoroughly several times a week. Save your back and get one.

▼ Nail clippers (guillotine type) or nail grinder.

▼ Good quality scissors.

▼ A baby gate. This will help to keep your puppy confined to certain rooms. Some companies make ones specially designed for dogs.

First Things First

Before you even bring your new puppy in the door, make sure you take him to the place where his latrine will be. He probably won't make it that far, but at least he won't start right off urinating in the house. You'll get enough of that over the next few days. Take him to the same spot every time until he gets the idea.

Feeding Your Puppy

You'll want to keep your puppy on the same diet he has been eating at the breeder's. Sudden dietary change can be rough on a dog's digestive system, and in the case of a new puppy, the adventure of leaving his litter to live in his new home is about as much change as he can handle. His familiar food will be a source of comfort to him. If you do want to make a change, do so gradually over the course of several days by mixing the new food in with the old.

Go a little light on the first meal; the puppy will be excited with all the new sights and smells and you don't want him to get a tummyache. He won't starve.

Puppies require a much larger amount of food for their body weight than do adult dogs; their tummies are small, however, and can only hold a very limited amount of food at one sitting. Feed your new puppy 4 times a day; you can gradually reduce the number of meals to 2 daily as he matures. Some people feed adults dogs only once a day (which approximates their feeding schedule in the wild), but I have found that twice-a-day feedings make for a happier dog.

Feed your puppy in a quiet corner, away from kitchen traffic—and other pets, if you have them. However, you puppy should get used to your being near him while he eats, and should accept your petting him while he has dinner. You do not want to encourage food-guarding behavior; sooner or later, some kid will run up and try to grab something out of his mouth, and this is the time when a snap or bite is most likely to occur. Preventive training is the best defense. If your puppy gets used to surrendering whatever he has in his mouth to you, you'll have a safer pet. Luckily, because of their retriever heritage, Poodles have "soft mouths," which, along with their innate gentleness, makes them safe pets around children. Of course, you will counsel your children not to pester the puppy while he is eating.

Your puppy will normally eat his dinner quite quickly. If he seems very hungry, you may give him a bit more. It's impossible to say exactly how much to feed; it depends on the size and activity level of the puppy. Weigh him frequently and check with your veterinarian. If he seems to be getting pudgy, cut down on his food intake or increase his activity level until he appears fit.

Poodles and Children

Poodles, in general, make excellent family pets. If you take reasonable precautions, the introductions will go smoothly. Remember that the children and the new dog will be curious about each other—maybe too much so. They may knock each other over, roll on each other, and steal each other's toys. Never allow young children and dogs to play unsupervised. Clip your Poodle's nails; more damage to children results from scratches than from bites. Remember, however, that tiny puppies and Toy

Make sure your child understands that your dog is not a toy.

Poodles of any age are fragile. Teach your children to handle them properly and always supervise their behavior.

Training Children to Be Pet-Friendly

Children need firm instruction in how to be kind to animals. Some are just unaware of how annoying their teasing can be. They don't usually mean to be cruel; they just don't know any better. Sometimes children chase a small puppy relentlessly, or scream in its ear like banshees. Such behavior is inappropriate and potentially dangerous.

If children misbehave around animals, it is often the fault of their parents. I have seen adults sit around, seemingly oblivious, while their kids pummel, bite, scratch, or pull the hair or tail of a dog. Children copy their parents' behavior. If kids see their parents slap, annoy, or neglect a dog, they will do the same. Families like this are better off with Chia Pets.

Poodle Precautions

Don't allow young children to carry the puppy. Even a careful child can drop a dog, and your puppy could be seriously injured or frightened. 🐾

Poodle Precautions

Although most children's abuse of pets is unintentional, it is sometimes deliberate. Maltreatment of animals is not only dangerous itself, but also a warning sign of future problems that may escalate. 🐾

Most of the time, though, Poodles and children are born friends. Take advantage of their natural comradeship and reward your children for responding appropriately to the dog. This is why it's also important for your children to be a regular part of training sessions. Teach them the right way to praise, work with, and play with your Poodle.

Poodles and Other Pets

Poodles generally get on well with other dogs. Cats and Poodles are also amicable, especially if they are brought up together. An adult cat might conceivably scratch a too-inquisitive puppy, but little damage is usually done. Never force the two to get acquainted by restraining the cat; they will make friends independently, if ever.

Make sure the cat has a safe place to escape to that is out of the dog's reach. If you find the pets sleeping together, you can be pretty certain that they have become fast friends.

"Tug of War"   *Courtesy of Barbara Burdick*

Isaac (red) and Ascu (white)   *Courtesy of Lou Murphy*

The First Night

Of course, your new Poodle will sleep in the house with you. Poodles are house dogs. Although some breeds take quite well to outdoor living arrangements, the Poodle is not among them. Except in exceptional circumstances (and I can't think what they might be), keeping your Poodle outdoors night and day is a cruel practice.

The first night is traditionally an ordeal that owners and puppies must suffer through. But it does not have to be a dreadful experience. It can be terrible if you insist that the new puppy sleep in his own room, which is usually the kitchen, living room, or some other place of exile. No wonder he's miserable. He's been kidnapped from his mother and his littermates by a bunch of strangers. Then there's a lot of noise and confusion, and he's put in a strange room, alone, in the dark. Why shouldn't he cry?

The solution is easy. Allow your new puppy to sleep in the bedroom with you. It is neither necessary nor advisable to terrorize him by forcing him to sleep alone in a distant part of the house. Furthermore, it will ease your housetraining chores considerably if you are close to your puppy. When you sense he is beginning to stir, you can jump right up and head outside with him.

Having your puppy sleep with your in your bedroom will not spoil him. It will simply make him aware that you are his parent and will be there to comfort him the way his own mother did. Some people allow their dogs to sleep in the bed with them. If you are entertaining this idea, start him off snuggled by your pillow. Snuggling up to your puppy will make your dog more, not less, secure. However, since I strongly advise that you crate-train your puppy, you are best off letting him sleep alongside you in his own crate. That way, he won't fall off the bed, wander around the house and get into trouble, or dial 911 and claim he is being abused.

If your puppy cries during the night, talk to him quietly until he falls asleep again. Make sure he is warm. He may wake up a time or two during the night, but this is normal. He'll soon sleep contentedly throughout the night.

Teaching Your Puppy

Poodles are, by nature, interested in pleasing you. Your new puppy can only accomplish this goal if you help him. It is your job as his new parent to let him know the basic rules. Will he be allowed in every room? Will he be allowed on furniture? On the bed? Will he be given treats between meals? Should he bark, scratch, or come to you when he wants to go out? You need to determine the answers to these and many other questions first; then you can let your puppy know what you have decided. If you don't make these decisions for him, your puppy will come to his own conclusions on these matters. Don't blame him if your choices differ.

Learning his Name

You have to name your puppy, of course. James Thurber made the following insightful comment on naming Poodles: "The word Poodle itself is bad enough, but the kennel names of individual members of the breed are worse: Tiddly Winks Thistledown of White Hollow, Twinkle Toes the Third, Little Chief Thunderfoot of Creepaway, and other unlikely compounds of whipped cream and frustrated mother love." Some people prefer human names for their dogs, like Reginald, Thelma, or Arthur. Others prefer descriptive names, like Curly, Scooter, or Snowflake. Then there are the mysterious names, like Ballyhoo, Noondrop, or Wormright. It's entirely up to you—the Poodle doesn't care. If you own two dogs, matching names are fine: Fred and Ginger, Sweet and Sour, Fetch and Carry, Ups and Daisy, Better and Worse, etc. Names should not be too much alike, though. I'd nix Teeter and Totter, Helter and Skelter, or Oodle and Noodle.

Poodle Parlance

No matter what you decide to call your dog, he will inevitably wind up with some extremely stupid nicknames, of which "babykins" and "poo-poo" are not the worst. 🐾

Whatever your decision, your puppy should always associate the mention of his name with something pleasant.

Learning to Lead

Teach your puppy to accept the lead by leaving a short one on him while he walks around the house. Supervise him the entire time so he doesn't catch the lead on anything or chew it to pieces. He will probably fuss with it a bit at first, but he'll soon get used it. When you pick up the end of the lead, call the puppy to you gently. When he toddles up to you, give him a treat and praise him. Very soon he will be happily following you everywhere. When you first take the end of the lead, though, you should follow him around for a while. Later I'll go into more advanced lessons walking on the lead. At this stage, try not to struggle with your puppy. If he resists you, don't tug the other way, but don't give in either. Lure him to you with a biscuit—he'll soon catch on that it's fun to do what he's asked. Keep puppy lessons to about five minutes a couple of times a day. That's enough for him at this time.

The Poodle Pundit

If your Poodle puppy seems inclined to chew his leash, you may want to spray an anti-chew product on it, like Bitter Apple. 🐾

Poodle Puppies and People

Early socializing can take place at home by helping your puppy accept new things and strange noises. Vacuum cleaners and dishwashers are often alarming to dogs. Keep a treat in your pocket when you work with noisy equipment and offer it to your puppy; praise him expansively if he accepts it. Don't force the issue.

Even before your puppy is fully vaccinated, you can begin to take him on walks—as long as you are careful not to let him near dog feces or unvaccinated dogs. Walks are an excellent opportunity not only for exercise, but also to have him meet new people. Make every effort to be sure that walks are a positive experience for your puppy, even if you have to bribe friends (or strangers) to help you. Hand out treats to acquaintances and ask them to pet the puppy and offer the tidbit. Include people of all races, ages, and sexes. It's especially important for him to meet babies and children.

Include people on bicycles, in uniform, or pulling a wagon. You want your puppy to look out at the world with friendly and trusting eyes. Never allow your puppy to beg for a treat, however; make sure he is sitting quietly when he accepts it.

If possible, get the strangers to pick up his paws and look at his teeth. The more your puppy gets used to being handled by all kinds of folks, the easier life will be for both of you—at the veterinarian's office, the groomers, the show ring, or a kid's party.

He should meet some strangers once or twice a week in different environments. You need to take an active part in seeking out these places. Take your vaccinated puppy everywhere dogs are allowed—parks, sidewalks, pet supply stores. Go for car rides together. All these trips help cement your bond and make him into a more secure and friendly dog.

Visiting with your Poodle Puppy

Restrict the number of outdoor ventures with your new puppy until he has had his second set of shots. That doesn't mean you shouldn't take him out at all, but you should limit his contacts with other dogs. There are many contagious diseases lurking about. Be particularly careful when going for a walk in the park, since some people do not clean up after their dogs and many viral diseases are carried in feces. (This is a good reason to check your shoes when returning from a walk—you may have stepped in something unpleasant yourself.) Of course, your curious puppy will want to investigate everything he finds.

When you do make your first visit, don't feed your puppy immediately before venturing out. The intense excitement of going on a trip may cause an upset stomach with upchucking.

This is not the best way to impress your friends with your new puppy. It's also a good idea to exercise your puppy before taking him somewhere new. The thrill of being in a new house may well make him wish to christen it. Or worse.

Puppy Kindergarten

If possible, enroll your Poodle in a puppy kindergarten class. You can usually enter your puppy at 3 months, and he will graduate at 5 months. These classes are valuable because they help your puppy develop socialization skills with both people and other dogs. (Poodles excel at this, so you may have the class valedictorian.) Your puppy will learn some elementary skills, and you'll pick up a lot of basic obedience tips. Puppy kindergarten teachers can also give you housetraining advice.

The Pubescent Poodle

Each of the three varieties of Poodles matures at a different time. The tiny Toy Poodle is mature at about 7 months, and the Miniature between 9 and 12 months. The Standard Poodle, however, is not completely grown until he is at least 18 months of age. Until your pet has achieved physical maturity, be careful about his exercise program. Doing agility work, galloping up and down stairs, or leaping off beds can damage immature joints, tendons, and ligaments.

Poodle Precautions

The Toy Poodle is particularly at risk of developing leg disorders, like Legg-Calvé-Perthes disease, so you must be especially careful with this variety regarding jumping.

Housetraining

This is such an important element in training a puppy that I've reserved an entire chapter for it (Chapter 5). One thing you should know is that Poodles are among the easiest of all breeds to housetrain. Keep telling yourself this as you mop and gingerly tiptoe through the inevitable accidents.

Chapter 5

Your Poodle Goes Potty–Housetraining

Even the elegant Poodle has a digestive system, and knows how to use it. Therefore, appropriate (meaning human-approved) elimination skills are something you must teach your puppy.

The CRAPS System of Housetraining

Here is the key to successful housetraining. I call it the CRAPS system.

▼ Containment
▼ Resolve
▼ Attention
▼ Praise
▼ Scheduling

Containment

Containment equals crates. Should you use a crate? In a word, yes. A crate is a best friend to both you and your Poodle. This first step, containment, is the essence of housetraining—but it must be used in moderation. Forcing a dog to stay in a crate for too long a period defeats the very purpose of crate training. He can only control his bladder for so long, and if left in a crate for an extended period of time he will be forced to urinate in it. This, in turn, breaks down the natural inhibitions he has about urinating in his bedroom, and soon you'll have more problems than before.

Practice putting your puppy in the crate for brief periods when you are home with him. Give him a toy or snack to work on while he's in there. This will help him learn that the crate with a pleasant place to be. One enjoyable snack is a Kong toy filled with peanut butter or melted cheese.

The Poodle Pundit

It's a dog world axiom that a puppy up to 8 months can control his bowels and bladder for as many hours as his age in months, plus one. Thus, a 2-month-old puppy should be able to be continent for 3 hours. However, these estimations were developed for larger breeds. A Toy Poodle cannot hold out as long as a Standard in this regard, and it's unfair to expect him to do so. 🐾

Even if your Poodle somehow manages to hang on longer than is good for him, you may be courting future disaster in the form of bladder stones.

I think that 4 hours is the maximum time a dog should be left in a crate. There is more to consider here than whether or not the dog will urinate in the house. You need to consider his psychological needs and his need for exercise. Dogs are complex creatures, and the highly intelligent Poodle cannot bear the attendant psychological deprivation that accompanies long periods of being crated.

Poodles are also highly active dogs that need plenty of exercise; they don't get it in a crate. If you must crate your dog for longish periods, be absolutely sure that you exercise him both before and after his period of confinement. If this means getting up earlier in the morning to go for a walk or run with your dog, then do so.

If you must be gone for longer periods, please help your dog by hiring a dog walker to take care of his potty needs.

Resolve

Be patient. Your Poodle puppy has a tiny bladder and almost no bladder or anal sphincter control—which he won't have until he is at least 4 months old. When you combine these factors, it becomes clear that puppy housetraining is a job that requires your constant attention. But take my word for it, if you do everything (or even most things) correctly at the beginning, the entire process will not take long. Remember that you are dealing with an intelligent and eager-to-please pet. If you do your part and make clear what you want, your Poodle will go out of his way to do his part. A puppy is housetrained when he knows what you want and makes every effort to comply. The fact that he can't wait as long as an older dog doesn't mean he's not trained; it means he has reached his limit.

Attention

One mark of the astute dog owner is figuring out the signs of impending elimination. While the puppy is still learning how to tell you he wants to go, it's up to you to figure it out on your own. Can you outsmart your Poodle?

Common signs of an impending event include circling the floor, paw or mouth licking, and whining. The last behavior is especially useful and one you want to encourage, since you don't have to be in the same room with your dog to get the signal.

Puppies often don't think of going until it's an emergency, so you may just want to pick up your dog and carry him out. This will prevent an accident happening on the way to the door, which is a fairly common occurrence.

The Poodle Pundit

Toy Poodles have more difficulty in acquiring housetraining skills than do larger ones—not because they are slower on the uptake, but because their tiny bladders and bowels need more frequent relief. They also have a higher metabolic rate. You must take a small dog outside to eliminate more often than you would a larger one. 🐾

Praise

When your puppy succeeds in accomplishing his mission, praise him lavishly. A sedate pat on the head and a "good boy" will not do. You must go crazy with joy and exuberant praise. If you have time, let him play a bit before you bring him inside—this will function as a reinforcement and extra reward. If you take him directly inside afterwards, he'll respond by delaying the precipitating event as long as possible once outside, since he'll undoubtedly be enjoying himself.

Scheduling

Keep to a schedule. Eight-week old puppies should go out every couple of hours. Puppies new to the household should go out even more frequently, as nervousness and excitement stimulate their bladders. Most adult dogs can be left alone for 8 hours, but this is as variable as it is with people.

Poodle Precautions

Don't leave food out all day long for your un-house-trained dog; it can mess up his elimination schedule. 🐾

When your Poodle knows that he can depend upon you to take him out at regular times (dogs have clocks in their heads), he'll be more inclined to wait for that moment. If he doesn't have a clue if or when you're going to take him out, he may feel as if he has nothing to wait for. Might as well go now as later.

A strict schedule should apply to eating times as well, since the two events—eating and elimination—are connected. If you have to leave your dog alone all day and he isn't able to wait that long, think about hiring a dogwalking or petsitting service. Or take some of your unused vacation time. Your Poodle will appreciate the company, too.

It's best to select a particular spot you want to Poodle to use as his bathroom. This reduces lawn stains and the chance that you will step in something unpleasant.

Accompany your puppy outside; do not let him wander aimlessly in the yard. If you do that, you won't know whether he has succeeded or not. Also, if left outside unsupervised, your puppy will undoubtedly find it such an interesting and exciting place that he'll completely forget why he went outdoors in the first place. A less adventuresome puppy may just sit down on the back steps and wait for you to join him.

The best plan is to slip a lead on the puppy and walk outside with him. He'd rather be with you anyway, and your company will make his outdoor duty seem less like an exile and more like a walk. It isn't a walk, however, so don't allow him to toddle around aimlessly; keep him focused. I find it helps to encourage the puppy to walk in circles in the area you have selected as his bathroom. Praise him when he succeeds.

The Poodle Pundit

On hot summer days, remember that your Poodle will undoubtedly be drinking more water. Consequently, he'll need to go out more frequently. Do not remove his water dish in hopes that he won't need to urinate so much; you'll only succeed in tormenting the poor creature with thirst. However, feeding your dog dry food rather than canned will reduce his need to urinate frequently. 🐾

If you cannot teach your Poodle to bark when he wants in or out, you can buy a Doggie Doorbell designed to prevent scratching. With such devices, a pad is placed on either side of your door at dog-height. When your pet touches the pad, a built-in wireless transmitter activates a door chime. Alternatively, you can install a pet door. Or you can train your dog to come and sit in front of you when he wishes to go out, as some owners do.

Paper Training?

This is not a good idea. Paper training adds another step (a generally useless one) to the housetraining project. In paper training, you are asking your puppy to learn two new behaviors, one of which is supposed to replace the other. First, you are asking him to use paper rather than the bare floor or carpet. After he gets that down pat, you then change your mind, get rid of the familiar papers, and tell him to go outdoors. It is much easier to teach him to go outdoors right away. It requires a little more work from you, since you must be ready to leap up and race to the door at the slightest hint that your Poodle's digestive process is in overdrive, but, if done correctly and consistently, the whole ordeal will be pretty much over in a week.

The Poodle Pundit

Toy and Miniature Poodles can be trained to use a "dog box," which is similar in design to a cat's litter box. 🐾

Accidents Do Happen

If an accident does happen, assume that it is an accident and don't go ballistic, or even scold your puppy. Wipe it up without comment. If the accident occurs on a rug, use an enzyme cleaner and follow the directions on the label. It's usually best to clean up the mess out of the puppy's sight.

Scolding your Poodle, especially after the fact, will just confuse him. He will assume that you are scolding him for pooping, not for going in the wrong place. Since he can't stop himself from pooping, he will be forced to find secret places to do it. Then you'll be wandering all around the house, wrinkling your nose and exclaiming, "I know there's dog poop around here somewhere!" Of course, you'll find it eventually—or perhaps your guests will.

Poodle Precautions

Never rub your Poodle's nose in his excrement; this is a form of punishment that is dirty, cruel, and ineffective. And never strike your Poodle for any reason—least of all for a household accident. Doing so will only make him afraid of you, and will do nothing to change the behavior. 🐾

I have a suspicion, although I can't prove it, that scolding a dog for pooping inappropriately encourages him to start eating the evidence himself. If this happens, you'll have not one but two unfortunate habits you'll need to help him break. Some dogs acquire this habit, called coprophagy, anyway, but I believe scolding a dog for housetraining mistakes can be a factor in producing it, especially in cases where dogs consume their own feces.

Correcting a Mistake

If you catch your Poodle in the act, grab a leash (you should have several, one hanging on each available doorknob) and cry, "Out, out!" Then race outside with him and praise him for finishing outdoors. If you actually pick up the puppy, he will probably stop going while you're en route—but I can't guarantee it.

Some people tout the advantages of household vinegar for cleaning up urine. This works very well if you don't mind a spot smelling of dog urine and vinegar. Your best bet is one of the newer enzyme cleaners like Nature's Miracle. They really do work.

Poodle Precautions

Never use an ammonia-based cleaner to remove a dog urine stain. Since ammonia smells like urine to a dog, you'll only succeed in making your dog think that's a good place to eliminate. 🐾

Walking Your Dog

Your dog will often find it necessary to eliminate while on your daily walk. Carry a plastic baggie with you to pick up the waste, then dispose of it in an appropriate container. If you don't see one, carry it home with you. Never, under any circumstance, leave the pile unattended to. Not only is it illegal to do so in many jurisdictions, but it is also thoughtless and rude. No one wants to even look at dog poop, much less step in it. So many dog owners ignore this basic principle that many localities now ban dogs from public parks and other places. If we dog owners were more responsible for our dogs' habits, perhaps we would be allowed to take them more places.

When Peeing is More Than Just Peeing

Unlike human beings (well, unlike most civilized human beings), dogs have discovered a use for urination that goes far beyond simple elimination. This is what I call the urination subtext.

Submissive Urination

This is a common behavior in rescued dogs, puppies, and dogs introduced into a household where there are dominant dogs. It can also occur when a shy or abused animal is placed among strangers.

If your dog is engaged in submissive urination, the first thing you should do is ignore it. Never scold the dog; in fact, don't pay any attention at all. Specifically, avoid eye contact with the miscreant. Dogs regard eye contact as a threat or a reward—and you don't want to give either message. Just walk off and clean it up later. The less response he gets to such behavior, the less likely she will be to repeat it. It may take a while, but gradually a submissive dog will acquire the self-confidence to break the habit on his own.

Dominant Urination

Unneutered males often develop the unpleasant habit of "marking" their territory. This can even occur in the house if there is another dog around. I have observed this behavior (although usually outdoors) in dominant bitches as well. It may also crop up if there's been a change in family structure and the dominant partner leaves. The dog may decide that it's his turn to lead.

Poodle Potpourri

The dominant urination subtext also applies—to a lesser extent—to defecation. I have seen many an unneutered male "dis" his rival by pooping directly in front of him, especially when the latter was penned up and unable to retaliate. 🐾

Exuberant Urination

Sometimes your Poodle, especially as a puppy, is so excited to see you that he just can't hold it another instant. The best way to react to this behavior is by not reacting at all. If you return the greeting too enthusiastically, your Poodle will get an incorrect message. Be calm, nonchalant even, as you greet your dog. Walk off into another room and examine your mail. In a few minutes, when the dog is a little calmer, pet him and greet him. Then take him out.

Medical Causes

Certain medical conditions manifest themselves through increased urination, urinary incontinence, or difficulty in urination. Elderly females often dribble, especially at night while they are sleeping. Cushing's disease, bladder stones, chronic kidney failure, brain or spinal cord injuries, diabetes, and certain medications can all affect urination patterns.

If you notice any changes or abnormalities in your Poodle's elimination habits, note them carefully and consult your veterinarian. Bring a sample to the office with you if possible.

Lawn Spots

Those yellow and brown spots you see all over your lawn are burns from urine and feces. They are just another reason for getting your Poodle to use one corner of the yard as a bathroom; at least you can reduce the damage that way.

Besides keeping your yard picked up regularly, you can add products like Grasssaver or G-Whiz to your dog's diet. They act to neutralize your dog's urine and control odors. Other products, like Spot Check and Green-Um, will help reestablish grass growth when sprayed or sprinkled on the damaged area. If you actually catch your dog in the act, rinse the grass—but not the dog—immediately with 2 or 3 gallons of water.

A good chemical remedy is K-9 Turf, which is safe for both pets and kids. It's an all-natural product that doubles as a lawn fertilizer. Use it once a month and your problems should be over. Other good products include Spot Check and Dogonit. Dogonit gets rid of winter salt damage, too.

Photo by Catherine Haake

Chapter 6
Poodle-Proofing Your Pad

All dogs get into trouble. Poodles, however, are far too smart to get into trouble; they get you into trouble instead. For example, a normal puppy is likely to chew up a houseplant and make himself ill; Poodle puppies are far more likely to pull an important contract off the kitchen room table, urinate on it, then rip it shreds, thus jeopardizing your job. So keep all papers (and houseplants too) out of the reach of your curious puppy.

Your entire house and yard present infinite opportunities for puppy adventures and misadventures. Although some dangers can be avoided by crating, you can't always leave your dog in a crate. Nor can you count on his resisting every temptation. You'll need to compromise by training him as much as you can while removing as many hazards as possible.

Imperiled Indoors

Electricity

Puppies love to chew; it's one of the ways they learn about their environment. Electricity is something, however, that you don't really want them to experience first-hand. Electrical cords are a great danger to dogs. Although Poodles are less likely to electrocute themselves than are other dogs, they are liable to chew an electrical cord down to the bare wire, stuff it behind the sofa, and wait for the house to catch on fire. To give Poodles their due, they will probably sound the alarm when the house begins smoking, after having removed themselves to safety via the dog door. All electrical cords should be attached to the baseboard where they are inconspicuous, or removed completely from your Poodle's reach.

The Poodle Pundit

Check around your local department or hardware store. Lots of items labeled as baby-proofers work equally well to protect dogs. 🐾

Extension cords that trail across the center of the floor are especially tempting. Safe Living/Smart Products makes a pet-safe extension cord called the Smart Cord, which sells for $14.95. It contains an advanced internal monitoring system that stops electrical flow in 25/1000 of a second, so that even if your Poodle's teeth sink into it, he won't get shocked. The Smart Cord also provides built-in fire protection.

Windows, Doors, and Accessories

Keep upper-story windows shut or screened and curtain cords tucked out of reach. Left to their own devices, puppies will often eat as much of the window cord as they can, not just the plastic ends. Puppy tummies, although seemingly made of cast iron, cannot digest the nylon these items are often made of. At the least you might have a very sick puppy; at worst, your dog could die.

Hazardous House Plants

Bringing the outdoors inside has its own built-in dangers. Poisonous and otherwise dangerous houseplants include cactus, English ivy, dumb cane (*dieffenbachia picta*), wax begonias, oleander, yellow calla, peace lily, and philodendron. Philodendron and dieffenbachia, both of the *Araceae* family, cause intense pain and allergic reaction; the latter can swell tissues in the mouth to the point of choking the dog, and can also induce kidney failure. Clinical signs of *Araceae* poisoning include salivation, head shaking, pawing at the mouth, and vomiting or diarrhea. Get your dog to a vet, and bring a leaf from the suspect plant with you. (See

Violent Veggies and Fearsome Flowers, below, for a list of dangerous garden plants.)

Not all plants are poisonous, however. Ferns, coleus, spider plants, and palms are harmless to dogs. On the other hand, your Poodle may eat them and destroy the plant.

You can keep dogs out of dried or artificial flower arrangements by spraying the arrangement with hairspray, then scattering pepper (white or dark, to match the color) on the flowers. Poodles hate that. And although Poodles do not usually indulge in glue-sniffing, it's best to keep craft supplies well out their clutches.

Poodle Precaution

Although it is common for a dog to consume his vomit, don't let him—even though it does make house cleaning easier. 🐾

Tobacco

Like people, some dogs have a weakness for tobacco. But nicotine is a poison, and devouring cigarette butts from a full ashtray will sicken your Poodle.

The Poodle Pundit

Marijuana isn't good for dogs, either. It can cause vomiting and diarrhea. Those who think it amusing to get their pets high are only being cruel. 🐾

Insect Traps and Bait

These are poisonous, of course. Dogs can easily be seduced by roach bait, snail bait, rat poison, or other anti-pest products. Take extra care to keep them out of the way.

Cleaning Agents

There is evidence that some popular household cleaners, such as Pine-Sol and Lysol, may be dangerous for dogs. They contain phenol or phenol derivatives that have been implicated in liver and kidney damage. Phenols are slow-acting toxins that may sicken your dog so gradually that you don't know what's happening. They are especially dangerous to puppies. Some experts recommend disinfecting with rubbing alcohol, which works fast and has no side effects. Caustics like Drano and Ajax, automatic dishwashing detergents, and toilet bowl cleaners are also extremely dangerous.

The Medicine Chest Menace

The American Veterinary Medical Association (AVMA) tells us that 70 percent of pet poisonings are due to the ingestion of drugs. Curious dogs will often decide to medicate themselves with over-the-counter drugs, prescription drugs, or vitamins. One of the most interesting aspects of dog ownership is that while you may have a lot of trouble getting a dog to swallow his own pills, the same creature will eat his owner's prescriptions without turning a hair.

I know of dogs that overdosed on Di-Gel, blood pressure medication, and tranquilizers. Childproof bottles are not dog-proof. Keep medications locked up and never give your pet human medication and unless instructed to do so by your vet. Tylenol and ibuprofin (Advil, Nuprin, Motrin) are particularly toxic to dogs, even in low doses. And even when dogs and people take the same drugs, therapeutic dosages can vary considerably. Don't gamble with your pet's life.

Other medicine cabinet mainstays, such as perfumes, eau de cologne, aftershave, and the like, are nasty when swallowed. Your Poodle will probably not drink them, but you never know. Keep the stuff out of the way.

Holiday Hazards

We all enjoy holidays, but they can be ruined in a heartbeat by a minor oversight.

Christmas

'Tis the Season to Be Careful! Glorious though they are, Christmas trees, ribbons, tinsel, and presents mean Poodle peril. For some odd reason, a dog who never does anything to a tree outdoors except urinate on it is instantly attracted to an indoor tree. He may not only christen on it, but will almost certainly wreak some sort of havoc upon it—and himself—when you're not looking.

Use only non-breakable ornaments for Christmas decorations unless you are absolutely sure your Poodle will not molest the tree. It's best to hang ornaments on the lowest branches with ribbon instead of hooks. If you do use hooks, buy plastic ones, which are safer if swallowed. Poodles also pull off and swallow popcorn-cranberry garlands. Hang these colorful decorations outside where the birds will enjoy them.

Poodle Precautions

Tinsel is extremely dangerous when swallowed—and even Christmas tree needles can perforate the intestines of a dog. 🐾

Chemicals (tree-fresheners or preservers) people sometimes put in the tree's water are dangerous to dogs. Christmas plants, like mistletoe, can produce vomiting and diarrhea. Holly and yew berries are extremely dangerous. Ingesting a few causes diarrhea; 20 or 30 holly berries can be fatal. Poinsettias, although overrated as a poison, may also produce unpleasant effects. It's the sap.

Poodle Potpourri

It's estimated that 79 percent of dog owners give their pets birthday and Christmas presents. Make sure you're one of those people. Food is the number one preferred present, followed by toys. Dogs are uninterested in municipal bonds, software, and gift certificates, except possibly as snacks. 🐾

Before putting your presents under the tree, find out if they contain food. Your Poodle's sense of smell is hundreds of times better than yours; if there's food under there, he'll find it. Besides, this will give you an excuse to eat the cookies while they are still fresh. (Fruitcake does not count as food and may be put under the tree with confidence. Even dogs won't eat it.)

We have a special Christmas room in our house that is animal-secure. If this isn't feasible for you, and you don't really want to put barbed wire around the tree, there is another solution. You can buy an electric tree skirt that delivers a mild, non-harmful shock that keeps the pets away from the tree. There is also something called a "scat mat" that works on the same principle, which can be used to barricade a room.

Another trick involves a plastic mat intended for placement under office chairs (to help them roll easily). Use one meant to be placed on a carpet, and place the mat upside down—with the plastic points upward—at the threshold of the forbidden room. Most dogs dislike the prickly feeling on their feet and won't cross it.

You may also corral the tree in a dog's "x-pen" (exercise pen) or play pen, or barricade a corner with a low decorative picket fence.

The Poodle Pundit

Always unplug (don't just turn off) your Christmas tree lights when you are not home. 🐾

Mardi Gras Poodles love Christmas!   *Courtesy of Jeanne Kennedy*

New Year's

Although the New Year is not particularly hazardous for your dog (assuming he's not suffering from a hangover), it is a good time for you to make a few New Year's resolutions—for the dog. Does he need to lose a few pounds? Get more exercise? More grooming? Get updated on shots or dental work? Need a friend or more attention? Make a New Year's resolution to do at least one thing better, then stick with it.

Easter Evils

Watch out for chocolate bunnies! Dogs love chocolate, but it's toxic to them. A chemical contained in chocolate, theobromine, is the culprit. If your Miniature or Standard Poodle chomps the ears off a bunny despite your precautions, don't panic. A medium to large dog can generally handle about 11 ounces of milk chocolate without serious effects; baking chocolate, however, is 9 times more toxic, so figure accordingly.

Jewish Religious Holidays

These are generally safe for pets. Matzoh balls, potato latkes, and challah are easy to digest. If your dog swallows the dreidels, however, you have a problem.

Fourth of July, Fireworks, and Thunder

The Fourth of July means firecrackers. Experiencing pleasure from extremely loud noises exploding in one's ears is confined to humans. Firecrackers and pets do not get along. Many dogs are terrified of loud noises, including thunder. Remember that dogs have much more sensitive hearing than we do—what is merely loud to us can be excruciating to them.

Don't take your Poodle to the fireworks celebration. If you are leaving for the evening, keep your dog safe at home. Neighborhood firecrackers, besides probably being illegal, may make your dogs extremely nervous.

Thanksgiving Tummyaches

Gluttony is a deadly sin for dogs, at least as far as turkey skin and fat go. They can give your Poodle a bad case of pancreatitis. Be generous and give him a nice plate of lean turkey breast instead. And never give a dog cooked chicken or turkey bones— they can get stuck or splinter in the esophagus, stomach, or bowel.

The Poodle Pundit

Throw bones away, if possible, in a large jar with a screw-on lid. This will keep the smells in and save your trash from being ravaged by the neighborhood animals, who don't need turkey bones stuck in their throats, either. 🐾

Turkey stuffing sometimes contains onions, which are poisonous to dogs. Apple seeds, green potato skins, rhubarb, moldy cheese, and cherry pits are also bad for dogs. Although your dog isn't likely to gobble down rhubarb, you never know.

Daylight Savings Time

Go ahead and laugh, but Daylight Savings Time can be dangerous—if not for your dog, then for you. Dogs used to eliminating according to a strict schedule may be thrown off by the time change and begin to forget their housetraining.

Dangers Beyond the House

Although most people are fairly good about dog-proofing their homes, their attention wanders when it comes to the world beyond, even if that includes just the garage and backyard.

The Garage

With all the deadly things that can be found in the average garage, it should be obvious that this is no place to keep a pet. Noxious car fumes and various garage poisons can kill them. Especially dangerous is the carbon monoxide in car exhaust, which has no odor.

Antifreeze

Without a doubt, antifreeze is the most dangerous item in your garage. Autumn, when people are changing their radiator fluid, is the time of greatest danger. Antifreeze is apparently sweet and pleasant-tasting, but the main ingredient of many brands, ethylene glycol, is a deadly poison to dogs, cats, and children. Its metabolites attack and destroy the kidneys, and the final results are coma and death. Unfortunately, once dogs start drinking the stuff, they don't stop.

Since antifreeze is a necessity, try using one with a propylene, rather than ethylene, glycol base. Although propylene glycol is considerably less toxic that ethylene glycol, it is still a poison. It affects the central nervous system but not the kidneys. A medium sized dog would need to ingest about 20 ounces of propylene glycol before getting seriously ill, while only 2 ounces of the more deadly ethylene glycol can kill. It also seems that propylene glycol is less tasty to dogs than its deadly cousin.

Most commercially sold antifreeze is 95 percent ethylene glycol. The safer alternatives, propylene glycol products, include Sierra (Safe Brands Corporation) and Sta-Clean (Sta-Clean Products).

Keep your pets out of the garage. If it's sometimes unavoidable, be sure that he is restrained by a leash, harness, or your arms. It's too easy for your dog to wander into the garage to supervise your work, fall asleep, and accidentally get locked in. Check your dog's whereabouts frequently anytime he has access to the garage.

The best solution is prevention. Keep antifreeze locked away from anywhere your Poodle might possibly get to. And, no matter what kind of antifreeze you use, clean up any spills immediately. You can use cat litter to absorb most of the liquid; follow up with rags. Dispose of the stuff carefully.

The Walk

Ice-melters are harsh on your dog's paws—and toxic to his insides. If your Poodle licks the stuff off his paws, he will be ingesting poison. Even salt is dangerous, since dogs will lick and lick at the place between their toes where it is lodged, which can cause painful sores (interdigital dermatitis). Always wash your dog's feet after a winter sidewalk stroll—baby wipes come in handy for this purpose—then dry them, since chronically wet feet can lead to secondary yeast infections. If the pads are dry and brittle, coat them with a little vaseline or Bag Balm.

Several ice-melting products now on the market, like Safe Paws and Eco-Safe Ice Melter, are non-toxic to your pets and can be used safely on concrete and lawns. Although these products are more expensive than regular ice-melters, they won't damage your shoes and don't track.

Best Buddies: Raven, Standard Poodle, (3 ½ months) and Meesha, Bichon/Cocker (2 years)

Courtesy of Jan Bradley

Some companies manufacture little Eskimo boots for dogs that protect their paws from salt, snow, and harsh chemical ice melters. They come in several sizes. Although it takes some encouragement to get your dog to wear booties, they will save him a lot of discomfort.

Yard and Garden Hazards

Evil lurks in your back yard. It manifests itself as both natural and manmade dangers. Natural hazards include yellow jackets, hornets, ticks, fleas, and mosquitoes. Manmade hazards are mostly chemical.

The Chemical Lawn

Pets and chemicals don't mix. We Americans pour, shake, powder, rake in, and dump 300 million pounds of pesticides on our lawns every year. This stuff is not good for your Poodles or kids! Most of these chemicals are not water soluble, which means that they're going to be in your yard for a long, long time. They're also poisonous, and consist of such ingredients as diazinon, cholorpyrifos, banvel, benomyl, daconil, and 2,4D.

If your lawn could double as a chemistry experiment, keep your dogs away from it. If your dog does inadvertently walk on freshly applied chemicals, wash his little tootsies with a gentle shampoo as soon as possible. Baby wipes work well when soap and water are unavailable.

Instead of harsh chemical treatments for your lawn, consider using organic pesticides like flea-eating nematodes and the seeds from the Asian neem tree. Both help rid your lawn of fleas and other pests naturally. Always dispose of yard product containers safely, away from pets and children. If you're out to get slugs, make sure the bait is safely enclosed.

Poodles are generally not terrible chewers. However, if you do have one who chews, make sure he can't get at treated wood. Such woods are soaked with poisonous insecticide. Anything soaked in creosote is also dangerous. Don't allow your Poodle to go chomping on the stuff.

Violent Veggies and Fearsome Flowers

It just doesn't seem fair. Ever since the Garden of Eden, vegetation has contained secret perils. Many plants, though ever so lovely to look at, can kill a dog or toddler. Having said this, however, I want to emphasize that the number of dogs who become seriously ill from ingesting garden plants is minuscule compared to the number who die every year from consuming household chemicals and drugs. Most plants are not palatable to dogs, so you don't have worry—much—about their eating them.

At any rate, here are the names of some common poisonous plants; more information may be obtained from the ASPCA's National Animal Poison Control Center.

▼ Aloe vera
▼ Amaryllis
▼ Azalea and rhododendron
▼ Bleeding heart
▼ Boxwood
▼ Buttercup
▼ Daffodils
▼ Daphne
▼ Delphiniums
▼ Dutchman's breeches
▼ Caladium
▼ Calla lily
▼ Elephant ears
▼ English ivy
▼ Foxglove
▼ Holly
▼ Honeysuckle
▼ Lily-of-the-valley
▼ Mayapple
▼ Monkshood
▼ Morning glory
▼ Mother-in-law's tongue
▼ Certain mushrooms (you never know which ones)
▼ Nightshade
▼ Rhubarb
▼ Skunk cabbage (which stinks and shouldn't be in your yard anyway)

▼ Tulip bulbs
▼ Tomato and avocado leaves
▼ Wisteria

Poodle Potpourri

Privet and yew, which many folks use for hedging, can be nasty plants. In our area, a kindly neighbor tossed his Japanese yew hedge clippings into a neighboring field, thinking that the farmer's cows might enjoy them. They did too, at least for a while. The yew killed them all, and we were treated to the sight of 25 dead cows in a field, their legs sticking straight up into the air. Luckily, adult dogs are not likely to eat yew, but it's wise to be one's guard anyway. Inquisitive Poodle pups need to be supervised. Yew contains an alkaloid that kills by depressing electrical activity in the heart. Two ounces of the stuff can kill a Standard Poodle. Signs of yew poisoning include trembling, staggering, diarrhea, and collapse. 🐾

If you have a compost pile, contain it in a Poodle-proof enclosure. In addition to making a mess in it, your Poodle could poison himself. Toxin-producing bacteria break down organic material in compost piles.

Cleaning Up Dog Messes

Dog messes are not just eyesores; they can be serious health hazards for your pet. Pick them up every day. This is especially important if you own more than one dog. Dogs re-infect one another with parasites such as hookworms, roundworms, tapeworms, and whipworms, which are just a few possible denizens of the average pile of doggy doo. If your dog has been infected, you'll need to disinfect the entire toileting area to prevent re-infestation. That's another reason to keep the bathroom area as small as possible.

Swimming Pools

The family swimming pool can be a death trap for your Poodle. Although many Poodles enjoy swimming, their heavy coats can weigh them down and even drown them. Never leave your Poodle alone—even for five minutes—in the pool. A good rule is that if you wouldn't trust a toddler, don't trust a Poodle. If you do allow your Poodle to use the pool, always show him how to find the stairs. Dogs sometimes get confused about which way is out, and so should be trained to enter and exit the pool by the stairs only. By the way, if your pool is vinyl-lined, a few sharp claw marks can lead to a very expensive pool repair.

Winter covers for pools can be dangerous. Unless you have a Loop-Loc-type cover, make every effort to keep your dog away from your covered pool. Dogs cannot distinguish pool covers from solid ground until it is too late.

You can purchase a life vest for your dog; they come in various sizes and are really handy, especially if you and your dog might be traveling to a lake or going canoeing. Unclipped Poodle fur soaks up a lot of water, and the weight can be deadly to a swimming dog.

Barbeques

While you're enjoying your outdoor barbecue, make sure your dogs are never left alone with the hot grill. Not only will they attempt to steal the steak, but they can also knock the grill over and spill hot coals all over themselves. It's not something you want to happen.

Fencing Your Poodle In

Standard and Miniature Poodles should have a safe, enclosed outdoor area where they can run—and even Toys appreciate such a luxury. The best arrangement is for the dogs to have their own fenced area away from the door, where visitors are apt to enter and leave. Many a dog has escaped because the mail carrier didn't see it, and the dog made a break for it. Gate latches are too easily left open. A large area off the side or back door is ideal, so you can let your dog in or out without leashing him up first.

Chapter 7
Provisioning Your Poodle

More ink has probably flowed over the issue of nutrition than any other single canine topic. Commercial dog foods versus homemade, raw vs. cooked, people food vs. dog food, bones or no bones, chicken wings or no chicken wings, supplements or no supplements. All these options have stirred dog fanciers to varying degrees of frenzy. The good news is, you can relax. Dogs (even Poodles!) are scavengers by nature and can survive—and thrive—on a remarkable variety of foods. A good commercial dog food will probably satisfy his nutritional needs, but the exciting elements that make for good discussion are cancer prevention, immune system enhancement, and overall life improvement. For more detailed information on canine nutrition, see my book *Feeding Your Dog for Life: The Real Facts About Proper Nutrition* (also published by Doral Publishing, Inc.).

The important thing to remember is that dogs, although technically classed among *Carnivora*, or meat-eaters, are really omnivores. They'll eat anything. They'll eat garbage if you let them.

Doggy Digestion

Although we won't be going into the whole digestive system of your dog, we will take a quick look in his mouth. That's where the digestive process begins.

Teeth

Dog teeth are multi-purpose tools. Wild dogs and wolves use them for fighting, catching and killing prey, and gobbling said prey when caught. Although it may be difficult to think of civilized Poodles gobbling prey, they can do it, believe me.

Most adult dogs have 42 teeth, up from the 28 needle sharp milk teeth they had as babies. Toy Poodles (along with other small breeds) often have fewer teeth and more dental problems.

Poodle Precautions

Every once in a while, some milk teeth don't fall out and have to be removed by the vet. They should not be allowed to remain, since they can affect the bite and thus the whole digestive process. This is a particular danger with Toy Poodles. 🐾

Most adult dogs have the following arrangement of teeth:

▼ **12 incisors**: To nibble, groom, catch, and crack fleas.

▼ **4 canines**: To hold and tear.

▼ **16 premolars**: To cut and shear.

▼ **4 top molars and 6 lower molars**: To chew and grind non-meat products.

These teeth should meet in a "scissors bite" (the top teeth slightly overlapping those on the bottom) for both best functioning and to meet the breed standard.

Like Caesar's Gaul, each tooth is divided into three parts. What you see most easily is the enamel-covered crown. The part that indents a little at the gumline where the enamel ends is called the neck, and the root is the unseen part that embeds the entire tooth in the socket. The roots of the canine teeth are really long—about twice the length of the crown. Some teeth, like the first premolars, have small peglike roots, while the last premolar in the upper jaw has three long roots. These huge premolars are the carnassials, or shearing teeth.

All dogs should have their teeth brushed regularly, but this is especially important for Toys. Small dogs, with their tiny jaws, tend to have crowded teeth that must be looked after carefully.

Otherwise, they will accumulate tartar, which will eventually cause gingivitis. If tartar does develop, take your Poodle to the vet for a thorough cleaning. Brush your Poodle's teeth often—once a day if possible—and use a toothpaste designed especially for dogs. Giving your Poodle dog biscuits helps, although not as much as you might hope.

Taste

Poodles don't have as many taste buds as people do, but they can detect sour, sweet, and salt tastes. (Cats, in contrast, have no sweet-detecting taste buds.) This comparative lack of taste buds makes dogs more adventuresome eaters than humans—in other words, they tend to gobble anything down. In the wild, where dogs lived in packs and competed for food, this was a valuable trait; in today's world, however, this is a habit that can get dogs into trouble.

Feeding Your Dog Right: Home Made Dinner

If you really want to go all out, you can't do better than a home-prepared diet of meaty raw bones, cooked eggs, raw meat, and a variety of vegetables, with occasional additions of rice and yogurt or fish. Green beans, carrots, and cooked potatoes are all fine for dogs.

Although some claim that it is difficult to concoct a home-made diet that can match the years of research represented by commercial foods, this is not really true. You've been cooking for your family all these years, after all, without resorting to pre-packaged kid-kibble. At any rate, what you cannot match is the inexpensiveness and convenience of commercial foods. A good quality commercial food will be the choice of many pet owners for that reason alone.

If, however, you are really dedicated to making your dogs' meals yourself, you can do so—there are some excellent books on the subject. For more exact formulations, the Hill's Company provides free recipes for home-cooking pet meals. The big advantages of homemade diets are that you can tailor the diet to your dog's particular needs, and you will be using higher quality ingredients than found in any commercial food. But it can be a lot of work, and nearly all dogs do very well on commercial foods.

Poodle Precautions

Avoid high-fat dairy products, processed meats, candy, and chocolate. Don't give any to your dog, either. 🐾

Nutritional Needs

Is variety the spice of life? Some nutritionists insist that the canine system does better on one complete food, and that switching around can upset the digestive tract. They compare a dog to a finely-tuned car, saying that once you find the right brand of gas with the right octane, there's no point in changing. Others maintain that switching dog foods makes a dog finicky.

Some people, who cite the fact that dogs are natural scavengers, believe that dogs not only enjoy variety, but also thrive on it. They argue that since we don't yet know everything about canine dietary requirements, it's safer to change a dog's diet occasionally to increase the chances that he's getting everything he needs. The proponents of the variety school think dogs are a lot closer to humans than they are to cars. I agree with them.

My own 7 dogs eat a little dry food, a little canned food, and a lot of people food. They are all quite healthy. This could be coincidence, but I do believe that dogs like and need a variety of different foods for their spiritual and their physical well-being. (This is just my gut feeling.)

We know for certain that dogs, like humans, need the following components in their diets: protein, fat, vitamins, minerals, water, and maybe carbohydrates (for lactating bitches and dogs under lots of stress).

The Poodle Pundit

Puppies need more total protein, amino acids, fats, and minerals in their diet than do adult dogs. Senior dogs have their own special needs, too. 🐾

Protein

Proteins contain the important amino acids that mammals need to grow and thrive. Dogs need more protein than people do; although no optimum level has been established, even 30 percent of their total calories is not too much. Protein is found in many foods, including meat, fish, eggs, and soybeans. However, not all proteins are digestible proteins, and some are more digestible than others. This digestibility factor is what is really important, rather than the total amount of protein.

Poodle Parlance

Digestible proteins are those that can be absorbed through the gut wall and used by the body. 🐾

The digestibility factor of some cereals commonly found in dog food is only about 50 percent. Dogs do best on meat- or fish-derived protein; vegetable-derived protein can cause diarrhea. In general, a dog's diet should be about 75 percent meat and the rest vegetables.

Fat

Fat is not bad for dogs; on the contrary, it's an important energy source. Most commercial dry dog foods contain between 5 and 10 percent fat, which is sufficient for sedentary dogs; working Poodles require at least twice as much. Fat also makes food taste better, which is why most dogs prefer any canned meat to dry kibble.

Fats also help deliver the fat-soluble vitamins A, D, E, and K. Too much fat, however, especially when given all at once, can result in pancreatic problems.

Carbohydrates

Scientists are still trying to figure out the place of carbohydrates in a dog's diet. Dogs can use them to make energy, but are they necessary? Test results suggest that they may be, at least for pregnant and nursing dogs. It's not a major issue, however, since nearly every dog food and dog biscuit available is loaded with carbohydrates.

Fiber

Fiber, or roughage, is an indigestible carbohydrate. There is much controversy about whether fiber is necessary in a dog's diet at all, and, if so, how much. The right kind of fiber regulates a dog's bowel function. Most veterinarians agree that diabetic dogs, especially overweight ones, can benefit from eating fiber because it slows the absorption of glucose in the intestine. This helps control blood sugar. Some kinds of fiber, however, may decrease the absorption of some critical minerals.

Dog food labels don't adequately reveal how much fiber is contained in the product. The guaranteed analysis may list "crude fiber" as an ingredient, but that term refers to what's left over from the food manufacturing process. The dietary fiber contained in the product can be several times higher.

Vitamins

Vitamins come in two kinds: fat-soluble and water-soluble. The fat-soluble vitamins (A, D, E, and K) can be stored in the body (and too much of A and D can be trouble). Water-soluble vitamins are excreted in the urine. The ones your dog needs are thiamin (B_1) riboflavin (B_2), niacin, pyridoxine (B_6), vitamin B_{12} (cobolamin), folic acid, pantothenic acid, biotin, and choline (not strictly classified as a vitamin, but an essential nutrient nonetheless).

Poodles are smart enough to manufacture their own vitamin C, another water-soluble vitamin. (Humans can't do this. Neither can guinea pigs.) Still, a vitamin C supplement may lower cancer risk, and many holistic veterinarians suggest its use in managing the care of a dog diagnosed with cancer. Vitamin C also seems to reduce the side effects of some anti-cancer drugs.

Vitamin A and its precursor, beta-carotene, seem to enhance immune functioning and may help to prevent some kinds of cancer. Be careful not to oversupplement, however. Large amounts of Vitamin A are poisonous. A couple of carrots a day will do just fine.

Poodle Precautions

Puppies are particularly vulnerable to the dangers of over-supplementation. Do not add minerals or vitamins to your puppy's diet without a recommendation from your veterinarian. 🐾

Minerals

Dogs need the following minerals in their diet: calcium, phosphorus, potassium, salt, magnesium, iron, copper, manganese, zinc, iodine, and selenium—just like people do. Zinc is especially important as it is necessary for normal metabolism. A diet deficient in zinc will result in thin hair and a crusty dermatitis.

Poodle Precautions

Never give a Standard Poodle puppy a calcium supplement; it can contribute to hip dysplasia, osteochondrosis, and enlarged joints. It also binds zinc, resulting in zinc deficiency and a poor coat. 🐾

Reading the Labels

Although most dog owners feed their pets commercial foods, few know how to read the label. It may come as a surprise to learn that as far as federal regulations go, very little is required of pet food manufacturers. Companies are required to accurately identify the product, provide the net quantity, give their address, and correctly list ingredients. That's it. Additionally, pet food companies are not subject to quality control laws. The feds do not require them to list the ingredients in any particular order, although some states do. A little security can be found by looking for the Association of American Feed Control Officials (AAFCO) label. This organization provides model regulations that pet food manufacturers must follow in order to carry the AAFCO label.

AAFCO labels provide a guaranteed analysis of the food, as well as calorie and nutritional adequacy statements. This doesn't necessarily mean the product is good, however; it just means that it's properly labeled. Critics claim that AAFCO testing is not particularly stringent and is in no way equivalent to a controlled scientific study.

The good news, however, is that the highly competitive dog food market is driving up the overall quality of commercial foods. Owners now have more quality choices than ever before; however, they also need to educate themselves in order to know what they're buying.

"Meat" Labels

If an AAFCO labeled product has the word "beef" as its simple name (like "Diane's Beef Food for Dogs"), it must be 95 percent beef, exclusive of water needed for processing. Counting the water, it must be 70 percent beef. The same goes for chicken, fish, or lamb. These foods are all canned; no kibble is 95 percent meat.

"Dinner" Labels

If the word "dinner," or a similar word like "platter" or "entree" is used, each featured ingredient must compose between 25 and 94 percent of the total. Therefore, "Diane's Sawdust Dinner for Dogs" must contain at least 25 percent sawdust (or whatever the named ingredient is).

"With" Labels

If the word "with" is used, the named ingredient must compose at least 3 percent of the total. So "Diane's Sawdust Dinner for Dogs with Liver" must contain 3 percent liver. "Diane's Sawdust Dinner for Dogs with Liver and Sirloin" must contain 3 percent liver and 3 percent sirloin, as well as at least 25 percent sawdust.

"Flavor" Labels

If the label reads "beef flavor," rather than "beef," it need only contain enough beef to be taste-detectable (as if you were going to eat it). The word "flavor" must appear in letters as large as those of the named ingredient.

Guaranteed Analysis

AAFCO also requires that ingredients must be listed in order of their weight in the food. Inherent water content is included in this calculation.

Poodle Parlance

You may see the words "crude" fat or "crude" protein on the label. These terms refer to the method of testing the product. It doesn't mean that the protein or fat in the food is "cruder" than any other kind. You will notice that levels of crude protein will be lower in canned foods than in dry foods. This is due to the large amount of water present in canned food. 🐾

Caloric Content

Pet food labels may include a calorie count, but they don't have to. If there is calorie count, it will be expressed in "kilo-calories per kilogram," a singularly unhelpful number. A kilogram is 2.2 pounds, and kilocalories are just regular old calories. Thankfully, most pet foods also include the calories stated in relation to English measures.

"Premium," "Light," "Gourmet," "Natural," "Organic," "Performance," etc.

Some of these terms, like "light," have recently been standardized. Others, like "natural," have not. Read the ingredients panel carefully.

Types of Dog Food

Your choice of what to feed your Poodle is practically unlimited: dry food, canned food, semi-moist, people food, or any mixture thereof. I am not going to tell you that only one kind is right for you and your dog. Many factors come into play, including convenience, expense, nutritional value, taste, availability, allergies, and other things. What's right for one dog is not right for all. One rule I do apply is, don't feed your Poodle something he dislikes. Yes, he will eat almost anything if he gets hungry enough, but so would I, rather than starve. That doesn't mean I'd like it. Mealtimes should be pleasurable for everyone, so why not shop around until you find something nutritious that your dog really enjoys? If he seems to like something for a while, then gets bored with it, just change his food.

Dry Food (Kibble)

Kibble is a convenient, nutritionally adequate food for dogs. Dry food helps reduce tartar buildup on teeth, but not as much as brushing does, and it doesn't do anything for cleaning the canine teeth (the fangs), since chewing (if any) is done with the back teeth. In comparison with other food choices, dry food is the least expensive, largely because of its high grain content. Dry food tends to be low in fat. This can be dangerous if your Poodle is a performance dog, but good if he is overweight or inactive. Don't be seduced by fancy colors and shapes. Shape doesn't matter, and the colors come from vegetable dye, not food nutrients.

Most, but not all, dry foods are preserved with BHA or BHT. They used to use ethoxyquin (originally a rubber hardener), but were asked to stop due to potential health problems. Although BHA and BHT have been established as safe by the federal government, many people question this finding. If you don't wish to feed your dog food containing these preservatives, you can find some dry foods that don't use them—but they are pricey and sometimes hard to locate.

Some people like to feed their dogs a basic diet of kibble and add different foods every day, such as green beans, carrots, gravy, or canned meat. A plan of this type gives your dog adequate nutrition and variety.

Canned Food

Canned food is much more expensive than kibble, yet is usually about 75 percent water. The maximum amount of water allowed in canned, AAFCO labeled products is 78 percent, unless the food is labeled as "gravy," "sauce," or "stew." In that case, the water content can be even higher! Canned foods are also high in fat. They can be useful for mixing with dry food, however, since most dogs find them highly palatable. Dogs who have urinary tract infections often do better on canned food than kibble, mostly because of the increased water.

Some canned dog food contains grain products, while others have only meat. Whether or not grain products are good for dogs is controversial, as mentioned earlier. Dogs do need a vegetable element in their diet, so if you feed a pure meat dinner you should supplement it with dog biscuits or fresh vegetables. Fresh meat is sometimes deficient in calcium.

Poodle Precautions

As a rule, don't give raw egg whites to dogs; they contain avidin, which can destroy the B vitamin biotin. Giving a raw whole egg is okay, if your dog will accept them. 🐾

Semi-Moist Food

Semi-moist food is about 25 percent water, and can be just as high in sugar (in the form of corn syrup, beet pulp, sucrose, and/or caramel). Your dog does not need this stuff, which only promotes obesity and tooth decay. The shelf life of these products is lower than that of canned or dry food.

The Poodle Pundit

Food should be served at room temperature if possible, not directly from the refrigerator or a hot oven. Very cold food eaten rapidly can make a dog upchuck, not to mention that ice cream headache. On the other hand, some food seems more palatable to dogs if slightly warmed. 🐾

Beef, Dairy Products, and Gluten

Some Poodles are allergic to these products commonly found in commercial dog foods, so monitor your pet if feeding them—especially gluten. Check the labels. You may have to switch to higher-priced food. Gluten is found in barley, oats, rye, and wheat.

I don't recommend giving lots of dairy products to dogs; after weaning, they are usually unable to digest them properly. Yogurt is an exception—most dogs benefit from a teaspoon of plain yogurt in their food, especially if they need extra calcium. Dogs like milk, too, but it gives most adult dogs diarrhea.

Omega Fatty Acids: Nutrition for the Coat

A thick, beautiful coat is one of the hallmarks of the Poodle, and you'll be happy to know that you can do a lot to keep that coat in peak condition by feeding your dog correctly.

The most important nutritional components for a good coat are omega fatty acids (they may confer additional health benefits as well). There are two important kinds of omega fatty acids: omega-6 and omega-3. Omega-6 (linoleic) fatty acids are plentiful in safflower and sunflower oil, and most dogs get plenty in their regular diet. Although omega-3 (linolenic) acids are not found in most commercial foods—probably because the best sources for them, marine fish oil and flaxseed oil, are expensive—a few commercial foods do contain them.

Most experts believe that 5 units of omega-6 fatty acids should be fed for every 1 unit of omega-3. Omega-3 fatty acids may help in the treatment of cancer, and can be given as dietary supplements.

Once in a while you'll see an omega-9 (oleic) fatty acid listed on a label. This is mostly an attempt to capitalize on the word omega. Oleic acid is the main component in olive oil and is usually simply referred to as a monounsaturated fat.

Supplements

A high-quality commercial dog food should be complete, although there is plenty of controversy about whether or not this is true. Some people believe that if you're feeding a good commercial product you need supply nothing else; others claim that we still don't know enough about canine nutritional requirements to be sure. My advice is to start with a high-quality dog food and keep a careful watch on your Poodle's coat, energy level, weight, and general health. Add or subtract ingredients as you find necessary—but don't overdo it.

Garlic?

Garlic (*allium sativum*), which contains over 100 chemicals, is a fad additive these days. Many owners, however, swear by it. *Allicin*, the substance responsible for garlic's characteristic smell, is considered to be the source of many of its pharmaceutical benefits. Proponents of garlic tout its alleged effects as an appetite stimulant, flea repellent, immune system booster, and treatment for arteriosclerosis. Most experts believe these claims are not warranted; however, a little garlic certainly won't hurt your dog. It does seem to be a flavor enhancer—but if you're feeding a dog a good diet, its flavor should not need to be enhanced.

Caloric Requirements for Dogs

Research at the Ralston Purina Pet Care Center indicates that a 50-pound adult dog requires 1,450 calories a day during the summer (if inactive), 1,800 calories during moderate work or training, and 2,160 during heavy work.

Remember, these calorie requirements are for dogs in general, not for Poodles in particular—let alone your particular Poodle. Age and activity level are important determinants as well; consequently, it's impossible to determine precisely how many calories a particular dog will require.

Luckily, you don't need to know how many calories your dog actually needs—just keep an eye on him. If he starts looking pudgy, reduce his intake, and vice versa.

Poodle Potpourri

Metabolic rates can vary among individual dogs by as much as 40 percent, so the information given here on caloric requirements is very general. It is not surprising that most commercial dog food manufacturers tell you to feed your dog too much. Obviously, that's in their interest, as it increases their sales. Don't fall for it. 🐾

How do you know if your Poodle is pudgy? For a quick check, just look at him from above. A working dog of the proper weight will have an hourglass figure. If your dog looks like a rectangle from an aerial view, he's overweight. You can also view your dog from the side; his belly should tuck up neatly. When rubbing your hands along his sides, you should be able to feel—but not see—each rib. You should also be able to feel the layer of subcutaneous fat beneath. Weigh your Poodle regularly, too.

If your dog is overweight, he's not alone. Recent studies show that 80 percent of household pets are overweight. The American

Animal Hospital Association rates obesity as the number-one nutrition-related health problem in dogs. Don't put your overweight dog on a crash diet, however. You can buy commercial dog food in "reduced calorie" varieties. Follow feeding instructions on the label for "weight loss," not maintenance. Incidentally, the amounts usually recommended are designed to maintain, not reduce, weight. It's a legal thing (even if it doesn't make any sense).

Or you could simply cut out the cupcakes, lower your Poodle's food and fat intake, and exercise him more. He'll love that.

Poodle Potpourri

It is possible to feed your dog a vegetarian diet. I've seen one composed largely of rice and tofu, but even that had some bone meal tablets thrown in. He won't be crazy about it, but if your dog is allergic to meat products or you have strong philosophical objections to meat consumption, it can be done. But be extremely careful. Dogs can only digest about 60 to 80 percent of vegetable-based protein, as compared to 90 to 95 percent of meat-derived protein. You can a buy a commercial vegetarian dog food, or you can devise your own diet by carefully monitoring nutrient levels. I generally don't recommend a vegetarian diet for dogs, but I do know people who have managed to feed their dogs this way for years. 🐾

Puppy Food

Although a Standard Poodle does not reach maturity until about 18 months of age, I don't recommend that he stay on puppy food for that length of time. Standard Poodles are one of the many breeds that are susceptible to hip dysplasia. Research has found a link between this condition and the higher levels of calcium found in many puppy foods, so it's better to switch gradually to an adult food at about 6 months. In addition, some Poodles of all sizes have adverse reactions to the dairy products often added to puppy food. The most common side effect of dairy products is very loose stools, which are not pleasant to deal with when you're housetraining your puppy!

Water

Always provide your Poodle with plenty of fresh, clean drinking water. Dogs need one-half to three-quarters fluid ounces of water per pound of body weight per day. This includes the water taken in through food. You don't need to calculate this; just keep plenty of fresh water available. Healthy dogs won't drink too much; be aware, however, that excessive water consumption can indicate diabetes or other ailments.

Feeding More Than One

Chow time!   *Courtesy of Leslie Sims*

Poodle Precautions

Some plastics emit strong odors that permeate food and make it unpalatable. If your Poodle enjoys his food when it first comes out of the bag but seems to go off feed after it's been stored, it could be the smell. 🐾

If you are feeding more than one dog, be sure that each dog has his own special room or corner to eat in. "Alpha" dogs (the top dog in the pack) may bully submissive dogs away from a bowl, and two alpha wanna-bes may fight over food. Even if you have peaceable dogs who eat well together, it's better to feed them separately. That way, you'll notice if one or the other goes off his feed, which is often the first indication of illness. Also, if your Poodle dines undisturbed, will be less likely to bolt his food, which decreases the danger of choking or bloat.

Timing

Food should be offered at a regular time and served in the same place every day, if possible. Dogs enjoy routine, and keeping to a regular feeding schedule reduces stress. It also prevents many housetraining problems. Most dogs should be fed 2 small meals a day rather than just 1 large one. This helps prevent bloat and keeps your dog more content.

Automatic pet feeders are a godsend on a busy day, and some dogs do well on a free-feeding schedule. If your Poodle doesn't pig out, this may be a satisfactory arrangement. It is trickier to monitor food intake this way, however, and impossible if you have more than one dog. I generally advise against it.

Chapter 8
Primping and Preening Your Poodle

"Some of us have hopes that the show trim will be abandoned one day, giving the poodle a chance to establish its true identity and its real nature." —James Thurber, *Christabel: Part One*

The Dark History of the Poodle Cut

Despite what many people think, the Poodle's traditional trim is not the product of modern fashion, but rather an ancient practice designed for practical ends—primarily to improve swimming ability. Gervase Markham, whose book *Hunger's Prevention, or the Art of Fowling* was mentioned earlier, explained that the famous Poodle cut is essential to the well being of the dog. "These Water Dogs," he writes, "naturally are ever laden with hair on the hinder parts." Being ever laden with hair on one's hinder parts is a grave disadvantage, both then and now.

Markham concedes that in winter the dog's hair is protective, "yet this defense in the summer time by the violence of the heat of the sun, and the greatness of the Dog's labor is very noisome and troublesome, and not only maketh him soon faint and give over his sport, but also makes him by his overheating, more subject to the mange." Although today we might disagree that overheating produces mange, it nonetheless remains true that the Poodle's extraordinarily heavy coat can indeed be "troublesome." Still, Markham advises that the foreparts of the Poodle not be shaved, fearing that the dog would freeze. "But for the shaving of a dog quite all over from foot to nostril, that I utterly dislike, for it brings such a tenderness and chillness over all his body that the water will grow irksome to him." The hindquarters tended to become wettest and soggiest, so that was the part to be shaved.

Puffs of hair called "bobbles" were left around the joints also, in hopes that the extra hair would warm up the joint enough to prevent arthritis (or rheumatism, as it was then known).

As for the *pompom* on the tip of the tail, there are two, not mutually exclusive, explanations. One claims that the pompom acted as rudder for the Poodle, while the other states that it enabled the hunters to see the animal splashing around in the swamp more easily. The rudder concept doesn't make much sense, but it's possible that the extra tuft of hair did make the Poodle more visible.

Thus the famous (or infamous, depending on your taste) Poodle cut is rooted in ancient hunting practices. Early Poodlers even tied colored ribbons to their Poodle's topknot—not for decoration, but to help tell one Poodle from another as they splashed around in the marsh-grass. It also kept the hair from falling in the animal's face.

Poodle Potpourri

Poodles became *à la mode* at precisely the same time that fashion was rising to dizzying heights with wigs, satin, ribbons, make-up, and other beguiling items—for human males. It was only natural that dogs would follow suit. The French, ever fashion-conscious, even clipped their family crests into the Poodle's coat, as well as rosettes and clever designs. They often finished the job by adding strange outfits and bejeweled ribbons—to the Poodle, too. 🐾

Fashion Clipping

As Poodles became more prized as companions, people forgot the original uses of the Poodle cuts. For many, the clips became a fashion craze, but others, who disliked the fantastic trims, derided them mercilessly. The same is true today. Although the traditional lion and continental clips grow on you, some people never learn to like them. In any case, they are much too difficult for the average pet owner to take of properly. The wonderful thing is that you can enjoy having a Poodle no matter what clip you choose.

Grooming the Modern Poodle

A good-looking Poodle is a high-maintenance dog. Even if you decide to go for the simplest of trims, your Poodle should be bathed and clipped at least every 6 weeks—and much more often if you want his coat to remain in top condition. In the interim, your dog will require thorough brushing.

Poodle Potpourri

Suz Dalton, who owns a tracking Poodle named Cassis, compares dog grooming to flower gardening. "You can take some flowers, like daffodils, and just slam them in the ground and forget about them. Others, like roses, require pruning, fertilizing, spraying, and lots of attention, but the spectacular results are worth all the effort. Poodles aren't daffodils."

Even though it's a lot of work to care for a Poodle's coat, your Poodle will help as much as possible. Most of them actually enjoy being groomed (or at least the attention that goes with it) and easily learn to stand, sit, lie down, and give a paw upon their groomers' request. Even those who don't like it will generally acquiesce with grace. 🐾

Despite the complexity of the job, groomers like to work with Poodles, who are used to it. It's better than dealing with wild, hairy animals who enter the grooming shop once every year or so—and then only after they have rolled in a combination of tar and garbage.

Choosing a Professional Groomer

For Poodle people, choosing a good groomer is almost as important as selecting the right veterinarian. Although most professional pet groomers are able to groom a Poodle (they account for a large proportion of their business), some are much more competent than others. You can ask your veterinarian for recommendations, or check with breeders, boarding kennels, or Poodle-owning friends who are pleased with their groomers.

Call the prospective groomer and check on prices, products, and procedures. Also ask if the groomer requires proof of vaccinations.

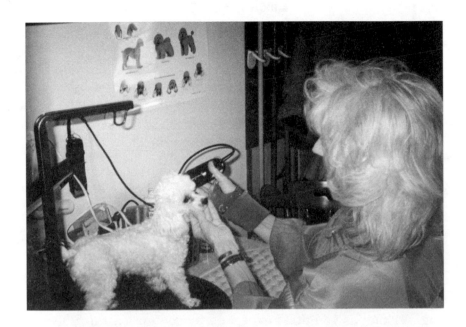

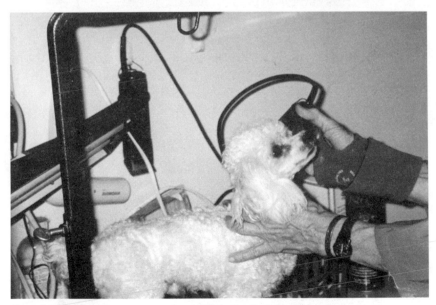

Grooming photos on these pages courtesy of Linda Currie, Cabin Companions

Poodle Precautions

Although a professional groomer can make your Poodle look truly professional, only you can do the regular ear, eye, foot, and tooth care. Your groomer should be an enhancement to your total dog care, not a replacement for it. Take time to watch the groomer with the dog. Any groomer who is rough with your Poodle should not be patronized.

It is your responsibility to inform the groomer if your Poodle is fearful of being groomed or doesn't like being left. If he has ever growled or snapped during the grooming process, the groomer needs to know this as well. Likewise, inform the groomer if the dog has arthritis, a heart problem, epilepsy, or any other condition that could be aggravated by the grooming procedure. 🐾

Grooming at Home

You may decide to take the plunge and do you own grooming. As long as you don't expect perfection (at least for the first few times), this can be an enjoyable experience.

Realize, however, that a good grooming job takes practice. Be prepared to accept the fact that your first attempt or two may result in your Poodle's looking a little odd. The best plan is to watch your groomer carefully while he does the job. Ask questions and take notes, especially about blade types, etc. Second best is to buy a videotape or book devoted to this intricate art.

The Poodle Pundit

If you decide to learn to groom your Poodle, don't start with a wiggly puppy. Choose instead a sedate older dog who is used to being fooled with. 🐾

Before clipping your Poodle, brush and comb him carefully to make sure there are no mats (you may need to use a "mat-rake" or "mat-breaker" for this purpose), bathe him, and then clip him.

Grooming anytime, anywhere...Cassis

Courtesy of Suzanne Dalton
Photo by Clyde Foles

Equipment

▼ Grooming table: Use the smallest size your Poodle can stand on comfortably to reduce fidgeting. If you don't have a grooming table, you can use any waist-high table. Add a car mat to prevent the dog's slipping.

▼ Hair dryer: Special commercial canine dryers are most effective, of course, but these are prohibitively expensive for most people. A good hand dryer will do nicely in a pinch, but it's best to have a dryer with a stand, since it takes more than one hand to groom a Poodle. Keep it on low or medium heat.

▼ High-quality electric clippers with interchangeable blades: Good ones can be expensive ($200!), so look around and see if you can get one second hand. You'll need at least two blades—a coarse one for the body and a finer one for the face, tail, feet, and between the toes. With clipper blades, the higher the number, the closer the cut. Clipper blades can cost $20 each.

▼ Assorted combs, mat rake, scissors, and brushes.

▼ Towels.

▼ Grooming glove.

Howie's head shot on the last day of "Big Hair"

Courtesy of Steven Chin

Brushing and Combing Your Poodle

This is something you will be doing yourself, even if you use a professional groomer. If you are totally committed to your Poodle you will brush him daily, but a minimum of 3 times a week will get you by. Brushing your Poodle helps condition his skin, remove dead hair, and improve blood circulation. It encourages the sebaceous glands to produce healthy oils. And it's a good way to spend quality time with your dog.

The Poodle Pundit

Always brush your dog before you bathe him, even if your Poodle is very dirty and smells. Otherwise you will turn ordinary mats into Gordian knots that can be removed by the sword alone. 🐾

Your brush inventory should include a slicker brush for short, dense hair, a pin brush for longer hair, and a bristle brush for the mane, topknot, and ear feathering. Some people prefer the pin brush for ear feathering. Experiment with different kinds of brushes until you find the combination that suits you and your Poodle best.

The Poodle Pundit

A slicker brush works well with hair that is somewhat matted, but is generally harder on the coat than a pin brush. 🐾

Develop a brushing routine that covers the entire dog. Most groomers begin brushing at the rear and move forward. The critical thing is to use the same routine every time so you don't forget anything. When both you and your Poodle get used to the whole procedure, he'll probably sleep through it.

The Poodle Pundit

Professional groomers usually do the left side last, since that is the side that will face the judge. 🐾

Brush out a little at a time, and be careful not to scrape the skin. White Poodles in particular have delicate skin that can be damaged by rough brushing.

The Poodle Pundit

If your black Poodle has a reddish tint to his coat, check his food. Some people speculate that beet pulp, which is used in many commercial dog foods, creates this undesirable effect. On the other hand, beet pulp has been credited with improving a red or apricot coat. 🐾

When brushing, make sure you brush outward to fluff the hair, rather than trying to straighten it. Don't forget the tricky areas behind elbows and ears. If you are not assiduous about grooming very frequently, your Poodle's coat will mat.

Poodle Precautions

Even though Poodles don't actually shed, the texture of the coat does undergo a change in the spring and fall. These periods call for extra-thorough grooming. 🐾

Your most frequently used comb will be made of steel, with medium spaced teeth on one end and more finely spaced teeth on the other. This indispensable tool will allow you to get through all kinds of hair without changing combs.

Bathing Your Poodle

Bathing your Poodle often and thoroughly is the key to a good coat. Clean hair is less apt to mat and break than dirty hair. It also keeps the skin in good condition, which further enhances a beautiful coat. You can use any mild shampoo intended for humans or for canines. It's best to use a fragrance-free shampoo; this will decrease the chances of your dog rolling in muck immediately afterward to rid himself of the smell. Remember, don't bathe your Poodle until you have combed out all the mats!

Bath time for Mardi Gras Poodles   *Courtesy of Jeanne Kennedy*

Begin at the head and work back. Some people like to protect their Poodle's ears with cotton balls before bathing, and this is certainly acceptable. On the other hand, if you are reasonably careful, you won't be pouring water down his ears anyway.

It helps to place a non-slip mat on the bottom of the tub. This helps your Poodle feel more secure, and will make your job easier.

The critical thing is to rinse, rinse, rinse. It should take you at least as long to rinse the dog as it did to soap him up. If you do not remove every trace of shampoo, your Poodle will suffer. Follow with a conditioner, and then rinse, rinse, rinse again.

Drying the Coat

Dry the dog's coat slowly to reduce the possibility of matting. It usually works best to put the dryer on medium heat. Dry one small area at a time, and try for a fluffed, rather than curly, look. A fluffed coat is much easier to clip and looks beautiful as well.

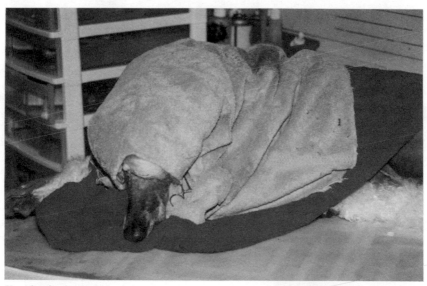

Xanadu after her bath   *Courtesy of Jeanne Kennedy*

The Poodle Pundit

Start drying at the topknot. While doing so, pin a towel closely around the rest of the Poodle so that his hair doesn't dry curly. The topknot is the ball of hair on the head; the mane is the thick covering of hair on forequarters; the bracelets are the puffs on both front and back legs; the pompom is the tail tuft. The clipped areas on the back legs are called bands, and the clipped area of the hindquarters is called the pack. The two puffs of hair on the back on a dog in continental clip are known as rosettes, or more prosaically as kidney patches. 🐾

Pet Clips

Most pet clips can be handled quite nicely by your neighborhood groomer. Your Poodle will need to be trimmed every 6 or 8 weeks. Set up the appointment well in advance, since trimming a Poodle takes time. The best plan, of course, is to befriend a professional Poodle groomer. Become close friends. Very close.

Most common is the sporting or lamb trim. More rarely you will see the Dutch or royal Dutch trim, but these trims, while very handsome, require frequent attention. Other trims include the town and country (clown), retriever, teddy bear, modified continental, and a whole host of others. Follow your own wishes.

The Poodle Pundit

In general, clip your Poodle in the same direction that the hair grows, except for the feet, which you should clip in the opposite direction. 🐾

As mentioned, the lamb trim is the most common clip. A special variety of lamb trim, known as the sporting trim, is permissible in the Brood Bitch and Stud Dog classes. This trim is neat and easy to look after. Your goal in clipping is a nice, evenly-trimmed coat with an understated topknot, beautiful ear fringes, and a pompom for the tail. The feet, face, and tail are clipped close, while the hair on the neck, ribcage, and back is left a bit longer (about one inch) to show a little curl. The leg-hair is

Ferrous, a red/apricot standard Poodle with a non-traditional clip

Courtesy of Vikki Kaufman

scissored (not clipped) to about two inches, then blow dried and shaped to make neat pantaloons. The ears are combed and the hair on them is left long, but evened out. The topknot is combed outward and scissored.

Some people shave the face completely, while others like to leave a handsome little mustache. Sadly, the mustache is out of favor at the moment, perhaps because it is thought to be unhealthy (attracting particles of food, etc.). Some, however, consider it rather distinguished.

The Poodle Pundit

Wherever you encounter loose skin on your Poodle, particularly on the face, stretch it out smoothly with your hand before clipping. This will greatly reduce the chance of a nick. Hold the dog's jaws firmly together while clipping. 🐾

Facial hair trims come in three basic styles. The "doughnut mustache" features long hair in front of the muzzle (grown out from the center of the nose) with a long chin-beard. A variation omits the beard and includes a side mustache of scissored whiskers. The third choice keeps both whiskers and a beard, but the top of the nose is shaved.

Poodle Precautions

If the clippers start to get hot, take a break. Hot clippers can burn your dog and give him a case of clipper rash. 🐾

Assuming your Poodle has a traditionally docked tail, the pompom should cover about half of it (don't just clip it into a little ball on the end.) When clipping or trimming your Poodle's feet, hold each foot firmly as you lift it for grooming. Remember to trim the hair between his toes; you should be able to do it with the clipper edge. Clip against the grain on the feet.

One nice thing about the lamb clip is that if you change your mind and decide to show your Poodle after all, the lamb clip can be grown out and easily converted to an English saddle or continental clip.

If you have decided that showing is not for you or your Poodle, you may have him clipped in any way that appeals to you. In fact, such "fantasy cuts" have been popular for centuries. Find yourself an imaginative groomer and have fun.

Ready for a trim?   *Photo courtesy of Jeanne Kennedy*

Show Clips

Poodle Precautions

If you're going to show your Poodle, you'll need a professional handler—not a pet groomer—to do the grooming. Handlers can spot the strong and weak points of your dog, and know how to enhance or downplay them. 🐾

The aim of the show clip is to give the dog a balanced and elegant appearance, showing off his graceful neck and head and accenting his stylish movement. Most pet groomers are not qualified to give a show-quality clip to your Poodle; you'll need to speak with your breeder or handler to find a competent person.

Poodle Precautions

In all show clips, the topknot may be secured with rubber bands if desired. Rubber bands are not allowed to be used anywhere else. 🐾

The Puppy Trim

Poodles between the ages of 6 months and 1 year are eligible to be shown in this trim. The face, throat, feet, and base of the tail are shaved, but a pompom is scissored at the tip of the tail. The hair on the body, head, and legs is combed and scissored to present a smooth outline.

Although it sounds easy, this is a difficult clip to maintain. The hair is left long enough to grow into an adult clip; however, this saving of hair often creates problems of its own. Some groomers advise owners to forget about what the puppy will look like later on and concentrate on how you want the puppy to look now.

The Continental Trim

This clean, elegant clip is currently the favorite among show exhibitors in the United States. In this country, all three sizes of Poodle are shown in this clip. In England, however, only the Standard is commonly seen in it. It is considered a very fine clip for dogs having a particularly nice derrière.

Puppy clip   *Courtesy of Leslie Sims*

Poodle Potpourri

Curiously, the modern continental clip is much closer to the Poodle's original haircut than is today's sporting clip, which looks sporty enough but would only bog a dog down in the mud. The continental clip one sees in the conformation ring is an extreme example and wouldn't be very useful for hunting, either. 🐾

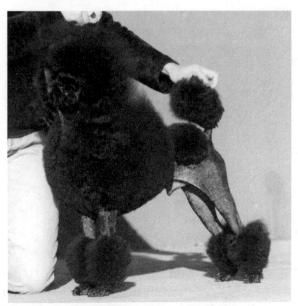

Ch. Silverado Howard Huge, CGC at 2 years. Howie is in a continental clip
Courtesy of Steven Chin

The face, throat, feet and base of the tail are shaved, as are the hind legs, except for the bracelets. Puffs are left on the front legs. The rosettes are optional; some groomers create them by placing a saucer over the appropriate spot, then clipping around it.

The Lion or English Saddle Trim

In my opinion, this is one of the handsomest of trims. It's difficult to care for, however, so it usually seen only in the show ring—and not often there. The face, feet and base of the tail are clipped very short or shaved, while the rest of the coat is left to grow out at least 3 or 4 inches. A perfect lion trim can usually be accomplished only by a professional show groomer with many years of experience.

Poodle Precautions

One advantage of the lion clip is that if you decide it's not right for your Poodle, you can easily switch to the continental. The reverse is not true. 🐾

There are two shaved bands on each hind leg. Del Dahl, the well-known Poodle expert, says that the puffs on the front legs should resemble rolls of toilet paper. I prefer to think of them as muffs instead, like the ones ladies carried in days gone by.

The Sporting Trim

This trim is similar to the pet lamb clip. The face, throat, feet and base of the tail are shaved. There is a scissored "cap" on the top of the head, and a pompom at the end of the tail. The body hair is clipped to an inch or less, with the lower leg hair left a bit longer. Veteran dogs can be shown in this clip.

The Corded Poodle

The Poodle's coat is heavy, harsh, and profuse. If you decided not to groom your Poodle at all, he would develop some awful mats that, if carefully cared for, would develop into cords. At one time, the corded Poodle was considered the very height of fashion.

The Poodle Pundit

If you want to see a corded dog, go to a dog show and take a look at the Puli or the Komondor. Then envision your Poodle in the same style. 🐾

Suppose you're adventurous and like the look of cords. Can your Poodle be corded? Absolutely! Charla Allman of Somerset Standards has a beautiful corded Poodle named Carlie. (You can also check out the Poodle Club of Canada on the World Wide Web to see some very handsome corded Poodles.) Here are Charla's directions for Poodle Cording 101:

▼ NO brushing—ever. Use your fingers to separate cords (some people call them mats) into pencil-sized hunks.

▼ NO straightening—instead of using a slicker brush to make the hair straight, use a spray bottle of water to make it curly. A hose works well outdoors.

▼ NO conditioner—you want the guard hairs to be wiry so they wrap around the undercoat making those glorious mats/cords.

▼ NO drying with heat—just plunk your clean, wet, unconditioned dog in a crate and use fans to dry him.

▼ DO buy a wardrobe for your dog. A turtleneck helps keep the body cords clean and tightens them up. Socks keep bracelets clean and protect from scratching. Pony tail wraps are less damaging than rubber bands. Use lots of colors!

▼ DO have a lot of patience. If a dog scratches, it takes a long time to recover the missing cords.

▼ DO enjoy a dog that looks very different!

Grooming–Besides that Coat

Nails

Hair is not all that needs to be tended during Poodle grooming. The nails mustn't be neglected. A pet Poodle's nails should be short enough that they don't click on the floor. Show dogs often have very short nails, but those extremes aren't necessary for a pet.

If your Poodle spent all day running around on concrete, he probably wouldn't need to have you trim his nails. However, since it's extremely unlikely that he spends that much time on the mean streets, it's up to you. White nails are usually easier to trim than black ones, especially since the dark quick is more visible. However, if you use a Dremel grinding tool as I do to trim nails, both white and dark nails will trim with equal ease. Using a Dremel greatly reduces bleeding, even if you hit the quick by mistake, because it also acts as a cautery.

Poodle Precautions

Brittle nails can be a symptom of thyroid problems. If you notice this, consult your vet. 🐾

If you prefer conventional clippers, choose the guillotine rather than the pliers-type. The latter tend to squeeze or pinch the nail. (However, I must state that some people feel just the opposite. You'll need to experiment.) If you are nervous about trimming nails, take your pet to the groomer for a nail trim. (If the nails click on the floor when the Poodle walks, it's time for a trim.)

Most problematic are nails that have been allowed to grow too long; they can't be cut all at once, but rather just a little bit every other day or so. The quick will recede as the nail is shortened.

The Anal Sacs

Worse than nails (at least as far as smell goes) are the anal sacs, which can sometimes fill up with an awful-smelling brown liquid. If you notice your Poodle scooting his rear along the floor, it's probably because his anal sacs are full and uncomfortable and he is trying to empty them. These can be emptied by you, your vet, or your groomer if your dog is unsuccessful in his efforts. You can easily do it yourself if you don't mind the smell. Get a professional to show you how. Remember—at all costs—to cover the anus with a small rag so the discharge goes into that instead of onto your clothes or skin. Don't, however, empty anal sacs as a matter of course; that could lead to infection.

Eyes

Bathe the eyes in cool water, and note any discharge or discoloration. Clean your Poodle's eyes every day with a soft clean rag. Do not use a cotton ball—the tiny fibers can embed themselves painfully in your dog's eyes.

Poodles who have habitually runny eyes may be suffering from an allergy or other ailment. In some cases, tear stains can be caused by the minerals present in hard water. If tear stains are a real problem, try having your Poodle drink only bottled or distilled water. Think of the remarks your friends will make.

The Poodle Pundit

On the other hand, some people believe that adding yogurt or cottage cheese to the diet will reduce or eliminate tear stains. They think that the stains are caused by bacteria, not minerals. The bacteria causing the stains are killed by the yogurt. Neither method actually eliminates tearing—just the accompanying stains. 🐾

Ears

Poodles naturally have hair growing inside their ears. Although people have different opinions about the advisability of plucking it, most groomers do so every 6 weeks. You can buy a chalky ear powder to make removal easier if you choose. Talk to your veterinarian about whether or not it is best to pluck the hairs from your Poodle's ears.

The Poodle Pundit

Some experts recommend plucking the hair from the Poodle's ears only after he is about 8 months old. Just the hair near the surface should be plucked. You can buy a hemostat at the groomer's to use for this purpose. 🐾

All Poodles need to have their ears cleaned regularly. Your best bet is to use a non-alcohol commercial cleaner made specifically for this purpose. A vinegar-and-water mixture is also fine, provided that you dry the ears carefully after application. If you notice a brown, greasy, waxy exudate in the ear, your Poodle may have ear mites. There are commercial products to get rid of them, too.

Teeth

Dental care is a must for dogs. Since adult dogs have 42 teeth, it's an imposing job. Regular cleaning of teeth and gums will help your Poodle avoid plaque and tartar buildup. Plaque buildup can result in periodontal disease, just as in humans. Periodontal disease not only leads to tooth loss, but can also release dangerous bacteria into the bloodstream. These bacteria then have the potential to lodge in the heart.

Brush your dog's teeth at least once a week (although it's best to brush daily). Use a toothpaste designed for dogs—they come in a variety of dog-pleasing flavors like chicken and beef.

Even though puppies are usually problem-free toothwise, puppyhood is a good time to get them used to brushing. You may use one of the following to brush his teeth:

▼ A baby's nylon bristle toothbrush

▼ A specially designed canine toothbrush that fits over your finger (or a regular-looking one from the grooming supply store)

▼ A washcloth

▼ A piece of cotton gauze wrapped around the finger

▼ Your bare finger.

It's often best to start with your finger, as your dog will probably accept it fairly readily. When he gets used to the idea, you can switch to a toothbrush, which will get into the groove along the gumline where plaque can build up.

Aim the toothbrush at about a 45-degree angle and brush in a circular motion. Scrub the tooth from crown to gum. Most of the plaque buildup occurs on the outside of the tooth, which is a good thing, since the insides are a lot harder to reach. Brush both the upper and lower teeth, especially the big canines and carnassials (shearing teeth) towards the back of the mouth.

Halitosis (bad breath) and inflamed gums can be a sign of dental trouble. (Halitosis can also be caused by stomach disorders, as well as decayed or abscessed teeth.) You can buy an oral cleansing solution like Nolvadent that removes food particles and helps keep breath fresh. Hydrogen peroxide also works well to clean along the gumline.

Even with consistent, thorough brushing, you'll still need to take your older Poodle to the vet for a thorough ultrasound cleaning every year or so.

The essence of Poodle puppy: Ch. Silverado Howard Huge, CGC at 8 weeks of age

Courtesy of Steven Chin

Chapter 9
Poodle Parasites

It's hard to believe that any creature could wish a Poodle ill, but that is apparently the case with parasites. Even the elegant and sophisticated Poodle can fall prey to these beasts, so it behooves you, the Poodle person, to keep your pet free from them.

Those Fierce Fleas

Fleas are the most common and annoying of canine parasites. They love heat and humidity, and they can lay eggs anywhere, from Poodle fur to Persian rugs. Fortunately, we have fewer problems with fleas today than in the past, largely because of responsible pet owners and very effective new anti-flea products.

The Poodle Pundit

The most impressive thing about fleas is their jumping power. They can jump 200 times their body length, right onto your pet—or your leg—from almost anywhere. Fleas are partly made up of a remarkable substance known as resilon, which provides the bounce. 🐾

Flea development includes four stages: egg, larva, pupa, and adult. Only the adult feeds on your dog. The cycle takes 17 to 40 days to complete, depending on the time of year and where the fleas live. Midwestern fleas, for instance, complete their cycle in less than 3 weeks in the summer, but take more than a month in the early spring. Florida fleas usually live for a bit over 2 weeks. The flea population is usually about 50 percent eggs, 30 percent larvae, 15 percent pupae, and only 5 percent biting adults. It's a tough life. Once on your dog, the flea bites down and gets a drink of blood. She then lays her eggs, usually on the dog. The eggs, which are smooth and slippery, fall to the ground. Between 2 days and 2 weeks later, the larvae enter the world. They eat whatever they can find, but seem to prefer the feces of big fleas. Now that is truly recycling.

Flea Potpourri

A female flea can lay 40 or 50 eggs a day—up to 2000 during her lifespan. 🐾

After another week, the larvae make themselves little cocoon-like jackets, called pupae, and go to sleep. When they wake up, they have become adult fleas, ready to leap onto and bite the first creature they encounter. There's actually a theory stating that the footsteps of the prospective victim is the stimulus that awakens the fleas!

Flea Types

There are over 600 species of fleas, but only 4 of them affect your dog: the dog flea (*Ctenocephalides canis*), the cat flea (*Ctenocephalides felis*), the human flea (*Pulex irritans*), and the sticktight flea (*Echidnophaga gallinacea*), which prefers poultry. Don't be fooled by the names. All four species will bite anything, preferences notwithstanding. In fact, the cat flea prefers dogs—when it can find them.

Flea Lifespans

Fleas try to live as long as possible. This is usually only about 50 days, with just a week or so of that time spent as blood-sucking adults. But some have managed to hang on for 6 months or so by hibernating in their cocoons. Scientists have learned this disturbing fact from controlled studies, made more difficult by the fact that every flea looks pretty much like every other flea.

Flea-Borne Diseases

Despite the many admirable qualities of fleas, most pet owners are not enamored of them—with justification. In worst-case scenarios, fleas carry typhus and bubonic plague. They carry tularemia, too, and have been implicated in the spread of Lyme disease. More commonly, fleas are an intermediate host to tapeworm. They itch and are annoying at all times, although they are most active in the summer.

"How Do I Know When My Poodle Has Fleas?"

He will probably scratch, for one thing. If you see your dog scratching, look closer. Darkness-loving fleas stick close to the skin, so you may need a fine-toothed flea comb to find them. They tend to be worst on the head, stomach, and neck, which are difficult for the dog to tend.

Gritty, blackish specks in Poodle fur are another sign of fleas. These are flea feces, composed of partially digested blood. You can test this yourself—drop a bit of water on them, and they will turn red. You can turn this into a science fair project for your child, if you like.

Many dogs are allergic to flea bites, or, more precisely, to the protein in flea saliva. A flea bite can turn into a "hot spot," a raw, oozing area on the dog's skin that is often complicated by a staph infection.

Farewell to Fleas!

Luckily, fleas are a treatable problem. However, you have to de-flea your house and dog at the same time to avoid re-infestation.

▼ Carpets make a wonderful flea nursery. Get rid of them and install washable rugs, vinyl tiling, or Pergo flooring instead. If you must have carpets, those with deep pile.

▼ Try new products available from your veterinarian, like Program, Advantage, and Frontline. Program works to get rid of both flea eggs and larvae by preventing the fleas from laying eggs. However, it does not kill adult fleas or ticks. If your dog is allergic to flea bites, try Frontline or Advantage. These are applied to the dog's skin, but are not absorbed into the bloodstream. I like Frontline best—it lasts for 3 months and is the only product that works on ticks, too. Unlike Advantage, it does not need to be reapplied after swimming or bathing.

▼ Use traditional flea-remedies like dips, powders, and sprays. Many of these contain pyrethrins, which kill adult fleas. Their effects are short-lived, however. A genetically altered form of pyrethrin, called permethrin, lasts longer—about 10 days. Read the labels carefully. Many products can't be used on puppies. And never use a canine flea killer on a cat.

▼ Vacuum frequently, after applying a flea powder/carpet freshener combination to the area. Put mothballs inside the vacuum bag to kill the fleas. Be sure to hit all those tiny crevices where fleas hide. Vacuum the drapes, car, and dog at the same time, and wash your dog's bedding the same day, too.

▼ Sprinkle diatomaceous earth (available in hardware stores and pool supply places) in dark, flea-friendly crevices. Diatomaceous earth is a collection of fossilized seashells and similar microscopic creatures. It's all-natural and kills fleas by piercing their little body parts and drying them to death.

▼ Call Orkin.

What Doesn't Work

▼ Flea collars. They are useless against fleas in heavy-coated breeds like Poodles. Many also contain neurotoxins. Besides, dogs may develop contact dermatitis from a flea collar.

▼ Electronic or ultrasonic devices that are supposed to rid your house of fleas. They don't.

▼ Garlic. No matter what you've heard about the magical properties of garlic, there is no evidence that it has any effect, positive or negative, on fleas. It only affects vampires.

Flea-Proofing the Yard

To help rid your yard of fleas organically, buy nematodes at your garden center. A can of them contains about 100 million microscopic nematodes, which is plenty. Nematodes are little creatures that feed on flea larvae. The nicest thing about them is that after they've eaten all the fleas, they die from starvation.

Lice

There are two kinds of lice—biting and sucking. Both are awful. Lice are a pinky-gray color, and tend to collect on the inside of the ears. Lice can be intermediate hosts to tapeworm. Luckily, it is rare to find lice on an indoor Poodle, but if you do, you need a special shampoo to get rid of them. Check with your vet.

What Makes a Tick Tick

Ticks are 8-legged, blood-sucking parasites. They are all dangerous, and even those that don't inflict a deadly disease at the time they bite can cause local inflammation, anemia from blood loss, toxic reaction, and skin disorders.

Although there are over 850 species of ticks, most have the same modus operandi: they're out for blood. Most dine on blood several times during their lives, usually between every progression in the life cycle. Ticks mature via the same four phases that fleas do.

Poodle Potpourri

Many species of tick have more than one host. The more hosts a tick has, the more dangerous it is. Ticks carry Lyme disease (Borreliosis), Rocky Mountain spotted fever, tularemia, canine ehrlichiosis, heptatozoonosis, haemobartonellosis, and babesiosis. Unfortunately, illnesses transmitted by ticks are notoriously hard to diagnose, mostly because their earliest symptoms mimic those of other diseases. 🐾

Once a tick becomes an adult, it climbs a bush and waits for a hapless host; they've been known to do so for 17 years in a kind of suspended animation. Suddenly, your Poodle walks by. Dinner! The tick leaps on the host and begins feeding. It manufactures its own cement to glue itself to the dog. After lunch, the tick drops off, lays her eggs (up to 6000 of them), and the whole process is repeated. Sometimes during this period the tick mates, but I'd rather not talk about it.

Tick Season

Although you see more ticks in the spring, they are not limited to any one season. Ticks can become active any time the temperature rises into the forties—even in February.

Tick Watching

Although hundreds of tick species exist, you need to watch for just a few. Among these are the Brown Dog Tick, the American Dog Tick, the Northern Deer Tick, the Rocky Mountain Tick, the Black-Legged Tick, and the Lone Star Tick.

The **Brown Dog Tick** is found virtually everywhere in the United States. It's a long reddish-brown tick that is often seen in backyards and kennel areas. You may find it around your house, too, although it is not particularly fond of biting people.

The adult Brown Dog Tick prefers to dine between your dog's toes or in his ears, but in larval and nymphal stages may be found on the dog's back. These ticks can cause anemia, paralysis, ehrlichiosis (tick fever), and piroplasmosis. They also cause Hepatozoon canis, a fatal, slow-developing ailment. Symptoms include fever, eye discharge, muscle inflammation, partial paralysis, and weight loss. This disease is transmitted in an unusual way—apparently only dogs who eat infected ticks are stricken. Human beings are not affected. But then, humans are not in the habit of eating ticks.

The **American Dog Tick** is found primarily in the east, although it's now been spotted along the Pacific Coast. It's a big brown tick with white markings. Despite its name, the American Dog Tick is the one you are most likely to find on yourself.

The **Rocky Mountain Tick** is common in western states. It carries tularemia and Rocky Mountain spotted fever, as well as Colorado Tick and Q fevers. It is a paler version of the American Dog Tick.

The **Northern Deer Tick** is tiny—no bigger than a pinhead as a nymph. It has a 2-year life cycle and lives mostly in the eastern half of the country. The Deer Tick carries Lyme disease, particularly as a nymph. The Black Legged Tick and the Western Black Legged Tick are the southern and western subspecies of the Northern Deer Tick; they are a bit larger and easier to spot.

Poodle Peril

The ultimate source of Lyme disease is a tightly coiled bacterium (spirochete) named Borrelia burgdorferi. Lyme disease is a debilitating illness in both dogs and people, although it is more serious for us than for canines. Less frequently, it affects cats, cows, and horses. Deer and mice are classic carriers of Lyme disease, although dogs may harbor it as well. This doesn't mean that you can catch Lyme disease directly from your dog; it means that your pet could infect more ticks, which may then pass it on to you—or others. 🐾

If you suspect Lyme disease, ask your vet to perform a full "tick panel" on your dog. Lyme disease is difficult to diagnose, but if caught early, it's treatable with antibiotics. Your dog can be vaccinated against Lyme disease, although the vaccine is only about 85 percent effective.

The Lone Star Tick is bigger than the others, like Texas itself. It also carries Lyme disease. The Lone Star tick is not confined to Texas; it can be found throughout the United States. It's brown with a yellow square on its back.

Deticking

During tick season, check your dog daily, especially if he has been in the woods or tall grass. The ears, toes, neck, and head are tick target sites.

Remove all ticks as soon as possible with tweezers or gloves. Never touch a tick with your bare hands—the Lyme disease spirochete can penetrate directly into your skin. Make sure you grab the tick by its head. If you squeeze the body while it's still attached, you may eject the tick's contents (including all disease-carrying material) into your dog.

Discard the tick in the toilet and flush. Wash both the affected spot and your hands thoroughly. The area where the tick was attached may look nasty—it may scab over or swell up—but it's probably not infected.

To prevent tick infestation, use Frontline or another anti-tick product.

Poodle Precautions

Never use cigarette lighters, gasoline or matches to burn a tick; it's too dangerous. Smothering a tick with petroleum jelly or nail polish is also a bad idea; it takes too long. The longer the tick is attached, the more likely it is to transmit disease. It takes 24 to 48 hours for disease transmission to begin. 🐾

Cheyletiella (walking dandruff)

I cannot resist writing about this creature, partly because of its whimsical name. The Cheyletiella mite is big as mites go, but you still need a microscope to get a good look at it. It skims along the surface of your Poodle's skin and causes intense itching and a yellowish dandruff. You can catch it as well, so it's something you want to get rid of right away. A good insecticide, applied over the course of three weeks, should do it.

Scabies (mange)

Talk about itchy—nothing is worse in that department. The scabies mite is a nasty burrowing creature that bores into the upper layers of the skin. People can get a temporary (about 6 days) case from their pets, although these mites do not actually reproduce on us. Puppies and young children are more likely to be affected than adults of either species. A good insecticide needs to be applied to the entire area where the dog lives.

Worms

In general, worms are divided into flatworms and round-worms. Each requires a different dewormer.

Poodle Precautions

If you need another reason to keep your dog worm-free, be aware that it's possible for some Poodle parasites to become human parasites with very little encouragement. Roundworms and hookworms are particular offenders. Always keep your yard picked up, and never allow young puppies to lick your child's face or share food. Interestingly, freshly shed eggs are not infective—they take 2 or 3 weeks to become so. 🐾

The best test to see if your dog has worms is a fecal float, which can be performed at your veterinarian's office.

Tapeworm (*Dipylidium caninum* and *Taenia pisiformis*)

Tapeworms, which infest your dog's intestine, are classified as flatworms and require an intermediate host for transmission. Hosts include lice, feces, rodents, garbage, and raw meat, but by far the most likely candidate is the flea. Lots of fleas mean a greater chance of tapeworm infection.

Dogs and cats can pass tapeworms to each other through ingested fleas; the eggs are shed with the feces in segments that look like grains of rice. The segment degenerates outside the dog, and the eggs that are released are then gobbled up by flea larvae. The ingested eggs form an infective cyst inside the adult flea. When your Poodle crunches down on the fleas in an effort to kill them, he may swallow the cyst and so perpetuate the cycle.

Let's say a mouse eats the flea instead of a dog. Well, the clever tapeworm somehow knows that a mouse is not its proper host. It simply waits in the infective cyst state, hoping that a dog will eat the mouse. If it does, the tapeworm becomes an adult in the dog's small intestine, where it absorbs nourishment.

If your dog has tapeworms, see your vet. No over-the-counter treatments exist. Heartworm drugs like Interceptor, although effective against roundworms, do not prevent tapeworm. The medication of choice for tapeworm is Droncit. Luckily, tapeworm is not a major threat to your dog's health.

Roundworm (*Toxocara canis* or *Toxocara leonina*)

Most puppies are born with roundworms (ascarids), but they can also contract them by eating infected feces or dirt. A roundworm can lay 80,000 eggs which then hatch in the intestine, pierce the intestinal wall, and enter the blood stream. Some of these become encysted in the body of the dog, and are reactivated if the dog becomes pregnant, which, in turn, infects the puppies.

Symptoms include a bloated-looking tummy, a dull coat, vomiting, and diarrhea. Roundworms can be eliminated by worming puppies at 4, 6, and 8 weeks. The treatment works only on adult worms, which is why it must be repeated.

Hookworm (*Ancylostoma canimum* and *Unicara*)

Hookworms, a variety of roundworm, are common in hot, humid areas. These tiny creatures make their living by devouring blood and tissue through the wall of the small intestine. They are called hookworms because they "hook" themselves into the intestinal wall.

Hookworms hatch in feces and generally enter the body through the mouth, although they can work their way into the dog via the pawpads or even the area between the animal's toes. Some kinds of hookworms can be passed from cat to dog and vice versa. In larval form, they can penetrate the skin and cause severe itching and bumps. A mother dog can pass them on to her puppies. A puppy can die of blood loss with an infestation of only 100 hookworms.

Hookworms cause bloody diarrhea, itching, anemia, a dull coat, weakness, and weight loss. You can't see hookworm eggs without a microscope, so if you suspect your Poodle has them, take a stool sample to your vet.

It is possible for human beings to be affected by hookworms. This is usually manifested as a skin irritation that lasts 3 weeks. It is extremely unlikely that they will get into a human's digestive tract.

Whipworms (*Trichuris vulpis*)

Whipworms are yet another variety of roundworm. Their eggs are transmitted through feces and hatch in the dog's intestines. Whipworms lay their eggs in the cecum, the first section of the large intestine; from there, they are passed along in the feces.

They are one of the most common parasites in dogs and are very contagious. Unfortunately, whipworms present few symptoms, but can be fatal if left untreated. Signs of whipworm include bloody or mucusy stools, weight loss, pain, and straining at stool.

You need to be especially careful to pick up dog droppings if your dog has contracted whipworm so he won't be reinfected. Whipworms have a 3-month life cycle, but the eggs can survive in contaminated soil for years. Human beings cannot be infected by this parasite.

Heartworm (*Dirofilaria immitis*)

Heartworms are hideous creatures that live in your dog's heart. They restrict the blood flow and eventually destroy the heart itself. They are transmitted by mosquitoes, then make themselves at home in the right atrium and ventricle of the heart. They can grow to be up to a foot long, and an infected heart can have dozens of them. The infestation process can take as long as 6 months. Symptoms include weakness and wheezing, and untreated heartworm is fatal. Heartworm is endemic in many parts of the country, particularly on the east coast.

You absolutely must put your dog on a monthly heartworm preventative like Interceptor, which has the added benefit of killing other roundworms. Before your veterinarian will prescribe the treatment, however, he will do a heartworm test to be sure your dog is not currently infested.

Keep your Poodle indoors as much as possible during mosquito season. Heartworms can be passed between cats and dogs as well as through intermediary mosquito bites.

Ringworm

Ringworm is not really a worm at all, but a fungus that affects humans (especially kids), dogs, and cats, and is contagious among us. You'll notice a whitish ring beneath the skin's surface. If your dog gets ringworm, have him treated, then clean your house. This includes getting the air filters changed and disinfecting animal bedding. Ringworm spores can float around in the air for years.

Giardia

Giardia are single-celled organisms that live in your dog's intestinal tract. They contaminate fresh water, and infection is caused by swallowing the protozoan cysts. Symptoms of giardia infestation include diarrhea and vomiting, although the infection may be asymptomatic for many months. Giardia must be diagnosed by your vet and treated with prescription medication. A new vaccine has been developed against the disease, but is recommended only for dogs at high risk.

Parasite Medications: A Summary

▼ **Program**: Prevents adult flea reproduction.

▼ **Advantage**: Kills adult fleas quickly.

▼ **Frontline**: Kills adult fleas and ticks.

▼ **Interceptor**: the medication of choice to rid your dog of heartworm, whipworm, hookworm, and roundworm. Does not kill tapeworm.

▼ **Droncit**: Kills tapeworm only. This expensive medication is used only when tapeworms have been diagnosed, not as a preventative. Although Droncit kills the tapeworm on the day it is given, your dog can become reinfected.

▼ **Sentinel**: Combines Interceptor with the insect growth regulator Program.

My Recommendations

Use Interceptor once a month and Frontline during flea and tick season. That should take care of things. If necessary, Droncit can be used for tapeworm. However, since tapeworm is primarily carried by fleas, keeping your dog flea-free reduces the possibility of infestation. Also, see the Resources section at the end of this book for sources and resources on canine parasites.

Chapter 10

Poodles in Peril: Dealing with Emergencies

You, your vet, and your Poodle will form a lifelong partnership in the interest of your dog's good health. Find a vet you like and trust. It's a plus if your vet is especially familiar with Poodles and their most common health problems. However, when an emergency occurs, realize that you will probably be alone with your dog.

Recognizing an emergency is a necessary skill in dog ownership. It can make the difference between life and death. Dog sicknesses can be serious because dogs are stoic creatures; by the time the dog is actually showing distress, the illness may be far advanced. Besides, dogs can't tell you when they're sick—they can only show it through their symptoms.

You must pay attention to small signs, such as lack of appetite, increased drinking, or lethargy. These are often the first symptoms of something seriously wrong. I tend to be conservative with my dogs; as soon as I notice something amiss, I rush them to the vet.

Sometimes, however, you may need to undertake certain measures to help your dog before you can get him to the vet. This chapter is designed to recognize emergency situations and equip you with first-line defense skills.

Keep a complete first aid kit on hand, as described in Chapter 4. It can save your dog's life. The Red Cross, in cooperation with The Humane Society of the United States, offers a pet first aid class. Every pet owner should take it.

Serious Symptoms

The following symptoms are serious enough to warrant an immediate call to your vet:

▼ Blood in feces, urine, or vomit.
▼ Pale, dark red, or yellow gums.
▼ Persistent coughing.
▼ Seizure or shaking.
▼ Prolonged lethargy.
▼ Unexplained weight loss.
▼ Refusal to eat (for 48 hours) or drink (for 12 hours).
▼ Difficulty breathing.

First-Aid Firsts

Because you are your Poodle's first-line health care provider, you should know how to do the following:

▼ Give a pill or liquid medicine.
▼ Take a dog's temperature, pulse, and respiration.
▼ Examine gums.
▼ Determine capillary refill time (CRT).
▼ Induce vomiting.
▼ Stanch bleeding.
▼ Give basic artificial respiration.

Giving a Pill

The classic way is to take the pill, stick it far back in the dog's mouth, then gently hold his mouth shut and stroke his throat at the same time to encourage him to swallow. Be careful not to tilt the dog's head too far back, or the medicine may go down the windpipe rather than the gullet. It's a lot easier just to stick the pill in plenty of peanut butter, put it on the end of your finger, and offer it to the dog. If your dog is odd and doesn't care for peanut butter, try some soft cheese.

For liquid medicine, use the syringe that comes with it. Insert it into the side of the dog's mouth while holding his jaws gently shut so the medicine doesn't dribble out. In an emergency (if you need to administer hydrogen peroxide to induce vomiting, for example), use a turkey baster.

Examining Gums

Gums should be pink (except where there is natural dark pigmentation). Pale gums can indicate anemia, dark-red ones fever or poisoning, and a yellow tinge can signify liver dysfunction.

Taking Temperature and Pulse

The normal temperature for a healthy Poodle ranges from 100–102.5 degrees Fahrenheit when taken rectally. Use a lubricated canine thermometer, shake it down to 96 degrees, and gently insert the bulb about 1 inch into your Poodle's rectum. Hold it there for about a minute. Do not allow the Poodle to sit down! You may need a helper to do this.

Poodle Precautions

Don't forget to disinfect the thermometer with alcohol. 🐾

The normal pulse rate for adult Standard and Miniature Poodles is 60–169 beats per minute. Toys' pulses run higher—up to 180. A puppy's normal pulse may go as high as 220. The key is to find out what is normal for your dog, so check him when you know he's healthy. If you don't want to count for a full minute, just count for 10 seconds and multiply by 6.

The best place to take a dog's pulse is on the femoral artery, which runs along the thigh bone on the inside of the rear leg, about halfway between the hip and the knee. Be sure to use your fingers, not your thumb, to check the pulse—your thumb has its own pulse, and you may get a false reading.

A relaxed dog's respiratory rate runs from 10–30 breaths a minute. Very rapid or labored breathing can be a sign of shock.

Poodle Parlance

Shock is a condition in which the circulatory system largely shuts down. Causes include trauma, drowning, burns, loss of blood, and severe allergic reactions. Shock can be deadly if not treated immediately. Cover your dog to keep him warm, but don't give him any water to drink. Get him to a vet right away. 🐾

Determining Capillary Refill Time (CRT)

This the length of time it takes for blood to reach the capillaries, which measures how well blood and oxygen are getting to the cells. Prolonged CRT (more than 2 seconds) indicates circulatory problems, shock, or dehydration. Test this by pressing your thumb on the gum near the canine tooth. (You can practice on yourself by pressing a fingernail.) Remove your thumb and note how long it takes for the white mark to return to pink. Again, the refill time should be no longer than 2 seconds.

Artificial Respiration

Lay the dog on his side and pull his head forward (if there is no neck injury). Pull the tongue clear of the throat and clean out any debris in the mouth with your fingers. Hold the dog's mouth closed and apply a loose muzzle. Take a deep breath, and, placing your mouth over the dog's nose, make a tight seal. Blow your breath gently into the dog's nose. Sit back and watch the dog's chest deflate. Repeat 10–15 times per minute. If you know how, apply heart massage between breaths.

Poodle Precautions

Dogs recovering consciousness may suddenly bite, so always use a muzzle. You can make one from a strip of cloth, or even a sock. 🐾

Bleeding

Major wounds may require stitches; you can handle minor ones yourself. Penetrating wounds in the abdomen or chest areas are major emergencies.

The Poodle Pundit

Always wash your hands with plain soap and water before treating a wound. 🐾

Clean the wound carefully, removing any hair or dirt in it. Hydrogen peroxide is no longer recommended to clean wounds because it can damage tissues, so use Betadine solution (not surgical scrub or skin cleanser) or Nolvasan (a veterinary wound cleanser. If the wound is a puncture type or an abscess, contact your veterinarian.

Poodle Precautions

Don't try to stop rectal, vaginal, or oral bleeding. These can signal internal injuries, pyometra, parvovirus, or some other internal infection. Get the dog to a vet immediately. 🐾

Stopping Bleeding

Using a clean pad or towel, apply firm pressure to the wound without dabbing or wiping it. If the blood soaks through, just get another towel and place it on top of the first one. Minor bleeding should stop in 5 minutes. For major wounds, keep applying pressure until you get the dog to a vet.

If and when you get the bleeding controlled, clean and dress the wound. Don't slop antibiotic preparations all over an uninfected wound; it's not necessary, and actually works to weaken your dog's immune system in the long run.

Accidents

In case of accidents, you'll need to restrain your dog. This may mean muzzling him or binding his feet. If you have no muzzle handy, use a strip of cloth or a nylon stocking crossed over his nose and tied behind his neck. Loosen it periodically to allow him to pant or vomit. In severe cases, you may need to throw a blanket over him. Avoid moving the dog unless you have to.

If your dog has been struck by a car, assume the worst, even if it looks as if he has only been sideswiped. He may have internal injuries, so take him to a vet just to be safe.

Serious symptoms include bleeding from the nose, mouth, and/or ears. Be aware, though, that some internal injuries are slower in making themselves noticed. More subtle warning signs include pale gums, weakness, and/or general listlessness. By the time you notice such symptoms, it may be too late. Get the dog to a vet immediately.

Bloated Abdomen

The Poodle Pundit

If your dog gobbles broken Christmas ornaments, hooks, pins, staples, or any pointy object, pop a few cotton balls down his throat; the sharp items will embed themselves in the cotton and pass safely through the digestive system. Soft bread works, too. 🐾

A hard, swollen abdomen is a sign of bloat, especially if it is unaccompanied by vomiting. It is most common in Standard Poodles, rather than Miniatures or toys. Unless you have a "bloat kit" and know how to use it, nothing you can do is likely make any real difference. Get to a vet immediately; there is no time to lose. Bloat is a life and death situation.

Broken Bones

If it's an injured leg, tie it to a temporary splint made of a board or something similar. Place the leg in as natural a position as possible, but don't try to set it yourself.

If the back, pelvis or ribs seem broken, stabilize the dog as quickly as possible without repositioning him (slide him gently onto something flat that will allow you to transport him) and get him to a vet.

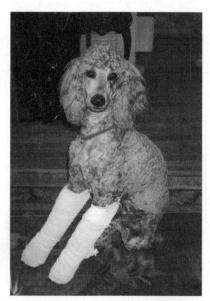

One plate in each leg; six screws in one, eight in the other.
Courtesy of Paula LeFavor

Burns

Superficial burns can be treated with ice packs; don't use butter or oil. Deep burns require veterinary attention. If your dog chews through electrical wire, the superficial burns around the mouth are much less serious than the damage to his internal organs and nervous system. Treat him for shock and get him to the vet. Chemical burns can be caused by acids or alkalis. If you don't know the cause, wash with plain water. If it's an alkali burn, use vinegar and water; if it's an acid burn, use baking soda and water. Get him to the vet.

Choking

If your dog suddenly begins pawing at his mouth while playing or chewing, he could be choking. Other signs include, of course, struggling or gasping to breathe.

If your dog has choked, do not try to retrieve the offending object unless part of it protrudes far enough for you to be able to grasp it firmly to remove it. Just put one finger in the dog's mouth—gently—and see if you can feel the object. Be careful. Overzealous prodding with your fingers could force it back into the throat.

If the dog is small enough, pick him up by the hind legs and shake him. If the dog is too large, pick up his hind legs until his head hangs down. If you're lucky, the object will dislodge itself.

The Poodle Pundit

One of the primary objects that dogs choke on, believe it or not, are cherry tomatoes. Dogs can live perfectly happy lives without this food item. 🐾

If nothing happens, get ready to perform a Heimlich maneuver on the dog. First, open the dog's mouth and pull the tongue forward to open up the airway. Next, stand behind the dog. Applying equal pressure with your arms or hands (depending on the size of the dog) behind the ribcage and using a fist (or, with a small Poodle, the heel of your hand), squeeze the dog sharply. Don't use too much pressure; you could rupture the liver or spleen. Repeat several times. If this doesn't work, cup your hands and try thumping each side of the dog's chest.

If the dog is lying down, you can still perform the maneuver. Turn the dog to his right side if possible, and brace his back with your right hand. Use your left hand to press the abdomen.

If the dog is still choking, you'll need to perform rescue breathing (similar to artificial respiration). Cup you hands around his muzzle and exhale gently into his nose. With small Poodles you can cover his nose and mouth. Getting air into the lungs will not only help your dog get oxygen, but will also make abdominal compressions more effective.

A sharp whack between the shoulder blades may dislodge the offending object. (This doesn't work on people, who, for some reason, tend to be standing up when they choke.)

Coughing

Coughing is a symptom rather than a disease, and can indicate anything from heartworm to exposure to second hand smoke. Pay attention to the elements of the cough. Is it hacking or wheezing? Gagging? How often does your dog cough? All this is important information for your vet to know.

Gastrointestinal Problems: Diarrhea and Vomiting

I am going to discuss these together, since they often occur simultaneously. Diarrhea may result from a simple digestive upset, but it may also be a sign of something more serious. If a bout of vomiting or diarrhea doesn't last more than a day or so, it probably isn't anything to worry about. If your dog experiences continuing or frequently recurring digestive upsets, however, he should be examined by a vet.

Dogs have the ability to throw up with ease, and almost anything can precipitate it: eating trash, a change of diet, poison ingestion, allergies, infections, and so on. Bloody feces, bloody urine, or straining to defecate, however, are all indications of trouble.

A little Pepto-Bismol works wonders to help your dog over a simple bout of vomiting or diarrhea. Fifty-pound dogs require a little over a tablespoon. The liquid kind seems to work better than the pills, but is harder to administer. Have your dog skip a meal or two afterwards and follow with a bland, low-fat diet.

If the diarrhea continues, take your dog to the vet along with a stool sample. The more you can tell your vet about the episodes of vomiting and/or diarrhea (timing, frequency, severity, etc.), the more help you can be in making the diagnosis.

Heat-Related Illnesses

Heat Stress (Hyperthermia)

Dogs are much less efficient in dealing with hot weather than people are, so you must exercise caution in the summer. When your dog is outside, he needs plenty of shade, plenty of water, and plenty of ventilation. Light-skinned Poodles can get sunburned, and so should not be shaved down. Your Poodle will be perfectly comfortable with a thorough brushing to keep his coat fluffy. If your Poodle is in a continental clip, keep him out of the sun entirely or cover him with a shirt. Although sunscreen works well, many dogs lick the stuff off, which precipitates more irritation.

The Poodle Pundit

In very hot weather, you can put some Gatorade or Pedialyte in your Poodle's water to help restore his electrolyte balance. There's even an athletic drink for dogs called Rebound! that does the same thing in a dog-friendly drink. 🐾

Signs of heat stress include staggering, loud panting, vomiting, bright red gums, and a bleary look in the dog's red eyes. The body temperature may rise above 104 degrees. If your Poodle exhibits these symptoms, immediately provide water, submerse the dog in a tub of cool water, or apply cold wet towels. Then call your veterinarian. Heat can also increase the chances of your dog's getting a fungal infection.

Heat Stroke

Symptoms of heat stroke include panting, staring, dilated pupils, salivating, and vomiting.

If your dog does suffer a heat stroke, place cool (not cold) wet towels on his head, neck, and chest. If the towels are too cold, they will constrict the surface blood vessels and lock the heat inside. Try to get him to drink water or Gatorade, but don't force him to do so. Get him to a vet as soon as possible.

There's an old saying that a cold, wet nose means a healthy dog. This is not necessarily true. However, a hot dry nose may indicate the first stages of dehydration; offer your dog some fresh, cool water. If his nose stays hot and dry and there are other symptoms, consult your veterinarian.

Poisoning

The Poodle Pundit

For help, call your vet or the National Animal Poison Control Center hotline at 800-448-2423 or 900-680-0000. 🐾

For most poisonings, **other than those caused by caustics like Drano**, the first thing to do is make the dog vomit.

To induce vomiting, force down a solution one of the following:

▼ half water and half hydrogen peroxide;

▼ lukewarm salt water (2 or 3 tablespoons of salt per cup of water);

▼ 1 tablespoon of dry mustard in a cup of water.

If the dog does not vomit soon afterward, repeat the dosage while waiting for veterinary care. After the dog has vomited (or in place of vomiting if you can't get him to do so), give him 4 tablespoons of activated charcoal mixed in water to absorb the remaining poison.

Poodle Peril

Do not induce vomiting if the dog has swallowed a sharp object or a caustic substance like drain cleaner. 🐾

Antifreeze Poisoning

Ethylene glycol, the principal ingredient in most antifreeze, depresses the central nervous system, damages the kidneys, and enters the cerebrospinal fluid. Symptoms include vomiting, diarrhea, and a staggering gait, which may lead you to wonder if the animal is drunk. Unfortunately, these symptoms may not appear for 8 to 12 hours after ingestion; all the while, irreparable damage is being done to your pet. If you suspect that your dog has ingested antifreeze, get him to your veterinarian immediately. Do not wait to see if the dog gets sick. Treatment is most effective if given within 4 hours after your dog drinks the fluid. The best antidote for dogs now on the market is 4-methylpyrazole, which is sold as Antizol.

Chocolate Poisoning

Dogs love chocolate, but it contains theobromine, which is toxic to canines. Theobromine is most concentrated in baker's chocolate, which is 9 times more toxic than milk chocolate. It is also present in tea and cola.

Symptoms of chocolate poisoning include vomiting, diarrhea, crazed running around (worse than usual), and frequent urination. You'll also notice a faster, more irregular heartbeat if the dog will let you take his pulse, which I doubt.

Hydrogen peroxide can be used to make the dog vomit if he has eaten the chocolate within the previous two hours. In any case, call your veterinarian immediately.

Onion and Garlic Poisoning

Onions can destroy canine red blood cells by oxidizing the hemoglobin inside them; this reduces their ability to transport oxygen throughout the body. A quarter cup of onions or garlic can do a job on a medium-sized dog, and it makes no difference whether the vegetable is cooked or not. An onion-poisoned dog may become anemic and need a blood transfusion. The condition is not permanent, however. Although dogs generally aren't crazy about onions, some people do sprinkle garlic on their dog's food as an aperitif. A little bit used in this way won't hurt your dog.

Rat Poison and other Rodenticides

Rat and mouse poisons are highly toxic to dogs as well as the rodents they were designed to kill. Most of them are anti-coagulants (warfarin, fumarin, diphacinone, bromadiolone) that interfere with the blood's clotting ability. Your dog can bleed to death internally right before your eyes. Unfortunately, the dog may exhibit no symptoms for 3 to 5 days after ingestion.

You need to keep rat poison away from pets, of course, but accidents do happen. The dog next door, Buddy, was poisoned in just such a way; he managed to jump against a not-very-securely-latched door and eat two cakes of poison. Rat poison is extremely palatable to dogs, as well as to rats, cats, and kids, so it's imperative to keep it locked up.

Remember two V's here: Vomit and Vitamin K. If you even suspect your pet has ingested rat poison, induce vomiting immediately and get him to the veterinarian. The vet will probably begin Vitamin K injections—3 times a day for a couple of days—which are followed by Vitamin K pills for 1 to 3 weeks afterwards. This regimen saved the life of Buddy, who never showed a symptom from his unorthodox eating habits.

Bites

Your curious Poodle is forever poking his nose where is doesn't belong. He will occasionally be rewarded with a sharp—and sometimes poisonous—reprisal.

Snakebite

A number of dogs get popped in the nose or leg every year by snakes. The bites of most American snakes non-venomous, but even a non-venomous bite can lead to infection.

Venomous snakebites, like those from rattlesnakes and copperheads, can be deadly. Snake venom is a complicated mess of enzymes, peptides, and proteins. It can affect the nervous, muscular, and urinary systems. To make things even worse, snakebites really hurt.

Treatment includes intravenous fluids, antivenin, steroids, and antibiotics. Do not try to cut the wound and suck the poison out! It's probably too late for that, and you'll only end up making yourself sick. In as many as 1 in 3 cases, a bite from even a venomous snake is not poisonous because the snake has complete control over his venom sacs. He may wish to save his good stuff for real prey, and just bite to frighten your dog.

As if snakes aren't bad enough, some amphibians can also give a dog problems. The Colorado River toad (*Bufo alvarius*), for instance, has poisonous elements in its skin.

Bee and Wasp Stings

Your curious Poodle may end up with a bee sting. Most cases respond well to a quick dose of Benadryl (about 50 milligrams for a 50-pound dog). This reduces swelling and itching. Severe allergic reactions require veterinary intervention.

The Poodle Pundit

When purchasing Benadryl, make sure you buy Benadryl (diphenhydramine) only. Benadryl for Colds and other such over-the-counter medications can also contain ibuprofin or other medications that are dangerous—or fatal—to dogs. 🐾

Spider Bites

There are as many as 100,000 different species of spiders in the world, and sooner or later one of them will bite your dog. Almost every species of spider is venomous, but the venom of most is very weak—good enough to paralyze a fly, but only a minor irritant to people and dogs. In the United States, we now have two kinds of dangerously poisonous spiders. We used to have just one, the black widow, but due to international travel, we are now host to the brown recluse spider as well. The bite of the brown recluse is especially nasty, since it not only makes a dog sick, but also results in ulcerated flesh around the bite. Often the skin becomes necrotic (black) and sloughs off. I have a friend whose dog recently died from this creature's bite. She had spent 6 months and $3,000 trying to save her dog's life.

If possible, capture the offending spider and bring it with you to the veterinarian. Of course, it is unlikely that you will be present or notice the bite. If you even suspect a spider bite, get your Poodle to the vet as soon as possible.

Porcupine Quills

It's possible for your Poodle to run afoul of a porcupine, a slow-moving denizen of the northern woods. Get to a veterinarian if possible, but if not, you can try to extract the quills with pliers. It's important to get the entire quill out so there's less risk of infection.

Seizures

Many factors can causes seizures: epilepsy, sleep deprivation, food allergies or overuse of supplements, toxins like heavy metals and flea dips, previous head trauma, hypoglycemia, and dehydration. Signs include staggering, head tilting, sudden blindness, snapping, jerking, or unaccountable aggressiveness.

During a seizure, the dog is unaware of himself and his surroundings. Remove dangerous objects from around him, but try not to touch the dog. If he is banging his head against a hard floor, slip a thick towel underneath it.

Stay calm. Seizures are frightening, but rarely life threatening. After the seizure is over, the dog will usually come to you for reassurance and love. Sit quietly with your dog and soothe him.

If your dog has a seizure for the first time, or if a seizure continues for more than 30 minutes or the dog has multiple seizures, it's an emergency. Take the dog to the veterinarian immediately. Devise a makeshift stretcher with a blanket.

The Poodle Pundit

If your dog has seizures, note the date and time of the attack, its length, severity, symptoms, and your thoughts about what may have precipitated the attack. 🐾

Photo by Catharine Haake

Chapter 11

The Poodle as Patient

L et's talk first about the most common and important medical procedure your Poodle may undergo.

Spaying and Neutering

Unless you have a show-quality dog you are planning on exhibiting, you will want to spay or neuter your pet. Here's why:

▼ It's safer and healthier for your dog. Mammary and testicular cancers are serious risks for unneutered animals. Unspayed females are also at a serious risk of pyometra, an infection of the uterus.

▼ It's easier on you. Unneutered dogs tend to wander and can be generally annoying around the house, often marking every piece of furniture. A female in heat is a real nuisance.

▼ It's your only ethical choice. Millions of animals are euthanized every year in this country. Most of them are the products of people who carelessly bred their animals, thinking (erroneously) that dog breeding is the way to riches, or people who just didn't bother with neutering and simply dropped off the resultant puppies at the pound. Even people who think they have found good homes for their puppies would be amazed at what's happened after the animals are placed. A minority of pets stay in their original placement home.

Vaccinations

It is important that your dog be vaccinated against the following diseases:

▼ Rabies
▼ Canine parvovirus
▼ Distemper
▼ Coronavirus
▼ Leptospirosis
▼ Hepatitis (canine adenovirus-1)
▼ Lyme disease (where the disease is endemic)

Your veterinarian will develop a vaccination schedule that is right for your dog and your area. A great deal of controversy rages about when and how often to vaccinate. If you have any concerns, talk them over with your veterinarian and decide together on a protocol for your Poodle.

Rabies

Rabies is a lethal viral disease. The virus is carried in the saliva of the affected animal, and it is usually transmitted through bites. A person or animal bitten by a rabid animal has about a 75 percent chance of contracting the illness.

Any mammal can contract Rabies. The virus attacks the central nervous system, and is 100 percent fatal once symptoms appear. An unvaccinated dog is at great risk of getting the disease if bitten by a rabid animal.

Skunks and raccoons are particular carriers of rabies. If you notice one of these nocturnal animals wandering about in the daytime, especially if it seems disoriented or in poor condition, call your local animal control. It may well have rabies.

The incubation period for rabies is 5 days to 10 months. Getting a rabies vaccination for your dog is not only safe and sensible, it is mandatory everywhere in the United States. Puppies should be immunized against this disease between 16 and 24 weeks of age.

Canine Parvovirus (CPV)

This disease was first reported worldwide in 1978. It is apparently a mutation of a parvovirus that previously affected only cats, but crossed the species barrier. It is a great killer of puppies between 6 weeks and 6 months of age, although dogs of any age can get it. Parvo is transmitted through dog feces; from there it can be carried on dog hair and on people's shoes. It is resistant to most disinfectants other than bleach, so get out the Clorox. Susceptibility is increased by keeping puppies outdoors where parvo can live in the soil for up to two years. Puppies should be completely immunized against CPV at between 16 and 18 weeks of age. Human beings are immune to CPV (so far).

Parvovirus is not curable, but a promising new treatment is being developed. It involves injections of canine immunoglobulin IgG, which is extracted from the serum of dogs who have recovered from the disease.

Symptoms of parvovirus include vomiting, abdominal pain, bloody diarrhea, high fever, and depression. The diarrhea can be so severe that an infected dog can literally waste away from it. Another form of the disease (*canine parvovirus myocarditis*) affects the heart. It, too, is often fatal.

Canine Coronavirus

This disease, related to the human cold, was first identified in 1971. It is transmitted by food that has been contaminated by the feces of an infected dog. It is very contagious and produces vomiting, diarrhea, and depression—symptoms similar to those of canine parvovirus. It's most serious in puppies.

A vaccine is available, but many vets regard the vaccine as more dangerous than the disease and recommend against its use. However, a new modified live virus vaccine has been developed. It induces rapid antibody development in the animal and induces immunity with a minimal risk of allergic reactions.

Canine Distemper

Distemper remains the main killer of dogs worldwide—50 percent of unvaccinated adult dogs infected will die from its effects. In puppies, the percentage is almost 80 percent. This extremely contagious disease is caused by an airborne measles-like virus that can survive for years. The incubation period is 7 to 21 days. The disease affects the dog's nervous system, and initial symptoms include lethargy, fever, runny nose, a yellow discharge from the eyes, labored breathing, and lack of appetite. Later symptoms include a nervous twitch and thickening of the pads and nose. (The disease used to be called "hardpad" for this reason.) Dogs progressing to this stage are unlikely to make a full recovery.

Puppies should be immunized between 12 and 14 weeks of age.

Pinnaped Peril

Believe it or not, sea lions carry distemper. Poodles should be kept well away from them. I admit that sea lions and Poodles are seldom found in conjunction, at least in nature. However, they can both end up in the circus. It's something to consider. 🐾

Infectious Canine Hepatitis

This disease, too, is particularly dangerous to puppies. It is not related to human hepatitis. Dogs contract it by swallowing material contaminated with the saliva, urine, or feces of affected dogs. The incubation period is 5 days. It attacks the liver, kidneys, and blood vessels.

Canine hepatitis presents itself much as distemper does. It is especially dangerous because, even after a dog recovers from the disease, he can pass it along to other animals for a period of up to 6 months. Human beings are immune to canine hepatitis. Puppies should be immunized at 12 weeks.

Leptospirosis

This is a bacterial infection that can be transmitted to human beings. The agent is a spirochete that exists in at least 6 varieties. Recently, the disease has returned in a new and virulent strain, one that was previously seen only in horses and cows. Dogs contract it through direct contact with the urine of infected animals, but not all dogs who encounter it will be become sick. They may, however, become carriers and shed the organism in their urine, thus infecting other animals.

Lepto affects the liver and kidneys, and can cause total renal shutdown. Treatment includes antibiotics and, in cases of kidney failure, dialysis. A vaccine is available for some forms of lepto-spirosis; however, many vets do not recommend its use, especially for young puppies, because the older forms of the virus are seldom seen nowadays, and the vaccine can cause reactions in some dogs. A vaccine against the new lepto strain is being tested.

Kennel Cough (Infectious Rhinotracheitis/Infectious Tracheobronchitis)

Kennel cough is an acute respiratory disorder that is often found where dogs share close quarters, like kennels, shelters, boarding facilities, and veterinary hospitals. Kennel cough is a complex of symptoms rather than a single, specific disease; it can be caused by a host of agents, including viruses and bacteria. In adult dogs, it presents as a bad cold; the dog often shows no symptoms of ill health other than a runny nose and a cough. Some have fever or lack of appetite. For puppies the condition can be more serious. You can immunize your dog against *Bordetella bronchiseptica*, the most common agent for kennel cough. Puppies should be immunized at 16 weeks.

Lyme Disease (Borreliosis)

Although not so devastating an illness as in people, dogs can contract Lyme disease, which is transmitted by a bacterium found in ticks (and maybe fleas—the ticks got it from white-footed mice). This disease manifests itself in lameness and swollen joints; it is treated with antibiotics.

Dogs living in tick-infested areas should be vaccinated against Lyme disease. However, since the vaccine can cause reactions, it may not be advisable to administer it unless your dog spends a great deal of time in wooded areas.

Ear Problems

Poodles seem particularly prone to ear problems. One reason is that Poodle hair grows deep into the ear canal. Consequently, Poodle ears need to be cleaned often. Some people use olive oil, which is soothing but can collect at the bottom of the ear, while pure alcohol is too harsh. You can cut alcohol with vinegar to make a soothing astringent ear cleaner, or better yet, buy a commercial product (usually a mild antiseptic) specifically designed for the job. A dry ear is a healthy ear; you can also buy a drying agent for your dog's ears.

Some people remove ear-canal hair from their Poodles every month. They pull it out with a hemostat, then clean the ear.

Poodle Precautions

Never stick any sharp object into your dog's ears; it is distressingly easy to puncture his eardrum. Use a cotton ball or soft clean rag. 🐾

All dogs can get ear mites, from each other or from the family cat. Both prescription and over-the-counter medications are available to remedy the problem.

Hereditary Diseases

Every breed has a host of genetic problems; with new DNA research, however, careful breeding should eliminate most of them. We aren't there, yet, though. While they may make perfectly good pets, dogs with any of the following hereditary diseases should not be bred.

Patellar Luxation (Slipping Stifles, Loose Knee)

This condition occurs most commonly in Toy and Miniature Poodles, and to a much lesser extent in Standards. It is congenital and hereditary, and several different genes are involved. A dog with this condition has a kneecap that slips out of joint and tends to rest on the inside of the knee. Dogs with patellar luxation are intermittently lame and move with the bad leg held off the ground.

Veterinarians grade patellar luxation from 1 to 4. Grade 1 cases may be so slight as to be unnoticeable, while Grade 4 cases produce permanent lameness. Serious cases require surgery, followed by 6 weeks of forced rest. The results are usually excellent.

Legg-Calvé-Perthes Disease

This condition affects Toy and Miniature Poodles, as well as other small breeds. It is probably caused by a genetic defect. Symptoms most commonly appear between the ages of 4 and 12 months. In this disease, the hip receives an inadequate supply of blood; in about 85 percent of the cases, only one leg is involved. The dog will be lame and show pain when the affected leg is moved. Surgical removal of the femoral head is often necessary, since the condition will not abate on its own.

Patent Ductus Arteriosus (PDA)

This is a congenital condition in which the shunt that connects the aorta and pulmonary artery fails to close, as it should, when the puppy is born. This permits unoxygenated blood to mix with oxygenated blood, which leads to a general decrease of oxygen in the bloodstream. Symptoms include lethargy and weakness. Surgery is recommended for this relatively common defect.

Sebaceous Adenitis (SA)

This incurable skin disease, caused by a recessive gene, affects Standard Poodles. Some experts estimate that as many as 50 percent of all Standards are either carriers of this illness or are affected by it. The sebaceous glands become inflamed and deteriorate, which eventually leads to hair loss. The disease seems to be cyclical and appears most commonly in young adult dogs.

The Poodle Pundit

The test for SA is performed by taking two small samples of skin from an area near the dog's shoulders, which are then analyzed. It is performed for the first time after the second birthday, and every year after that in animals used for breeding. The sample must be evaluated by a certified veterinary dermatopathologist. 🐾

Poodle owners will first notice silvery scales clinging tightly to the hair shafts, which is often accompanied by a musty odor. Awful as it looks, SA does not lead to scratching or irritation;

however, the disease is sometimes complicated by a secondary bacterial infection. It progresses rapidly.

Treatment includes keeping the dog comfortable through long and frequent baths. You can use a bath oil first. Then wash the dog thoroughly with a hypoallergenic dog shampoo, followed by a good rinse. You will find that the water will turn gray with the loose scales you have dislodged.

This treatment sometimes seems to encourage regrowth of hair, and, in all cases, the dog feels more comfortable. SA is not medically serious—it is truly only skin deep. Your Poodle is perfectly fine otherwise, even though he may look odd.

The Poodle Pundit

Some dogs seem to respond to isotretinoin, a synthetic form of vitamin A. Omega fatty acid supplements have also proved useful. 🐾

Renal Dysplasia

This is a genetic defect of the kidneys. The form found in Standard Poodles is called Juvenile Renal Disease (JRD). Unlike many other forms of kidney disease, JRD affects very young dogs. Early symptoms include pale, dilute, almost odorless urine and the leaking of urine; later, vomiting, anorexia, lethargy, and muscle weakness appear. Sometimes a kidney biopsy is the only way to make an accurate diagnosis. Sadly, there is no cure for this disease, but early treatment and a diet low in protein and phosphorus can lengthen and improve your Poodle's quality of life.

If your dog develops this disease, inform the breeder immediately; it means that both parents carry the recessive gene responsible.

Eye Diseases in Poodles

Poodles are plagued with 22 heritable eye diseases. Most common are progressive retinal atrophy (PRA), juvenile cataracts, entropion, and ectropion. Genetic tests can be performed to find out if your dog (or his parents) carries the gene that causes the problem.

If your Poodle has runny eyes, suspect a blocked tear duct or perhaps a foreign body in his eye. However, if your Poodle suffers long bouts of runny eyes, the constant discharge will eventually stain his hair a pinkish-brownish icky color. You can apply a tear-stain remover, but unless you eradicate the source of the problem, the effect is only temporary. Tetracycline has been used with some success in removing brown tear stains, but it does nothing to stop the tears themselves. (See Chapter 8 on Grooming for more hints.)

Progressive Retinal Atrophy (PRA)

This incurable, inherited condition inevitably leads to total blindness. It is most common in Miniature and Toy Poodles, but has been seen in all sizes; it sometimes occurs in conjunction with cataracts.

In PRA the dog loses first night, then day vision. The disease develops when the light-sensitive cells in the retina receive an inadequate blood supply, which causes them to wither away. PRA affects both eyes and progresses slowly. Its presence can be detected by ophthalmoscopic examination. Such an exam, however, can tell only if the disease is present at the time of examination. A more complex test, the electroretinogram, can predict whether or not your Poodle will ever get the disease. Even this test, however, cannot tell whether or not your dog is a carrier.

The Poodle Pundit

Your local Poodle club may sponsor an eye clinic in your area to test your dog for PRA and other eye diseases. Experts recommend that your dog be tested for PRA after his second birthday and annually thereafter.

PRA is caused by a recessive gene, so a dog's parents should be screened. An organization known as the Canine Eye Registration Foundation, Inc. (CERF) was founded in 1974 to certify dogs regarding PRA and other eye diseases.

There is now a DNA-based test for progressive red-cone degeneration (PRCD), the major form of PRA, which affects Miniature and Toy Poodles. Dogs can be classified as normal, carriers, or affected with PRCD. This test is offered by Opti-Gen, a private genetic-testing company. The test also serves to separate PRCD-affected dogs from those suffering the other, less common forms of PRA.

Poodle Potpourri

The force behind CERF was Dolly Traumer, a Poodle fancier. She insisted that only dogs who had been examined by a member of ACVO (American College of Veterinary Ophthalmologists) could be certified as eye-disease free. CERF not only maintains a registry of dogs free from eye disease, it also collects data and distributes it to researchers around the world. 🐾

Bilateral or Juvenile Cataracts

This condition, variously called bilateral (affecting both eyes), juvenile, or developmental cataracts, is characteristic of young dogs. It is transmitted genetically and is common in Standard Poodles.

The disease presents itself as a cloudiness in the lens. It develops rather slowly, usually first in one eye, then in the other. Cataracts often first appear between 9 and 18 months of age, but some cases do not show themselves until the dog is between 4 and 6 years old; this is particularly unfortunate since most dogs are bred before that time. Severe cases of juvenile cataracts cause blindness; in some cases, there is considerable discomfort as well.

Poodle Potpourri

Cataracts in dogs can be treated with prosthetic lenses. This is an expensive option, but one that will restore your dog's sight. This surgery is available to dogs who have lost sight in both eyes—a one-eyed dog can see well enough to manage without correction. Cataract surgery requires extensive post-operative care, including administering medication frequently. 🐾

There is no treatment that will prevent or slow the development of cataracts. Surgery to remove the opacity is the only treatment. One new treatment, called phacoemulsification, uses ultrasound to shatters the bad lens, then removes the pieces!

Entropion and Ectropion

Entropion is a painful turning inward of the eyelid; in ectropion, the eyelid turns out. These are usually congenital conditions that require surgery.

Canine Hip Dysplasia (CHD)

Hip dysplasia is a malformation of the hip joint that occurs when the head (ball) of the femur (thighbone) does not fit correctly into the corresponding pelvic socket (acetabulum). The joint eventually becomes malformed, sometimes to the extent that it is completely unusable. A dog may have dysplasia in one or both hips. The earlier the disease manifests itself, the more serious it is. Hip dysplasia is an inherited condition. It's considered a polygenic disease, which means that both parents must carry the defective gene. Symptoms include difficulty in getting up and rear-end lameness. It can be accompanied by arthritis.

This painful, crippling disease affects mostly Standard Poodles, but has been seen in Miniatures and even Toys. No one has yet identified all the genes responsible for hip dysplasia. Not all dogs having a genetic predisposition will actually develop it.

The Orthopedic Foundation for Animals (OFA), a non-profit organization affiliated with the School of Veterinary Medicine at the University of Missouri, will, for a small fee, inspect the x-rays of dogs 2 years or older whom the owners wish to breed. They will then issue a report to the dog's owner, good for the lifetime of the dog, which evaluates the dog's hip joint conformation.

Although hip dysplasia is not noticeable at birth, the condition is progressive and causes pain, inflammation, and eventually arthritis, which can be severe. Rigorous exercise makes the problem worse. Dogs with slight hip dysplasia are frequently overlooked or misdiagnosed. The only way to know for sure if a dog has dysplasia is to have him x-rayed by a competent veterinarian. The diagnosis should then be confirmed by a veterinary radiologist. This condition is sometimes extremely difficult to detect, and unless the dog is properly positioned for the x-ray, a misdiagnosis could result.

Ask your veterinarian to perform an OFA- or Penn–Hip-style x-ray when your dog is being spayed or neutered. This will give you a baseline reading, so that if your Poodle develops hip problems later, you and your vet will be able to check the new x-rays against the early ones. Treatment options for dysplasia include diet (usually involving weight loss), enforced rest, exercise, stretching exercises (swimming is good), drug therapy (buffered aspirin, Naproxen, Adequan, and Cosequin), acupuncture, and surgery.

The surgical procedure itself varies from case to case. Possible procedures include femoral head excision, triple pelvic osteotomy, and total hip replacement. In femoral head excision, the ball part of the hip is removed, and a piece of muscle or joint tissue is placed between the femur and the socket. Scar tissue develops which then supports the leg. This procedure is best performed on dogs weighing less than 45 pounds, since the scar tissue will not support a heavier dog. Most vets will perform this surgery on both hips at the same time. The prognosis is good in most cases.

A triple pelvic osteotomy is a preventative surgery, designed to keep arthritis and pain from developing in the affected area. It is performed on dogs who are at least 7 months old. The bone is cut in 3 places, while the acetabulum (pelvic socket) is rotated and the femur set correctly in the socket. Plates, screws, and wires are permanently installed to hold everything together. This surgery can be performed on only one hip at a time. Afterwards, the dog must rest for 6 to 9 weeks.

In total hip replacement, the ball and socket are removed and replaced with stainless steel and plastic, respectively. This surgery can be performed on an adult dog of any age. It's a major undertaking, but the success rate is over 95 percent. Your dog should feel like a new man (so to speak) within 6 weeks after the surgery is performed.

A more non-invasive heat-based surgery is now also an option for young dogs. It's a prophylactic procedure best done during neutering.

Poodle Precautions

Some people say that feeding your dog megadoses of vitamin C will prevent hip dysplasia. There is no evidence to support this finding—but maybe it's true. 🐾

It's important to keep the diet of a young puppy, especially a Standard Poodle, balanced and not loaded with extra calcium. Feeding a growing puppy too much food in general, which results in rapid weight gain, can make the situation worse— although it doesn't cause the condition to begin with. Exercise and/or jumping don't cause hip dysplasia, either, although severe physical stress can exacerbate the problem.

Epilepsy

Unfortunately, this chronic seizure disorder is common in all three varieties of Poodles. In fact, epilepsy is more common in dogs than it is in human beings. Formally known as idiopathic epilepsy, this brain disorder is inherited. Other types of epilepsy may be acquired; a diagnosis of idiopathic epilepsy is made only when other possible causes for seizures have been ruled out. Scientists are currently trying to locate the specific gene responsible. The disorder usually manifests itself in animals between 1 and 4 years of age.

Symptoms vary from a mild, barely noticeable seizure (mistakenly called "petit mal," or "little sickness") to "grand mal" ("big sickness") episodes of frightening proportions. Seizures generally last less than 2 minutes. A few dogs experience "cluster seizures," in which a number of seizures occur within a short time. The seizures are punctuated by brief periods of consciousness.

Before the seizure starts, the dog may exhibit an "aura," during which he may pace, whine, and become fearful. The actual seizure is called the "ictal" phase, in which the dog loses consciousness and experiences random muscle contractions of variable intensity. He may also salivate and lose control of his bladder or bowels. Finally comes the "postictal" phase, during which the dog is conscious but may be confused or unresponsive.

Poodle Parlance

A seizure is a disturbance of brain function characterized by random muscle movement and a loss of consciousness. 🐾

Since there seems to be a relationship between stress and the onset of seizures, owners of epileptic dogs try to keep their dogs as calm and comfortable as possible. Some owners use natural or holistic remedies like flower essence of cherry, impatiens, or rock rose. There is no cure, but the condition is treatable with medication. Drugs used in the treatment of epilepsy include phenobarbital, potassium bromide, and Valium.

Poodle Potpourri

Not all seizures are caused by epilepsy. There is growing evidence that some seizures may be a reaction to certain vaccinations—which is why many people are rethinking the timing of such preventative measures. 🐾

For information on how to take care of your dog during a seizure, see Chapter 10, "Poodles in Peril."

Von Willebrand's Disease

Standard and Miniature Poodles are susceptible to this inherited bleeding disorder. (Cats, human beings, pigs, and horses can also be victims.) In this disease, spontaneous bleeding occurs, often from the mucosa of the mouth, nose, or gastrointestinal tract. A simple DNA check for this disease can be done with a cheek swab at any time after birth.

Addison's Disease (Hypoadrenocorticism)

This autoimmune disease, first described in human beings, affects Standard Poodles. The most common sufferers are middle-aged females. In this condition, the hormone-producing adrenal glands are destroyed or produce an insufficient amount of essential hormones. Symptoms include poor appetite, diarrhea, vomiting, abdominal pain, weakness, depression, and shivering. The symptoms are vague, however, and are often overlooked—especially since not every dog exhibits all symptoms.

Poodle Potpourri

President John F. Kennedy had Addison's disease, but, as with dogs, his symptoms were so vague that his doctors couldn't figure out what was the matter with him for years. 🐾

No one is sure, but it is suggested that Addison's disease is caused by a single recessive gene. In any case, the immune system attacks the hormone-producing cells. It can also be the result of a tumor, pyometra, distemper, or pituitary problems. A definitive diagnosis can be made only by administration of the ACTH stimulation test, which measures cortisone levels in the blood before and after stimulation of the adrenal glands.

Poodle Parlance

There are two adrenal glands, each located right in front of a kidney (ad + renal). They produce the hormones cortisone and aldosterone, both of which are essential to life. Cortisone is used by every tissue in the body, while aldosterone regulates sodium and potassium levels. 🐾

Addison's disease has no cure, but is treatable through replacement of the missing hormones, which are administered orally for the remainder of the dog's life. The deficient cortisone is usually supplied by a low dose of the drug prednisone. An injectable form of aldosterone, desoxycorticosterone pivalate (DOCP), which is given every 3 weeks, has been tried successfully and will soon be approved for general use. Untreated dogs die of this disease.

Poodle Precautions

Standard Poodles seem to be also affected by a rather large number of other autoimmune diseases, including hemolytic anemia and hypothyroidism. 🐾

Seasonal Allergies

While you're sneezing away with the first appearance of pollen in the spring, your Poodle is pestered, too. But he's not sneezing—he's scratching. And the more he scratches, the worse he looks and feels. Dogs can be allergic to a disconcerting variety of substances, the most common of which are pollen, dust, and dander (including human dander).

Luckily, Poodles are among the breeds less likely to be victims of inhalant allergies, but they can and do occur. They tend to show up when the animal is between 1 and 3 years of age. Although there is no real cure for inhalant allergies, they can be managed by keeping your dog as far away from the allergen as possible. Oatmeal baths are soothing and helpful in alleviating symptoms. Treatments with topical medications of hydrocortisone or oral antihistamines are usually helpful, and sometimes a short course of an oral cortisone treatment (like prednisone) is necessary. In a few cases, it may be worthwhile to have your dog undergo hyposensitization therapy, in which your vet makes up a vaccine that specifically targets the allergen afflicting your dog. To do this, he will need to perform a skin test to identify the offending substance.

Diet therapy may also be effective; try adding fatty-acid supplements to your dog's diet. Be sure to choose one that contains the all-important omega-3!

Squamous Cell Carcinoma

About one-third of all canine cancers are skin tumors. Squamous cell carcinoma is one of the most common kinds of skin cancer found in dogs. There are two types, both of which are common in Standard Poodles. One type is known as cutaneous squamous cell carcinoma, which is most often found in older dogs. Lesions commonly appear on the head, toes, abdomen, and perianal area, and appear as firm, raised bumps. They often look ulcerated. No one knows for sure what causes this condition, although many suspect the sun is to blame. White poodles with little hair on their abdomens are affected most often.

The other type, subungual squamous cell carcinoma, occurs most often in black Standard Poodles (as well as in many other black coated breeds). These tumors normally show up on the toes, and many dogs will have several appearing at once. It is a little more common in females than in males. Again, excessive exposure to the sun may be a factor.

The treatment for both types of squamous cell carcinoma is surgery. If the tumor appears on the toes, the toes will have to be amputated.

Gastric Dilation (Torsion)

Known colloquially as bloat, this fearsome condition affects Standard Poodles, as well as many other large dogs. Although what predisposes certain dogs to bloat is uncertain, it does seem to run in families and is more common in dogs aged 6 to 9 years. Some people suspect that some dogs are born with their stomachs slightly out of the normal position, which allows them to twist more easily.

Most bloat episodes seem to occur between 6 p.m. and midnight. For some unknown reason, the movement of food stops. The food begins to ferment and produces gas that, in turn, swells the stomach. The stomach then twists, which causes the trapping of air and the stoppage of blood circulation to the liver and spleen.

Symptoms include severe abdominal pain, pacing, whining, drooling, non-productive vomiting, and a hard abdomen. The dog will show signs of extreme stress. Bloat is deadly and any dog exhibiting its symptoms must be taken to the vet for immediate surgery. A delay of a couple hours can kill your dog. In most cases, the vet tacks the stomach to the abdominal wall (gastropexy), and removes any necrotic (dead) tissue. Unfortunately, once bloat occurs, it will almost certainly occur again. Male dogs, fearful dogs, and dogs who are underweight are most likely to get this disease.

Poodle Potpourri

One of the most famous show Poodles of all time, the white Standard Ch. Lou Gin's Kiss Me Kate, who won a record 140 Best in Shows (an extraordinary feat, especially for a female dog, who often lack the spectacular coats of the males), died of this disease in 1983. 🐾

Prevention techniques include frequent, small meals and the addition of vegetables to the diet. It doesn't hurt to give an antacid containing simethicone to susceptible dogs. Dogs who gulp their dinners seem to be in more danger than dainty eaters, so some people recommend spreading the dog's food over a larger area to help them eat more slowly. Others recommend putting large rocks (too big to be swallowed) or, even better, a heavy chain, in with the dinner to slow eating.

Chapter 12
The Polite Poodle

Every Poodle should be a trained Poodle. This doesn't mean he needs to be a circus performer (even though he may have ancestors who were). A trained Poodle is one who knows—and obeys—basic commands, and who acts in a friendly and civilized manner. Unfortunately, not all Poodles are trained Poodles. And, more unfortunately, their lack of training is not their fault. It's their owner's.

An untrained Poodle is an unhappy dog who is constantly and uselessly reprimanded by his owner, gets into trouble, and is not liked. Too often, he ends up tyrannizing a household—or worse—in an animal shelter. Be of good cheer, however. Poodles are almost infinitely sociable and trainable. They're just waiting for a teacher. That's you.

Before you can even think of training your Poodle, you must train your family. All too often, the family dog responds only to one member of the family. When that person is not home, then, the dog is essentially untrained. A dog who will sit or come only for one family member is not trained.

Training the dog needs to be a family project, even though it is best to have one person as the training leader. That person will do the actual teaching of new skills, then practice them with the dog—and the rest of the family. Everyone must cooperate in this task. A family member who allows the dog to do as he pleases undermines the entire training project.

Silver boys love to fly. Mardi Gras Kiyara Different Drummer ("Ringo")
Courtesy of Jeanne Kennedy

Training Methods

Poodles respond eagerly to positive reinforcement. The old "jerk and praise" method of correcting a dog went out years ago. It's cruel and works only at the expense of making your dog fearful of you.

Poodle Potpourri

Aversive, confrontational training methods were developed during World War II to train war dogs. Unless you plan to have your Poodle join the Marines, you will have much, much better results using praise and positive reinforcement. Your dog will like you better, and you will forge a loving bond. 🐾

Training Goals

You can't train your Poodle until you know in your own mind what you want from him. Make a reasonable list of everything you would like your Poodle to know and do (or not do). To accomplish this, you need to set up regular training sessions. Each one needs to have a specific goal. If you lack an objective, you won't know whether you've accomplished anything or not during a session. That won't help you—or your dog—learn anything from the experience.

Keep a logbook of your training sessions, and write at the top of the page the goal for each session. Afterwards, record how the session went. If you do this faithfully, you'll have a valuable record that will be useful in the future. It will also help focus your attention on the specific aim of each training session. Don't try for too much at any one time.

The Poodle Pundit

Always wait until you are calm and relaxed to work with your dog. Poodles are psychic when it comes to picking up on moods, and your dog's mood will echo your own. If you want your dog to associate training with happiness, you just have to be—well—happy.

Don't try training your dog right before dinnertime; his mind will be on his dish. A hungry dog cannot keep his mind on training. 🐾

Training Basics

Before you begin training, exercise your dog just enough to take a little of the edge off. Your energetic, life-loving Poodle has a lot on his mind. After exercise, practice in a quiet, restricted area where neither of you will be distracted or able to run away (even though each of you may feel like it).

Train frequently, but for short periods. I recommend about sessions lasting about 15 minute, 3 times a day. With a puppy, however, 5 minutes at a stretch is long enough.

Basic training requires only two items, both of which can be bought at your local pet supply store: a simple collar and a lead. And, while not absolutely necessary, a few treats are always helpful.

The Poodle Pundit

A small treat is something really tiny, not something like a dog biscuit. A wee bit of carrot or the thinnest sliver of cheese is enough of a training reward. You don't want to give him something that takes a lot of chewing—it'll keep his mind from his work. 🐾

Collars

Owners have numerous collar choices: buckle, choke, prong, head halters, and even harnesses (which aren't really collars at all). There are then varieties of each of these. You will find that each dog's response to each kind of collar is unique, so will need to experiment to find what's right for your Poodle. I recommend that you begin with a plain buckle collar. With positive reinforcement training, it's all you'll ever need.

The Poodle Pundit

If you decide that you would like your Poodle to do formal obedience, check the rules to see which collars are allowed and which aren't. In general, only buckle and choke collars are allowed—although the rules seem to be subject to interpretation. 🐾

Many people recommend the use of a halter-type collar like the Gentle Leader or Halti-Collar. These are wonderful devices. They are much more effective than traditional collars (after all, you can lead a Clydesdale with one), and they are gentler as well. Although they take some getting used to by both you and your dog, I think you'll be pleased with the result. The bigger and stronger the Poodle, the more effective you will find such a collar, but even a tiny Toy is happier (once he gets used to the idea) with being led gently.

The Poodle Pundit

The choice of collar depends on you, your dog, and your training methods. What works for one dog may not work for another. I have seen dogs fight Halti-Collars forever but adjust beautifully to prong collars. I've seen the opposite, too. I have seen dogs who ignored prong collars but responded to choke collars. And so on. Experiment, but start with the mildest correction first. If your dog is already using a severely corrective lead, try going back to simple buckle collar. You may be surprised. 🐾

If you decide you must use a choke collar with an older puppy or adult dog, put it on the dog correctly; if you don't, it won't work, and/or may injure your dog. Make the collar into a P, with the P-loop in your right hand and the tail hanging straight down. Approach the dog from the front and slip it on. The tail of the loop will now be on his right. Attach the lead and keep the dog on your left.

Poodle Peril

Never use a choke collar on a Toy Poodle or a puppy of any size. It is too easy to hurt his trachea—or even his spine. 🐾

A Poodle's fur can be a problem when using a choke collar. If the Poodle is in a lion trim, for example, the hairs poke through and can be caught or broken off. To prevent this from happening, you can make a cloth "collar wrapper" for the chain, or buy a collar known as a "Fur Saver," which is designed to protect against this problem.

The Basic Commands

All varieties of Poodles are incredibly quick learners. This, combined with their desire to please, makes them top contenders in every field of dogdom where high-level intelligence is required. Poodles excel in obedience and agility, as well as in the conformation ring. Given this enormous learning potential, training a Poodle to be a pleasant household companion is a comparatively easy task.

People who own Toy Poodles often make the mistake of simply picking the dog up and removing him from an unpleasant situation. All this does is teach the Poodle that he can yap or snarl or even nip from the safety of his owner's arms. If you own a Toy Poodle, one way to avoid behavior problems is to treat him in the same way you would a Standard Poodle.

It's best to work on only one command at a time. If you get 3 correct responses from your puppy—3 good "sits" or "downs" or "heels"— then it's time to call it a day. End all training sessions on a positive note—go out and have fun together.

Poodle Parlance

Please is an important word in Poodledom. I often include the word *please* with positive commands, since it helps me remember to keep my voice light and encouraging. Poodles are sensitive, courteous souls who respond well to politeness. 🐾

Paging your Poodle: The "Come" Command

Poodle Precautions

Never ever chase your Poodle, unless it's to save his life. It's too much like a game. Even though you can catch your little puppy, the fact that you're chasing him encourages him to run the opposite way. Encourage the dog to chase you instead, which reinforces the concept of "following." 🐾

This is the first and most important of all commands. If there is one thing that you would like your Poodle to do correctly every time, this is it. Dogs who do not come on command are at the least annoying, and at the worst in very grave danger. The trick is to make your dog understand how important this command is. If you fail here, your Poodle may well turn the "come" command into a game. Your part of the game is to call him, and his part of the game is to see you how long he can make you stand there looking like an idiot.

The Poodle Pundit

It's much easier to teach a puppy to come than an older dog, because puppies have an instinctive desire to follow their mothers. However, you can make use of any dog's pack instinct to teach the command. 🐾

Most books will tell you to use the same word every time you call your dog, but, with Poodles at least, it really doesn't make any difference. They can usually tell what you want, whether you say "come" or "here," or "come" sometimes and "here" others. Not only does the tone provide the clue, but dogs, especially Poodles, are also more adept at learning language cues than most people give them credit for.

The Poodle Pundit

If your dog doesn't seem to be paying attention to your firm and repeated commands, try whispering. Your lower tone and distorted voice will tend to make your dog look up, pay attention, and try to decipher what you're saying. 🐾

This becomes clear if you learn to think like a dog. Let's say you're running around in the field and you hear your owner call out something (anything). Unless you are specifically trained to do something else (like herd sheep), your first inclination is to assume your human wants you for something. After all, he's probably not telling you to lie down. Whether you actually obey the summons is something else.

When you first begin teaching the command, wait until the dog is already headed in your direction. In other words, don't initiate the command yourself. When he gets to you, give him lots of praise and attention, or even a treat if you have one. This can be whatever your dog prefers—a treat, a favorite toy, or lots of hugs and praise. I once had a stubborn dog to whom I taught the "come" command by offering him a ride in the car every time he complied, as that was his favorite treat.

The Poodle Pundit

It often works to put aside a special toy to use only for teaching this command. When your Poodle obeys, give him the toy and allow him to play with it. Keep the toy for this purpose only. 🐾

The key here is to look sharp and be prepared to call "come" (in a happy tone of voice, of course) every time you see your dog doing it anyway. This is positive reinforcement. This exercise is not just for your new puppy, by the way; do it periodically throughout your dog's life.

The Poodle Pundit

It's not necessary to holler at your Poodle—his auditory acuity is quite good. If he doesn't respond, it's not because he can't hear what you're saying. He simply chooses not to. 🐾

After your puppy understands that "come" is always rewarded, you can start more advanced training. Put the puppy on a long lead so he can't get away. (The puppy should be leash-trained by now.) I think using a harness rather than a collar is a good idea at this stage, because it's gentler and you won't yank on the dog's neck, even by mistake. The most important thing at this early stage is letting him know that disobeying is not an option. Pull the lead gently towards you as you call him sweetly—and don't forget the reward.

The Poodle Pundit

It takes between 3 and 5 months of work on the "come" command to insure that your dog is reliably trained. Most people think they have it down in 3 to 5 days. 🐾

When your dog is completely responsive on a lead, try the commands off-lead in a confined area. You may want to put the dog in a corner, which reduces the opportunity for avoidance. If your dog doesn't obey, don't chase him. Turn your back and walk in the opposite direction. He'll probably come to you. When he does, start again. If you have repeated failures off-lead, go back to lead training.

Remember, always call your dog in a happy voice and praise him when he comes to you, even if it's taken longer for him to respond than you'd like (maybe several minutes, or an hour). Never call your dog to scold or punish him. This can be trickier than you think. For instance, although giving your Poodle a bath may be just grooming to you, but to him it may be a fearsome punishment. The same goes for giving medicine. For such things, you should go to him. I know some very obedient dogs who will come to you on command even if they know something awful will follow. In that case, their loyalty to their owners wins out over their instinct to avoid pain. There is really no point to setting up an internal conflict of conscience in your dog.

"No, No, Nanette!"

Right up there with the "come" command is the "no" command. In fact, I thought of starting with that one, but didn't want to seem too negative.

Never add "please" to "no," as it sends the wrong signal. "No" means the following: "immediately desist!" You may combine it with a reference to what he's doing wrong, such as "no chew!" Some people think that saying "no" is a severe punishment and should be used sparingly. This is not true. "No" is just a guide to correct behavior. Your dog will learn what it means and won't hold it against you. If your dog is chewing something inappropriate, say "no chew" and hand him something more acceptable. Then praise him. There's nothing to it, really. You will not confuse your dog or destroy his psyche.

Many pet owners have more trouble learning the meaning of "no" than their dogs do. When saying "no," you must not betray your verbal command by your tone or body language. If you say "no" but are really thinking, "oh, the way he ate my slippers is so cute," he'll know you don't really mean it. Next time he'll eat your hundred-dollar cross-trainers. If you say, "no beg," and then relent a minute later, he's not the one experiencing "failure to communicate."

Poodle Parlance

"No" is a mysterious word to dogs unless you utter it when the dog is perpetrating the forbidden behavior. You can't walk into a room 5 minutes after the doilies were devoured, shake one in your Poodle's face, and shriek "no! no!" He will probably think "Gee, she's yelling no. She better put that doily down." 🐾

Your Poodle Plunks Down: The "Sit" Command

This is the easiest of all commands to teach. Use a treat and hold it up slightly above his eye level; this will encourage him to sit down. Praise him lavishly when he succeeds. Be careful to praise him as he sits down, not as he starts to get up. When you want your Poodle to get up, give him a "release" command. I use the word "break." Some trainers use "okay," but since that word is in constant use, it's easy for a dog to misunderstand it. You can even make up a secret release word that will amaze all your friends.

But here's the problem with "sit." It's not a particularly useful command unless you plan to do obedience, or you want the dog to take up less room. Most of the time, a quietly standing dog is just as good as a sitting one. People like to teach "sit" because it's easy and they feel they have more control of a sitting dog than a standing one.

Don't use "sit" to stop negative behavior. It doesn't teach the dog to halt the behavior—it only reinforces the "sit" command. Next time, he'll go right back to the same undesirable behavior until you tell him to "sit" again. You can spend the rest of your dog's life doing that. "Sit" should just mean "sit," and not "quit it." If you want a dog to stop a particular behavior, teach him to do that. If you want him to stop doing something one time, say "no."

The Prostrate Poodle: The "Down" Command

This command should be taught after the "sit" command. While he is sitting, take a treat and, holding it in front of his face, lower it slowly to the ground. The Poodle should follow suit. If he doesn't, while keeping him in a sitting position, very slowly pull the treat forward in front of him, close to the ground. He'll have to lie down to reach it. Praise him when he succeeds.

Of course you will use "lie down" rather than "lay down" as your command. Poodles are sticklers for good grammar in every language. The reason some do not respond to "lay down" is that they are too grammatically correct to comply.

The Poodle Pundit

Some people teach a separate "stay" command, while others prefer to simplify things by just assuming the Poodle will stay sitting or lying down until released. It's your preference; either works perfectly well. 🐾

Cassis in a "Down Stay"

Courtesy of Suzanne Dalton

"Please Leave"

I use this command to remove my dogs from the kitchen, especially when we are cooking or dining. I actually say "Aroint thee, beast!" but they get the picture. To teach "leave," take your dog's collar and remove him to the desired room. Then praise him. When he comes back, patiently say "please leave," and repeat. Do this until he gets the message. You may use treats to enhance your explanation.

Your Poodle is perfectly capable of understanding the function of doorways. Soon he will "leave" any room when requested. My own dogs enjoy asserting their independence in this regard. They lie as close to the threshold as possible, usually placing one paw in the forbidden room and gazing in with a stricken look. But they stay out.

"Off!"

This means "Get the heck off the couch! How many times have I told you not to get on the couch? But do you listen to me? Nooooo," etc. etc. You can use "no," but "off" is more specific. It tells the dog exactly what you want him to do right now, which is not "nothing" but "get off the couch." It is also a positive, rather than a negative, reinforcement. Besides, you can use "off" for other things, such as commanding him to jump out of the back of the van.

"Give It!" and "Drop It"

These commands mean what they say, and are not identical. A well-trained dog knows both of them. After all, you may want him to give you the stick he has unexpectedly retrieved for you, but you'd rather he just dropped the road kill he found. It's good practice for you to be able to remove anything your Poodle has in his mouth without his protesting.

The Perambulating Poodle

Little is more pleasant than a relaxed stroll along a quiet road with your Poodle pal at your side. Even a blaring city street can be made more bearable with the knowledge that your loyal friend is along. A lunging, charging, straining, or persistently lagging animal is no pleasure, however, and your walk deteriorates into a battle for leadership. To make every walk a pleasurable one, teach your dog the "heel" command.

A correctly-heeling dog is a pleasure to walk. The trouble involved in training him to move quietly at your side will be made up for later, when you are walking your Poodle with one hand and holding the baby/groceries/dog show trophy in the other. If you have a puppy, take heart. A puppy is much easier to teach heeling skills to than is an older dog. He naturally wants to come with you and has no bad habits to break. So far.

The "Heel" Command

Use a 6-foot nylon or leather lead for heel-training exercises. Never use a chain leash, which is too heavy and noisy.

If your dog works well on a plain leather collar, use that. The less control you need, the more pleasurable the exercise will be for both of you, and the better behaved your dog will ultimately be. You should be able to slip two fingers comfortably under the collar. If you must use a choke collar, adjust it correctly. Don't use a harness for this training.

Poodle Precautions

Don't wrap the leash around your hand. It's a less effective instrument that way. Besides, you'll have one painful hand if the Poodle suddenly lunges at something. 🐾

It's traditional for dogs to heel at the left side of their owners, but there's no law about it. If you want your dog to heel on the right side, be my guest. Some left-handed people prefer walking their dogs on the right side. However, if you're planning on showing your dog in conformation or obedience, it's best to go with the flow and use the customary left side.

Begin by reaching out and touching your dog. He will probably look up at you expectantly, which is what you want. You must get him to pay attention to you and keep his eye on you. Say "Mordred, heel," and begin walking. (If your dog's name happens to be something other than Mordred, use that name.) Keep his chest in line with your knee. Do not allow him to lead with his nose.

Am/Can Ch Uagl, UCD Ravendune Right On Q, Am Can CD, CGC, TT, VCX

The heeling exercise is not a potty break. Don't allow your Poodle to stop, lag, lunge ahead, or smell the roses while training. Every once in a while, after a successful heel, take a mini-break from training. Signify the break clearly by loosening the leash while saying "relax," or something similar. At these times, you can allow your dog to sniff about, but he should never be permitted to pull.

During a heeling exercise, stop at every curb. This is good practice for both of you. You don't want your Poodle to get the idea that it's all right to run across the street.

When you are finished with the heeling exercise, loosen the lead completely and say "break." This is the signal that your Poodle may now sniff around and be doggish.

Forging

Some dogs pull at the leash, or "forge." Forging begins long before you have attached the lead to the collar—it begins when your Poodle sees the lead. If you can't control him at this point, don't expect that the upcoming foray will be an easy one. Have your dog sit or stand quietly while you attach the lead. Do not put the lead on while he's dancing around—insist that he remain calm. If he starts jumping around when it's on, take it off and start again calmly. He will soon learn that the only way he's getting out the door is quietly. Otherwise, you will have a struggle on your hands before the walk even begins. There is no point to this.

Correcting Forging

If your Poodle starts to pull, just turn the other way without a word. Keep doing this. This will focus his attention on you. Since no one likes to be pulled, he'll start paying attention to you and try to anticipate your moves. Say "heel" in a quiet, firm voice as you turn.

Don't turn aimlessly, however, just to confuse the dog. Turn only in response to his pulling against you. (When your dog becomes more adept at heeling, you can practice more complicated patterns.)

You can also try walking backwards, which will make him stop to look at you. Do not allow your dog to pull you, ever. If you have to use an anti-pulling harness, do so, at least at first. The point is to break him from the habit of forging.

As his walking behavior improves, you can gradually loosen the lead so that you and he can take a struggle-free stroll together. When he is well-trained in heeling, you can allow him to wander a bit on the lead, sniff about and so on. But when you say "heel," he should immediately resume the correct behavior.

The leash is an extension of you. Never praise or treat your dog when the leash is taut. A taut lead indicates that your dog is resisting you, and you don't want to reward that kind of behavior.

Anti-Pulling Equipment

You may need a little mechanical help when you start training your dog to walk with you. This is especially helpful if you are working with an adult dog, particularly a Standard Poodle, who has had no previous heel training, and you are not very strong.

The traditional choke collar may not work at all, since some dogs automatically throw themselves against it. This is called an "opposition reflex," and yanking back induces the opposite effect.

If your Poodle is a puller and you can't handle him, try one of the following as a supplementary training device:

▼ A no-pull harness.

▼ A head halter like Halti-Collar, Gentle Leader, or Snoot Loop. As mentioned earlier, these attach to the dog's head and work by steering his head. Both are gentle and effective, and may be safely used in place of a regular collar. Many people prefer them, and they are especially useful when a child is walking the dog. Although it may take some time for your dog to get used to them, they are very effective and kind devices.

▼ Another kind of collar, known as a pinch, self-correcting, prong, spike, or "German" collar, looks frightening—but really isn't. Its action imitates the way a mother dog nips her puppies. Having said that, I'd like to add that the use of these collars is a signal that your dog is untrained and out of control. If you use one for more than a few days, you're doing something wrong.

Photo by K9s N Motion

Chapter 13

Poodle Pranks and Problem Poodles

Sadly, over 2.5 million dogs and cats are euthanized in the United States every year for behavior problems. What is even sadder is that most of the problems are caused by owners. Even the normally well-behaved Poodle can develop a fault or two. Naturally, this is not his fault; it's yours, since you let him get away with it.

There are six general ways to respond an unwanted behavior pattern in your Poodle:

▼ *Change your behavior.* It may be that you are doing something, consciously or unconsciously, that produces the behavior you are trying to correct. For example, cuddling a frightened dog is guaranteed to reinforce the fearful behavior. It's really easier to train yourself than to train your dog, anyway.

▼ *Change your dog's behavior.* This may include teaching him to accept baths, obey basic commands, release toys and food, and so forth. To get your dog to behave differently, you will probably have to do something different yourself.

▼ *Build a higher fence, confine the dog, etc.* Some canine behaviors are so ingrained that it may be impossible to train them out of the dog. If you can't retrain, you must restrain.

▼ *Medicate the dog.* Some bad behavior has a medical cause. If it does, there may be a medical solution.

▼ *Medicate yourself.* Perhaps a nice cup of herbal tea (or something) will put you in a better temper.

▼ *Get used to it.* This seems a bit harsh, but sometimes it's just easier for everybody. If your dog has a minor behavior problem that doesn't lend itself to any of the above treatments, just ignore it. I have a dog who growls, howls, and yelps every time anyone picks him up. He always done so, and I imagine will continue to do so. It's a terrible sound, and rather frightening—but there it is. He is 8 years old and has never bitten anyone. And never will. So we continue to pick him up to give him baths, move him from the couch, etc., and ignore the noise.

One size does not fit all. The cure that works depends on the target behavior, its cause, and your patience. Let's look at few of the more common problems Poodle owners may face, and some of the ways you can deal with them.

Casey, a black standard Poodle puppy   *Courtesy of Marsha Lorette MacDonald*

Positive Reinforcement

Most owners make the mistake of ignoring good behavior or taking it for granted. This is wrong. Most of the good behavior we demand from our pets is, to a greater or lesser degree, abnormal behavior for them. Jumping up, stealing, begging for or guarding food, barking, snapping, running off, and marking are perfectly normal behaviors—we just don't like them. So it's our job to encourage our dogs to adopt the patterns of behavior we prefer. That means positively reinforcing those good, albeit unnatural behaviors, like being quiet most of time, giving up food, and not biting even the most infuriating people.

Owners often unconsciously promote bad habits in dogs by permitting objectionable behavior sometimes and punishing it at other times. Such owners do not make clear to the dog when certain things are okay and when they are not. Dogs can, however, be taught to distinguish between even complex behaviors. For example, it is perfectly possible to teach a dog the difference between an old shoe that he may chew and the new ones he may not. But it's a lot of work, and you must be prepared to lose a few shoes in the process.

Poodle Pundit

If your Poodle makes a mistake and you have to scold him, do not make up with him immediately afterwards. Allow 5 or 10 minutes to go by; otherwise, he'll be utterly confused by the mixed signals.

If this sounds too complicated, just teach the dog that all shoes are off limits. This isn't, however, what usually happens. According to whimsy, the owner may suddenly decide it's okay for his Poodle to sleep on his lap—just this once. When the Poodle leaps up there the next day, the owner is surprised and annoyed. The solution? Teach your Poodle to come into your lap by invitation only. If you don't want to bother teaching him to accept an invitation, don't allow him on your lap at all.

Poodlish 101

Before you can deal with potential Poodle problems, you need to learn to communicate with your Poodle. We've already discussed the words your dog needs to learn from you; now it's time to return the favor. You don't need to be Dr. Doolittle to understand Poodle language—a few simple lessons should do the trick. Considering how much you expect Poodles to know about English, it's only fair that you should gain at least a rudimentary command of Poodlish.

The Poodle Pundit

Poodles respond to the tone of your voice. If you say "no" in a weak, thin, or high-pitched voice, your Poodle will regard it as "well, maybe." Be firm in tone and deepen your voice for negative commands. This is one reason why children, with their softer, higher-pitched voices, have a hard time training dogs. 🐾

Sometimes dogs talk to us in dog words—audible signals like barking, growling, and whining. Sometimes they use body language instead. All this can turn into a complex job of interpretation. To make it even more complex, Poodles have two handicaps; because they're lop-eared, they can't lay back their ears to show aggression, and because their tails are docked, they can't wag their tails completely, or put their tails between their legs.

So it's up to you to pay close attention to your dog. Your Poodle may be saying something other than what you think. Your dog may be trying to tell you that he is ill, or that he has delusions of grandeur, or that he really doesn't like your Maltese all that much.

Sniffing

This is the universal dog greeting. Dogs will also try to greet human guests in the same time-honored manner. Obviously, they need to be discouraged from doing this, usually by distracting them, or saying "Here, Rudy," in a firm voice. Between dogs, greetings begin nose-to-nose. If all goes well, the sniffing proceeds to the other end. It seems rude to us, but it isn't to them.

Mounting Behavior

Attempting to mount another dog—or even a human being—is not usually an expression of sexuality, deranged or otherwise. Females do it as well as males. It's an indication of dominance; your Poodle is saying that he's the boss. If he mounts other dogs in his household, you'll have to let them sort it out among themselves. Once the correct order of dominance is established, the annoying behavior should stop. But if your Poodle persists in mounting people, he may be thinking of becoming leader of the pack. Disabuse him of this notion immediately.

Pawing

A dog who places his paw on the shoulder of another dog is trying to demonstrate his dominance over that dog. He may try the same thing with a person. Discourage it.

Bowing

A Poodle who crouches down in front, wagging his tail quickly, is demonstrating "play-soliciting" behavior. He looks as if he were taking a bow. He may jump backwards and forwards while making weird little noises, or put his head low to one side and stare cock-eyed at you. It's playtime!

Nudging or Punching

Nudging or punching with his nose is also designed to get you to play with or pet him. It is a more dominant signal than bowing; in effect your Poodle is demanding, rather than asking, that you pay attention to him.

Mouth Licking

Mouth-licking is a care-soliciting behavior that youngsters use to seek food from their mothers. This behavior often persists into adulthood. Sometimes a dog will just lick the mouth of the other dog; sometimes he will actually poke around in there, lifting the corners of the mouth and sniffing away. The dog may be looking to see what his friend has been dining on. Most of the time, it is the submissive dog who licks the mouth of the more dominant dog.

Tail Wagging and Tail Carriage

Tail wagging in dogs is exactly analogous to smiling in humans. Usually it's because they're happy, but sometimes it occurs when they are nervous, threatened, or threatening. It all depends upon exactly how the tail is wagged. Although Poodles do have docked tails, the docking is usually not short enough to prevent a Poodle from clearly communicating his moods.

Fast, horizontal tail wagging means the dog is in a good mood. Nervous dogs also wag their tails, but usually in a more tentative manner.

Sometimes a tail wag can mean aggression or a challenge. Here are possible fightin' words in tail Poodlish:

▼ A slow, incomplete wag from an erect tail

▼ A short, sharp, stiff wag

▼ A tail carried very high or even starting to curve over the Poodle's back

Poodle Potpourri

It's true that Toy Poodles may be more aggressive than Standards. One can hardly blame them; it's probably the canine version of short-man syndrome. In an informal survey of some groomers, all agreed that Toy Poodles were much more likely to snarl and snap during the grooming process than Standards. Minis were somewhere in between. 🐾

Barking

Because dogs are social creatures, barking is a time-honored method of communication among them. Dogs sometimes seem to bark for the pure joy of barking, or as a warning; however, most of the time barking is associated with a particular need, such as food, territorial defense, play, or attention. To halt troublesome barking, see Problem Barking, a little further on.

Whining

A whine is a care-soliciting noise. It's also a sign of submission. Your Poodle wishes to come in, go out, be petted, or eat dinner.

Growling

Growling is best interpreted as a warning. It's commonly seen when Poodles are trying to protect their food from other dogs, or when something annoying is going on. Dogs usually growl before they bite, so this is a warning to be taken quite seriously. (This doesn't mean you should allow your dog to growl at you. It means be careful.)

Jumping Up

This a complaint one hears more often from owners of Standards than from owners of other varieties. This is not because Standards are more prone to jumping, but because it's more noticeable with a large dog.

Dogs jump for one reason and one reason only—they want your attention. They know that jumping up is a good way to get it. For most dogs, negative attention is better than no attention at all. Look at it from their point of view: you've been gone all day, or even for an hour (which can seem like all day to a dog), and he's happy to see you. But you have other things on your mind and don't notice the dog immediately—until he leaps on you. Voila! Your Poodle has finally gotten your attention.

The solution is simple. Greet your dog in a friendly way when he is calm, but ignore him when he jumps. Do not reward his behavior even by eye contact. Fold your arms and look away until you sense your Poodle has quieted down. Then pet him. When he learns that good behavior gets attention, he'll start being good.

Poodle Precautions

Never step on a dog's toes or knee him in an attempt to keep him down. That only confuses him, and it may hurt him, as well. Squirting water on your dog when he's trying to be friendly also makes him more insecure and even more likely to try to get your attention frantically. Simply look away and attend to other business. 🐾

It's worth noting, however, that bad behavior will probably get worse before it gets better; it's your dog's last-ditch effort to try for your attention the only way he knows how. This is called the "extinction burst."

Poodle Parlance

The extinction burst is the dog's final attempt to repeat his formerly successful bad behavior. If you can get through it, he should gradually start to improve. 🐾

Digging

Since digging is perfectly normal canine behavior, it's not something that can easily be trained out of your pet. Poodles are not known for relentless digging, but it can and does occur.

Your dog may dig for a variety of reasons: to escape the yard, to get cool in the summer, because he's bored, or because you've planted a new shrub and the loose soil is attractive. Digging, in pregnant dogs, is a nesting behavior. Notice where the hole is located—it will give you a good clue as to why he dug it. Holes close to the fence line indicate your dog is trying to run off; holes in the shade indicate your dog is trying to cool down.

If your dog digs, try to provide more exercise and company for him. You can also create a little garden patch of soft, loose soil for him, and hope he uses it instead of your lawn.

Destructive Chewing

Like digging, chewing is a normal behavior for dogs. Poodles are not in the habit of destroying their owner's homes, but some damage can occur—especially with younger dogs who are teething, or dogs who are left alone for long periods of time. The only sure solution is to crate your dog or separate him from valuable property while you are gone. Punishing him is wrong and doesn't work anyway.

Although your Poodle may chew things for many reasons, including playfulness and boredom, he does not do it for revenge. The link between ripping up the couch and getting even with a house-proud owner is too tenuous and silly for dogs.

Don't punish your dog for having chewed something inappropriate. It's tempting to hit the roof when you come home to find your living room in shreds, but doing so will only make your Poodle associate your return with something awful. He'll have no idea why you're angry with him. Dogs must be caught in the act in order to make the connection between inappropriate behavior and your displeasure. Sometimes you need to manufacture a situation in which you can correct your Poodle immediately.

Why Dogs Chew

As mentioned earlier, many dogs regard any attention as better than no attention at all. It will take some self-control on your part to refrain from responding to negative behavior with negative attention, but you must. Remove the target item (or the dog) with a minimum of fuss. Give him plenty of loving attention when he is behaving himself, but not when he's being a nuisance.

Your Poodle may be teething, and chewing helps relieve his discomfort. Ice cubes are a good chew toy at teething time; in addition to giving the pup something to crunch, they have a numbing effect on sore gums. You can even chill your pup's regular toys in the freezer, or give him a cold, rolled-up washcloth that has been soaked in beef or chicken broth.

Poodle Peril

Avoid rawhide chew toys made outside the United States; the ingredients in them are not made for dog consumption—but many dogs will eat them anyway.

If your older dog suddenly begins chewing, he may have dental or upper gastrointestinal difficulties. This is a problem that must be addressed, since the chewing can become habitual even after the initial problem goes away.

On the other hand, perhaps your dog is plagued with existential angst or ennui. Poodles crave companionship. A bored Poodle is a destructive Poodle.

I once got a letter from a dog who had this tale to tell: "I was forced to chew up 3 remotes, 2 pairs of gloves, a valuable textbook, and a watch before my slovenly owner learned to put her things away properly. She was a slow learner, but eventually, with positive reinforcement (I would lick her face as she stooped to pick up the chewed articles), she got the message."

Curing Chewing

Provide your dog with a variety of interesting chew toys—but don't have all of them out all of the time. If you see your dog chewing something inappropriate, substitute something better without fussing about it. When your puppy begins to chew the chair leg, offer him a favorite toy and praise him when he accepts it.

Exercise your dog before you leave the house; a tired dog is less apt to chew. If your dog is not on a regular feeding schedule, his instincts tell him to hunt for food wherever it may be. He may be eating the sofa because he's hungry. If your work prevents you from getting home at the same time every day, consider getting a petsitter or using a self-feeder.

Locking dogs in small, windowless areas is almost certain to result in destructive behavior, if your dog is not well-crate–trained. Dogs should be able to look out the window; they get endless amusement from spying on the neighbors, just like we do. Provide toys in the confinement area.

Most of us have to be away from our dog for at least some hours every day. To keep your Poodle from getting lonely, try leaving the TV or radio on.

A variety of bitter-tasting sprays and foams are commercially available to curb destructive chewing. Tabasco sauce also works nicely. So does Ban Roll-On, Listerine mouthwash, and cheap perfume. (Finally, a use for that cologne Cousin Mildred sent you last Christmas.) A product called Protex is designed to keep dogs from chewing fabric—or their own fur.

However, preventive products like Bitter Apple are, at best, temporary remedies. You can't expect to spray Bitter Apple on all your possessions for the rest of your days. The only surefire cure is steady, consistent training, or separation of the dog from your valuables.

There is another very simple solution. Get another pet. Two dogs can entertain each other for hours. Although two dogs are more expensive than one, they are not twice as expensive. They may knock over a few things in their runs around the homestead, but it's less likely they'll chew the furniture. They won't have time.

If one Poodle is enough for you, check with your vet. There are some anxiety-reducing drugs available, like Clomicalm, which can help reduce nervous tension and the destructive behavior that accompanies it. I recommend such medications only as a last resort, but they have produced some excellent results. Like Bitter Apple, they should supplement, not replace, training.

The Poodle Pundit

If your dog eats his bed, don't buy him another. He'll eat that one, too. 🐾

To protect your couch, try luring your dog into sleeping in his own bed. Good dog beds are probably more comfortable than your lumpy old couch, if only you can persuade your Poodle to use them. Some beds are even raised up off the floor for extra comfort and a more couch-like appeal.

Problem Barking

Although it's unreasonable to expect your dog to live his life in total silence, it is reasonable to expect your dog to be sensible about how much he barks. If he is not, it's up to you to find the cause and alter his behavior.

Some Poodle barking is an invitation to play. If you reward him for barking by playing with him, you'll get barking every day. Your Poodle may not understand when it is and is not convenient for you to play with him. Take note of the behavior and ignore it. When he is quiet and tries another ploy, like snuggling up to you or bowing, then by all means join in the fun. The trick is to reward the acceptable behavior (bowing) and not reward the unacceptable (barking). When he barks, turn away. Do not even reward him with eye contact. This is the same principle I spoke about regarding jumping, and it works just as well here.

As with all behavior problems, figure out why the dog is barking in the first place. Is he lonely and bored? Well, the key is to make his life less lonely—but not at the instant he's barking. Hard as it may be to do, you must ignore the barking until he's quiet. Be patient. He may bark for a really long time. At some point,

Poodle Precautions

It does no good to yell, scream, or spray water at a barking dog. That just makes him bark more. Likewise, aversive training collars that deliver a shock, a spritz of citronella, or noise to a barking dog are ineffectual and cruel. (Even the citronella collar, the least objectionable of the bunch, makes some dogs sick. Others just ignore it.) Also, once you start relying on such devices, you're stuck with them. The dog will continue to bark whenever he's not wearing the collar or sees that you have no squirt bottle in hand. You can handle the situation much better with a response that does not depend on fear or punishment for its effectiveness. 🐾

however, he will stop. Then you may reward his quiet behavior with play, and take care that in the future your dog gets more of your attention. This is also the time to provide plenty of interesting chew toys for your dog. Dogs find it difficult to chomp down on a peanut-butter-filled Kong and bark forlornly at the same time.

If your dog barks to warn you of visitors, that's fine. Praise him for barking and reassure him that all is well. If he continues to bark, ignore him until he stops.

If your dog is barking to request something, like treats or going for a run, deny the privilege until he ceases to bark— unless, of course, you want him to bark to request a walk. In that case, respond to his bark as soon as possible. Otherwise, reward quiet behavior. If your Poodle is barking for joy outside, bring him in the second he starts barking. He'll soon learn that barking results in being brought in the house.

The Poodle Pundit

As usual, Toy Poodles take a bum rap for being barky little things. In all probability, the average Toy Poodle barks no more than does any other kind of dog. It's just that the high-pitched bark is singularly annoying to human ears, especially, it seems, male human ears. 🐾

Running Away and Car Chasing

This is the most easily solved of all problems. Keep your dog safe in his fenced yard—he will never have the opportunity to chase cars or to run away. When I was kid, people took a more causal attitude. Dogs were let out in the morning and called in for supper. It was common sight to see dogs trotting down the street unattended. There were a lot of dogs hit by cars, too.

Nowadays, a responsible dog owner simply will not allow a dog to run free. This strategy is so simple that I wonder why no one ever thought of it before. Keeping your dog at home protects him from being hit by cars, shot by neighbors, mauled by tigers, poisoned by madmen, and tortured by kids. It will save you those phone calls, too. You know the ones.

Chapter 14

Poodle Panic and Other Peculiar Predilections

In this chapter we'll discuss two major kinds of Poodle problems: those arising from fear, and those arising from obsessive-compulsive disorders (OCDs).

Shyness

Shyness has a biological basis in both people and animals. We know that in Poodles it can be an inherited trait. Environment obviously plays a part in developing or inhibiting shyness, but the key factor is genetic predisposition.

The Poodle Pundit

Dogs who have a genetic predisposition toward aggression tend to become vicious rather than timid when abused. 🐾

A dog who has inherited a shy temperament will always be more timid than the average dog. This does not mean, however, that owners of shy dogs cannot do a great deal to make a timid dog less so.

To build a dog's confidence, you must present him with a series of gradually more challenging situations. As long as the program is very gradual, most shyness can be reduced to a manageable level.

One way to do this is to socialize your dog through an obedience class. Your main purpose here is socialization, so a puppy kindergarten is perfect if your dog is the right age. If not, explain the problem to your local kennel or Poodle club, and they will help you find a suitable class. After all, you don't want to get mixed up with a bunch of serious trainers who are working toward CD titles for their dogs (not yet, at least).

Don't rush or force the socialization process. It takes much longer with a shy dog. Don't allow strangers to rush up to your Poodle and begin petting him when you know that it will terrify him. Let your dog have his personal space; as he becomes more confident, that space will shrink. Ask strangers to hold out their hands (with a treat) and look away from your dog while offering it. For dogs, eye contact—especially from strangers—is threatening. If your dog absolutely will not take a treat handed to him, have the stranger place the treat on the ground in front of the dog, then back away.

The Poodle Pundit

Some experts recommend yawning conspicuously when your dog is faced with a nerve-wracking situation. This is supposed to calm him. 🐾

Don't pet your dog on the head. This is a dominant gesture that decreases your shy Poodle's confidence level even further. Gently scratch his chest and neck instead.

If you and your dog are faced with a situation he finds threatening, don't comfort him. Speak cheerfully and try to distract him by playing with him, feeding him, or trotting off with him. This isn't the same as running away—although it might feel like it. What you're doing is using his adrenaline in a positive way. The exercise should calm your dog and distract him at the same time. Don't run directly away from the feared object unless necessary; try going by it at a fast clip instead.

The Poodle Pundit

Shy dogs often work better on a harness than on a collar, and much better than on a choke chain or anything that would startle or frighten him in the slightest. Think like a dog. Would it calm your nerves to be led around on a choke chain, not knowing from one minute to the next when it's going to tighten around your neck? Give me a harness any old day. 🐾

Although it can be risky with alpha dogs, it's beneficial to play tug of war with a shy dog. Let him win; it will build his self-confidence. Owners of retrieving breeds have been doing this for years. Play other games too, particularly ones that enforce the prey drive—like chasing and catching things.

Many shy dogs take comfort in having their owners nearby when they eat. Stay near, but don't stare at the dog. Be sure that your alpha dog does the same.

Phobias

A phobia is an unreasonable, uncontrollable fear. People and dogs and horses get them. Wasps—and maybe cats—do not.

Thunderstorms

"I must confess that many poodles are afraid of lightning, slamming doors, pistol shots, high winds, and things that go bump in the night, but then so am I."
—James Thurber, *Christabel: Part One*

Some Poodles go mad when a thunderstorm arrives. No one is sure why. Answers range from ambient electricity, to the drop in barometric pressure, to the noise. What is certain, though, is that something bothers them.

Many dogs exhibit a perfectly normal, instinctive terror of thunder. Although you will probably never get your thunder-shy Poodle to enjoy accompanying you on a death-defying walk during an electrical storm, it is possible to avoid his having fits while safe at home during such an event. There may a biological reason for your Poodle's fear and discomfort; scientists are still trying to pin down the precise cause.

Let's talk about what won't work first.

▼ Coddling your dog during a thunderstorm. That will just confirm his suspicion that something is terribly, terribly wrong.

▼ Punishing your dog. This will just make him afraid of you.

What may work:

▼ Take a positive, cheerful attitude. "Oh, boy! A thunderstorm! Isn't that exciting!" Don't carry this too far, though. It would not be a wise idea to actually take your Poodle out for a walk in the storm. Thunderstorms are dangerous. Your dog knows this; that's what scares him.

▼ Anti-phobic drugs. Some dogs respond to tranquilizers like Valium, or antidepressants, in addition to other therapy. The anxiety drug buspirone may work. Clomicalm users are also reporting positive results.

▼ Homeopathic and herbal remedies. If you want to take a more natural route, you can experiment with one of the many products that contain valerian, a sleep-inducing herb. Melatonin, chamomile, St. John's wort, and hops are also candidates.

▼ Desensitize your dog by playing recordings of storms. Start at a low volume and increase it very gradually. You can include flashes of light to more fully approximate a complete thunderstorm experience. You may have to repeat the desensitizing procedure in several rooms. This method may take several months.

▼ Crate your Poodle. If your dog is used to being in a crate, it's a very comfortable place for him to be during fireworks or a thunderstorm. Putting a cover over the crate will also help assuage his fears.

Fireworks

Fireworks are a source of terror to many dogs. They are apparently too dumb to enjoy the sights and sounds of bombs exploding across the night sky, instead preferring the silent, unobstructed glory of the moon and stars. I can't say that I blame them. In my opinion, a dog who is not afraid of fireworks isn't exactly normal.

If you want to see the fireworks, go, but let your Poodle stay safe at home. Leave the TV on or provide other soothing, familiar sounds, and make sure the house is as secure as possible. Put your dog in his crate and turn off the lights. Dogs are more comfortable in the dark.

Other Loud Noises

Although fireworks are generally avoidable, the same cannot be said for other loud noises—vacuum cleaners and the like. You may, of course, wish to give up housecleaning altogether on the pretext that vacuums frighten and household cleansers endanger your Poodle.

If you feel you must go on cleaning, you should attempt to remove your dog from the situation or work to desensitize him the same way you would to thunder.

Separation Anxiety

Separation anxiety, although perhaps not strictly a phobia, is so much like a phobia that it can be addressed in this section.

Separation anxiety is one of the main reasons people get rid of their dogs. Affected dogs whine, bark unceasingly, salivate, chew the curtains, eat the couch, or tear up the rug. Many of these animals spent time in the pound or animal shelter; every time they move to a new home, their self-confidence weakens a little more.

According to one estimate, 14 percent of dogs have separation anxiety. This doesn't mean that the dog is mentally ill—it just means he wants to be with you all the time, a trait that we bred into our dogs. Perhaps, as a kid, you never heard of separation anxiety. The reason is that in days of yore, there was usually somebody home with the dog. And in cases when nobody was, the dog was put outside and left to wander around the neighborhood. Not any more. Today people get up, feed the dog, throw him in a crate or in the basement, and say "Be a good boy. See ya in 10 hours." Then they wonder why the animal seems distressed. Dogs need at least 2 hours of close human companionship a day to be happy and healthy. Walking, grooming, training, playing, and cuddling all count towards those 2 hours.

The Poodle Pundit

Research has also found that dogs who are left alone for a large part of the day suffer more physical health problems than do dogs with adequate companionship. 🐾

I am not suggesting that people throw their dogs out in the street or quit their jobs. I am saying that some sacrifices have to be made. Drug therapy is a new and very promising treatment for severe separation anxiety in dogs. But before medicating your pet, see what behavior modifications you can make in your own lifestyle.

Treatment for Separation Anxiety

Luckily, neither you nor your dog need suffer separation anxiety. Treatment is available.

▼ Get up. Arise a little earlier than you have to and spend some time with your dog. Play with him, run with him, groom him, brush his teeth.

▼ Sleep in. Let him sleep in your bedroom with you. He'll enjoy your company even while he's asleep.

▼ Go to work—with your Poodle. Try sneaking your dog into work with you once in a while. I did this for years under the pretext that the animal was having medical problems and needed frequent attention. It was true—sort of.

▼ Desensitize your dog. Start getting your dog used to being left alone. You can't take your dog with you to the opera, of course, but it is not unreasonable to expect to be able to leave him alone for a few hours without returning to a war zone.

▼ Be calm. Don't make a big to-do about departing or returning. Pay no attention to your dog for about 15 minutes or so
before you leave. This means you should avoid even looking at your dog, strange as it sounds. It has a calming effect.

▼ Prepare to leave, but don't actually do so. Jiggle the doorknob and jangle your keys. Do this several times a day.
Soon your Poodle won't necessarily associate your getting
out your purse with her being left alone.

▼ Change your routine. Stop giving the dog cues about when
you'll be leaving. The cues allow him to set himself up for
misery. One dog I knew began panting when his owner
put on her deodorant.

Leave your Poodle unsupervised for very gradually length-
ening time periods. Get him used to the idea of your being gone.
At first, leave and come back within a minute or so. Give him a
toy as you depart, and collect it when your return. He'll soon
understand that you'll always return, and he won't become destructive—at least not from separation anxiety. Destructiveness due to
boredom, however, is a possibility.

Most people make the mistake of not being gradual enough in
their separation training. If your dog behaves well for 1 hour
alone, do not assume he can be safely left for 8 hours. Increase his
periods alone by only 15 minutes a time.

▼ Get your dog used to being on his own—even when you
are at home. Discourage him from following you around
the house, and give him his own chores to do (like chewing
a bone). This doesn't mean ignore him; the concept is to
build up his confidence in the fact that he's part of your
life, even though you are not paying exclusive attention to
him. But don't forget; give your Poodle 2 hours of time and
attention every day.

▼ Crate your Poodle. For some dogs, crating may help create
a sense of security. Even if it doesn't, he won't be chewing
the furniture while he's in the crate. It's not safe to leave a
Poodle under 4 months of age alone, free, in the house; he
simply does not have the psychological poise to keep from
ripping things to shreds. Crate or kennel him. Don't leave

him in the crate for more than 4 hours, however. He needs both mental and physical stimulation he can't get in a crate. Be aware, however, that some dogs get worse when crated.

▼ Get another Poodle. Dogs are pack animals. Even though we have successfully bred them to think of us as their pack for thousands of years, there's no substitute for the real thing. Dogs naturally interact with each other. After all, the other dog won't give him a treat, make him sit, or tell him to fetch. They'll just run around and be doggy together. This natural interaction helps relieve stress. Your new dog doesn't have to be another Poodle; however, it usually works best if the 2 dogs are approximately the same size.

▼ Get a cat. If 2 dogs are too much for you, or forbidden by the landlord, consider getting a cat. Cats are elegant, clean, aristocratic creatures, like Poodles themselves, and they often become fast friends. Even a cat who steadfastly ignores a dog will surely draw his attention.

▼ Get a pet sitter or dog walker. If you must be away from home for an extended period of time, hire someone trustworthy to entertain your dog. This gives your dog something to look forward to. When you return, you'll find a much quieter, happier dog. This does not have to be an expensive proposition. Often, a responsible neighbor child will be happy to walk your dog for a nominal fee.

▼ Leave the radio or TV on. It's not much, but it's better than nothing. I suggest the Animal Channel. You can also call your dog on the phone and leave him a nice message on the answering machine. Don't be surprised if he calls you back. We are dealing with Poodles here!

▼ Get professional help—and medication. Along with behavior modification, new drug therapies are available. The best of all new medications for separation anxiety is the antidepressant Clomicalm (clomipramine hydrochloride), which was recently approved for use in dogs by the Food and Drug Administration. It comes in pill form, and is amazingly effective for both separation anxiety and OCDs.

Some people seem to object on principle to drugging their dogs—although these are often the same people who cram their dogs with unnecessary vitamin supplements and garlic (which contains a large number of chemicals). Although I empathize with those who want to treat their dogs naturally, there are times when modern pharmacology is the better alternative.

Clomicalm is a godsend for those people whose dogs do not respond to conventional behavioral therapy alone. It is neither a sedative nor a tranquilizer, and it won't change your dog's personality. It will just calm him down and enable him to learn positive behaviors more easily. It costs about a dollar a day. Clomicalm is designed to be used along with behavioral therapy; it's not a replacement for it. Owners using Clomicalm have noticed an improvement in their dog's behavior in about a month. Although a few dogs (especially those with OCDs) will have to remain on Clomicalm permanently, most can be weaned off the drug in 3 to 6 months.

Obsessive Compulsive Disorders

An obsessive-compulsive disorder (OCD) manifests itself in repetitive and pointless activities like tail chasing or paw licking. These behaviors are usually outgrowths of normal canine behavior, like grooming or the chase impulse; however, in the case of a true OCD, the behavior does not stop.

It is also possible that the precipitating cause may have been a raging infection, possibly not even diagnosed, that left an identifiable protein marker on the surface of certain cells. (This seems to be true in some cases of human OCD, as well.) The protein marker responds to antidepressant therapy. Certain diseases, like Cushing's syndrome, may also bring about the neurological changes that produce an OCD.

Constant Licking or Tail Chewing

In younger dogs, paw licking or chewing could be a nervous habit, which just indicates their need to use the bathroom. Chewing the base of the tail can mean fleas. A dog who spends a few minutes to an hour licking everything in sight may be nauseated; he is about to throw up. Get out the vomit bag.

If such licking behavior continues for weeks with no apparent organic cause, especially if carried to the point of raw or bleeding paws, however, I would suspect an obsessive-compulsive disorder arising from misplaced grooming behavior. In many cases, the final result will be a "lick granuloma," a scarred or ulcerated area on the inside of one or both legs.

Lick granuloma can be precipitated by separation anxiety, but the cessation of the anxiety (unless treated with antidepressants) is unlikely to cure the OCD.

Spinning and Tail Chasing

This chase-motivated behavior is most common in terrier and herding breeds, but any dog can be affected. There may be a genetic component, as well. The spinning dog ceaselessly spins or chases his tail. Some dogs carry this to the point of bleeding pawpads; they often pay almost no attention to any other stimulus. No one knows the exact cause, but it's likely that both genetics and environmental factors play a part.

Treatment of OCDs

Like OCDs in human beings, this is not a psychological problem. Although it may have been precipitated by loneliness, illness, or boredom, it cannot be classified as a neurosis. It has an organic component that is best treated medically. It is very seldom cured by getting another dog, mechanical intervention, or by giving your dog something else to do. Behavior modification doesn't work very well, either.

Behavioral Therapy

Mild, early-onset cases of OCDs can sometimes be contained or cured by conventional behavior therapies, diet, and exercise. Lots of play and perhaps a low-protein, additive-free diet may help. So will a regular schedule (to help relax the dog) and ignoring the behavior if it seems to be primarily an attention-getting device.

If you catch the behavior early enough, it may be possible to distract your dog by offering play or treats (like Kongs) in place of the behavior. It often helps to interrupt the unwanted activity and replace it with something more fun.

Drug Therapy

If neurological changes have already occurred, however, you'll probably need to ask your vet about prescribing an antidepressant. Antidepressants that help control OCDs in humans work for dogs; Prozac produces good results, although Clomicalm is showing very promising results as well. Substantial improvement is seen in 2 out of 3 cases.

Eating Nasty Stuff

For some reason, dogs revel in eating poop (coprophagy). This unattractive habit has some serious consequences. Dogs can contract bacterial or other infections, and the feces of wild animals are loaded with unpleasant little monsters. Cat poop is a particular favorite of many dogs, possibly because it is richer in nutrients (cats are not as efficient at processing food as dogs are).

Rolling in Nasty Stuff

Well, what's nasty is relative, is it not? It's a biological fact that even human beings are not born with the ability to distinguish between fair smells and foul. (Anyone with a baby can attest to this.) Only a few strong chemical odors seem to be instinctively avoided by both dogs and human babies. Various droppings, rotten things, and other loathsome objects found outdoors are of particular interest to dogs.

The Poodle Pundit

Rolling in foul treasures, like deer carcasses and cow manure, may be a scent-enhancement technique. Unlike cats, who depend on stealth to catch prey, dogs are uninterested in how they smell to their potential victims. In the wild, dogs rely primarily upon running their dinner down. Consequently, the smells they collect serve an intrapack purpose, perhaps to help establish dominance. 🐾

It may be that dogs roll in nasty stuff to disguise their odors from potential prey. This behavior is extremely common after a bath. I suspect the dog really hates the lemon-marigold-rosemary-coconut-oatmeal smell you have just saturated him with.

You cannot stop this behavior; it's completely normal. If you don't want your dog rolling in something awful, keep him on a leash.

Rubbing Face in Carpet

Usually this just means the dog has an itchy face, but constant face-rubbing may indicate an inhalant allergy.

Chapter 15

The Peevish Poodle:
Dealing with Aggression

A ll dogs are both dominant and submissive at various points in their lives. Whether they display dominance or submission may depend upon age, sex, temperament, environment, treatment, and relationship with the other party.

Serious Business: Dominance or Aggression

Dogs use dominance to find their place in the order of things. Left to their own devices, they even exhibit a substantial amount of aggression among themselves. In civilized society, however, we frown on such behavior, especially when it's directed against ourselves or other pets.

Signs of Dominant Aggression

Poodles can signal dominance vocally or through body language. Normally, canine physical signals include the rising of hackles (shoulder hair) and rump hair. However, Poodles have a problem in this area (so to speak). If your Poodle is in a continental show clip, you can't see his hackles, and he has no rump hair at all. But even pet-clipped Poodles have such thick/curly/fluffy hair that the hackles just don't raise very well. This may be a problem, so you need to look for other signs. The dog's lips may curl back, and he may stand on tiptoe. In dominant aggression, the pupils will contract and the dog will stare unblinkingly at his opponent. He may also growl or snarl (a snarl is a growl with a raised lip).

A dominant dog may also urinate frequently, defecate, or scratch the ground in the vicinity of the other dog with their hind feet. Dogs have scent glands in their feet; they want to spread their scent around as much as possible. This, accomplished by vigorously kicking up the dirt, means "I am King around this joint, and don't you forget it, Mister."

Poodle Potpourri

Owners of Toy Poodles have a particular responsibility. Because a tiny Toy isn't going to kill anyone, no matter how aggressive he may be, owners sometimes think that aggression is not a serious problem. Wrong. Not only is a nipping dog of any size a terrible nuisance, it's alarming to discover how much pain and suffering the tiniest of bites can cause—and how expensive it can be—in this litigious society of ours. Train your Toy as carefully as you would a Standard Poodle. 🐾

All signs of aggression toward people must be taken seriously, whether in a large Standard or a petite Toy. Even though serious aggression is rare in Poodles, you don't want it occurring in your family.

Submissive Body Language

Canine submission has its own language. A submissive dog will usually stand very still around a dominant dog, since running away elicits a chase-response from the dominant dog. The submissive dog will turn his head completely to one side. There is a myth that a dog does this to expose his jugular vein, but he's really just trying to avoid a fight by standing still and avoiding eye contact.

Submissive dogs also assume a lower stance than the dominant dog. He may crouch, lean back, or cower; he will certainly try to look away, and you'll see a lot of eye white. His pupils will be enlarged, and his tail will be rigid. Frightened and submissive dogs may turn sidewise to the dominant dog. In a final surrender, he may roll over on his side and urinate.

If, however, the fear is coupled with potential aggression, the dog will assume a classic approach-avoidance stance—alternately moving toward then backing away from the object of fear. If a less dominant dog decides to fight back, he will pull the corners of his mouth back until all the teeth are bared, but will not often snarl.

Poodle Potpourri

If your dog has done something wrong, like tearing apart the trashcan, he may seem to look guilty when you catch him at it. What you're really seeing is submissive behavior; he is nervous about your anger and anticipates punishment. Even before you open your mouth, he knows you're mad. In dogdom, a submissive stance often allows the miscreant to escape the wrath of the dominant dog; he's hoping it will work with you too. 🐾

Aggression Between Pets

Poodles are cheerful and gregarious by nature, and seldom get into fights. When it does happen, it is usually because the dogs involved have not established their places in the family hierarchy. A related factor, jealousy over the owner's attention, may also lead to infighting. This section is aimed at those who own more than one dog. Since Poodles are excessively charming, it is almost inevitable that everyone who owns a Poodle will sooner or later get 1 or 2 more. They can't help it.

The basic rule to establish is that the humans are the pack leaders. Most Poodles accept this axiom quite well—it is rare for a Poodle to attempt to dominate his owner. Quite a lot of jockeying for position can take place within the Poodle group, however, but if it is clear that you are boss it will be easier to sort out any disagreements within the pack.

Aggression Against People

Canine aggression against people is a growing problem. Reported dog bites are increasing at the rate of 2 percent annually. According to the AVMA, almost 4.5 million dog bites occur in this country every year, and 334,000 of them are serious enough to warrant emergency room treatment. About 2 million children are bitten annually, and half of them are under the age of 12. In fact, half of all children 12 and younger have been bitten by dogs. Every year, 16 to 20 people are killed by pet dogs. (None of them by Poodles, however!)

Dealing with Dominance

Most bites occur because the dog is trying to assert his dominance over a human. He hasn't learned the proper dominance-submissive pattern, which is all humans over all dogs. Sometimes the aggression has been growing for a long time; at other times, it seems to appear out of the blue. But there's always a reason, even if it's only in the dog's mind.

The Poodle Pundit

Obviously, no biting or aggressive behavior should be tolerated or ignored; if you make excuses for your dog, the situation will only get worse. 🐾

Perhaps something has happened within the family structure, like a divorce, which has upset the normal pattern. Perhaps someone is in the hospital, or has gone away to school. Maybe a baby has arrived. Dogs can experience stress from such changes, and may try to fill the gap that has opened in the domestic leadership structure. Dogs may suddenly become dominant, or, in rare cases, aggressive towards a lower status family member—usually a child.

Poodle Precautions

Even dogs who accept rough behavior from a family child may not put up with it from a visitor. It's your responsibility to monitor your dog's interactions with others. 🐾

Unneutered males between the ages of 18 months and 3 years are most likely to express this kind of aggression. Male dogs often seek, even if only briefly, to achieve the alpha position. Such dogs are really just as happy to lose, but many will make the effort just for form's sake. Obviously, this is an important time to assert your dominance.

Poodle Precautions

If your dog does bite a person, do not physically punish the dog. Immediately express your disapproval with a stern voice and remove the dog from the area. Striking a dog will only add fear to the complex of factors that induced the bite and increase the odds that he will bite again. Get him to a professional trainer or veterinary behaviorist specializing in aggressive behavior. 🐾

If your dog is bossy towards only some members of the family, those persons should take over feeding and training the dog. They need to make it clear to the animal that they are alpha over him. Obedience training is also essential.

On the other hand, never allow your child to pester a dog. If a Poodle walks away from a child, it means he doesn't want to be bothered any more. A more subtle indication of displeasure is the stiffening of the animal's body when he's being petted. A growl is an even stronger hint. Your child should be taught to know these signals.

The Poodle Pundit

Reward all signs of submissive behavior in dominant dogs with a treat, a pat, or playtime. Withhold these rewards unless the dog is behaving submissively. 🐾

Certain kinds of aggressive behavior respond well to drug therapy. Clinicians use anti-depressants, sedatives and tranquilizers, hormonal therapy, and anti-anxiety drugs like Prozac and Clomicalm to help aggressive dogs. Trainers have also been experimenting with holistic remedies for aggression. Herbs like St. John's Wort, valerian, and hops have a soothing effect on dogs, and certain flower essences (snapdragon, for instance) may be useful when used in conjunction with training.

Dietary changes, such as switching to a low-protein dog food with no additives, are helpful in some cases. Lots of exercise is important, if only because the dog becomes too tired to pick a fight. It also channels his energy into more constructive paths.

Other Aggressive Behaviors

Fear-Induced Aggression

Not all bites are provoked by aggression. Fear, pain, and over-stimulation may also play a part. Indeed, a combination of forces may be at work. Shyness, a genetic problem in some lines of Poodles, can lead to fear-biting. Fear-biting hurts as much as any other kind, and dogs who begin as fear biters and go uncorrected can progress to more dominant biting patterns.

As the name suggests, fear-induced aggression occurs when the animal is afraid—usually of something new. Fearful dogs often have a critical area of 1 or 2 feet surrounding them, which, if intruded upon, may elicit a bite response.

A human head or hand close to the dog's face is particularly threatening to a fearful dog. You can often cure this type of aggression by slowly desensitizing the dog to the frightening situation. Time spent in a loving and understanding home often decreases fearfulness in a rescue dog. Overprotection, however, is not the answer. Your Poodle must learn to cope.

The Poodle Pundit

Never corner a fear-biting dog. Allow him to come to you and praise him, or, better yet, treat him when he does so. If he refuses to come to you, allow him to walk away. You must not move, however. After a while, approach him with a treat. Don't make a big deal of it. This is part of the desensitizing process; he needs to learn that he has nothing to fear from you. 🐾

Some dogs fear certain kinds of people: men, people in uniform, people of a race different from their owners'. (In the latter case, dogs may be picking up clues from their owners.) The cure is to have these people (or reasonable facsimiles thereof) feed and pet the dog.

Territorial Aggression

Territorial aggression arises from a dog's natural predisposition to protect his area. Interestingly, many dogs who are not territorial in an open area become so when a fence is erected around their property! The bigger the dog's area, the less territoriality you are likely to see.

Possession Aggression

Guarding is a form of territorial aggression in some ways, but it's keyed to objects rather than to area. Obviously, this can be dangerous. Your dog should surrender any toy—or even his food—to you if you ask him. He may not want to do this, and may play keep-away with his toy, but growling must not be tolerated.

If your dog starts to display guarding behavior, you must reinforce your alpha position. Make your dog watch you while you pour the food into his dish. Pretend to eat some yourself first. Have him sit or stand away from the bowl, and do not allow him to approach it until you give him a signal. Keep a leash on him while training.

If your dog absolutely refuses to allow you near his food bowl, don't let him have one. This doesn't mean you should starve your Poodle, but it does mean that all his food is now going to come from you. Feed him by hand. This sounds like a lot of trouble, and it is, but it's better than being attacked by your Poodle. After a week or two of this you can start using the food bowl again, but you must drop just a few pieces of food in it. Put a few pieces more in a couple of minutes later. The idea is to get the dog to associate your approaching the bowl with a something pleasant—more food. Gradually add more food to the bowl, but then start approaching the bowl with something he really likes—such as chicken or liver. Gradually his terror at your approach will abate. Take your time with each of these steps.

Stand near him and pet him while he eats. Practice picking up his bowl while he's eating, then giving it back a few seconds later. Start with food he doesn't like very much, then work your way up to filet mignon. Gradually.

With both toys and food, you can also try swapping with him. Take away his toy or food, but offer him a preferred treat in its stead. When he learns to accept the fact that he'll get something in return, he'll be more likely to give up what he has. After a time, you can make the rewards more sporadic. Don't reward him every time, but only every third or fifth time. Go slowly. When you begin the swap-training, start with taking away objects in which he has little interest. Only gradually work up to the food bowl or favorite toy.

Food and toy guarding, if left uncorrected, will worsen over time as the dog acquires a larger and larger conception of what constitutes his food or toys. Sometimes a dog will allow his master to take away toys, but no other member of the family. This attitude must be corrected. All human beings should be alpha over all family dogs.

Pain-Induced Aggression

An injured dog may think that he can relieve his pain by attacking what he believes is the source of discomfort. This is really a self-defense bite, not true aggression.

In a few instances, it appears that aggression can originate from tumors, painful skeletal misalignments, or other serious conditions. Or perhaps the dog is simply old, grouchy, and tired. Peevish Poodles should be let alone. A dog's face, ears, and rectal area are very sensitive to pain, so take particular care around these areas. A normally friendly family dog that snaps suddenly while he is being moved or petted may be suffering from an injury or illness. Take him to the vet for a thorough checkup.

Genetically-Based Aggression

A few dogs are just born aggressive. Genetic aggression manifests itself at an early age by deep belly growls and an uninhibited bite response—usually by the age of 4 months. This form of aggression cannot be trained out of a dog; it must be bred out. Nearly all dogs exhibiting this behavior will have to be euthanized. This is another reason why you should know as much as possible about your dog's relatives.

Playful Nipping

Puppies frequently engage in play biting. They play rough with one another; it's a way for them to learn their limits. One of the things they learn is how hard they are allowed to bite without getting someone really angry at them. This peer-schooling period usually occurs between 5 and 8 weeks of age, which is one of the reasons it's important for a puppy to remain with his littermates that long.

This behavior is not true aggression; you will see young dogs wagging their tails and bowing to one another during play-biting sessions. In a natural extension, puppies usually attempt to carry play biting over to their human friends—and sometimes they nip hard. It never occurs to them that it's not all right, so it's up to you to discourage the behavior. Puppy teeth are much sharper than adult ones, but their jaws are weaker.

A young puppy will often take your hand or finger in his mouth. He is telling you he loves you; you are telling him you trust him. This is all fine, as long as he doesn't clamp down on you with those wicked little teeth. If he does bite down hard, squeal "ow!" in a hurt tone. He should withdraw his mouth. If he doesn't, pretend you're his mother. Snarl and give him a sharp tap on the nose. It's important that he pull his mouth away from your hand, not vice versa. You must emerge as the victor.

To halt actual nipping, grab the puppy by the nose or the nape of his neck. Shake it, and growl sharply, "no bite!" This behavior imitates what his own mother would do. Then walk away. He'll understand.

Establishing Your Dominance

If your dog exhibits symptoms of dominant behavior but has not bitten anyone, you can attempt to correct the situation yourself. However, if you have the least doubt regarding your ability to handle the situation, find a good animal behaviorist to work with you. Dominance always escalates if not controlled, and a dog's "bite threshold" is lowered with each uncontrolled bite.

The Poodle Pundit

Keep a short leash on a dominant dog when you are home; let him drag it around with him. If he exhibits incorrect behavior, you'll have a safe handle to grab him by. 🐾

Begin corrective training early. The longer you allow your Poodle to feel he's in charge, the more difficult it will be to teach him otherwise. You are not being cruel to your dog; you're doing him a favor.

Here are some general tips to establish your dominance:

▼ Never let your puppy nip or bite you, even while playing.

▼ If you feel challenged, stare coolly at your Poodle. Don't look away before he does. (However, never do this with a dog you fear may actually bite you.)

▼ Decide when games begin and end. Make sure you end up with the toys.

▼ Don't play tug of war or competitive games with your dominant dog. If it happens by accident, make sure you win.

▼ Keep dominant dogs off the sofa and bed. Dogs equate being high up with being the boss.

▼ Practice taking food away from your Poodle. He should accept your right to do so without complaint. To start, always trade him for something better.

▼ Initiate petting yourself. Don't let yourself be nudged into it.

▼ Have your dominant Poodle obey a command like "sit" before you feed, pet, or play with him.

▼ Reserve your praise for something done really well on command.

▼ Neuter your dog. Unneutered male dogs are 3 times as apt to bite as altered ones.

With a dominant dog, continually reinforce the concept that you are the alpha. If your Poodle is lying across your path, move him aside gently with your foot. If he is sitting in your favorite chair, move him out of it. Don't let him walk through a door before you do. Feed yourself before you feed him. Make sure he allows you to touch or remove his food.

Keep in mind that in the very unlikely case of a serious aggression problem, you should consult a professional animal behaviorist—not just a dog trainer. I prefer to use a veterinary behaviorist in case drug therapy needs to be prescribed.

Chapter 16
The Portable Poodle

P oodles are such good citizens that you will want to take them with you almost everywhere you go. Why travel solo when your best friend is just panting to go along?

Walking

Walking is a great exercise for both of you, as long as you walk together. Keep your Poodle attached to you with a leash at all times.

The Poodle Pundit

Remember—if you are attached to your Poodle, keep your Poodle attached to you! 🐾

Urban areas pose many hazards. Even well-behaved dogs may leap into traffic to follow something irresistible. In rural areas, unleashed dogs are likely to encounter skunks, snakes, rabid raccoons, horse manure, and other choice goodies. Our Poodle is a genius at finding excrement and rolling delightedly in it.

The Poodle Pundit

If your Poodle has a light-colored nose and he'll be spending some time in the sun, dab a bit of sunscreen on it to protect it from sunburn. The kind made for babies is best. You'll have to reapply it frequently if he licks it off. If you are in urban areas, remember that asphalt is blazing hot. If you wouldn't want to walk barefoot on the stuff, don't make your Poodle do so, either. 🐾

If you are a hiker, consider getting a lightweight nylon backpack for your larger Poodle. This way the dog can haul his own food and water. On the other hand, if you have a Toy, it wouldn't be a bad idea to get a special pack to carry him in.

If you are, by choice or necessity, a night walker, you might want to buy a Leashlight. This is a combination 16-foot retractable lead and flashlight. It's a tremendous convenience when navigating creepy dark alleys. It's sold by Black and Decker for about $35.

Biking

Larger Poodles enjoy tagging along while their owners ride. Since it can be dangerous to allow your dog to run free, you can purchase some nifty devices like the Springer or Canine Cruiser. These attach the dog to the bike while preventing him from running too close behind and getting hurt. They cost about $30.

Use your head about bike riding with your dog. Make frequent stops, don't go too fast, and don't go too far. Dogs will exert every ounce of energy to keep up with you, and more than one has died of heat stroke or exhaustion in his gallant efforts. Remember that dogs suffer more from heat than we do and can wilt at temperatures we find quite pleasant.

True Portability—Pet Carriers

Ideally, you'll have two kinds of pet carriers. The first is a strong, solid one suitable for airline transport; the second is a flexible, fold-up type that weighs almost nothing and can be kept in the trunk of your car. (The carrier, of course. I'm not suggesting

This Poodle enjoys her fold-up crate!
Courtesy of Kathie Kryla

you put the dog in the trunk.) Keep drinking water in the carrier, and line the bottom of it with a towel or cushioned mat. A good airline carrier, especially the larger ones, comes complete with wheels or casters. Newer carriers come in a variety of fashionable colors, including slate green, plum, and teal. Don't be the last on your block to get one.

Traveling By Car

Your Poodle's car trip should begin before your's does. Most dogs love to ride, but the excitement of the trip can have unfortunate consequences. Before you leave, exercise your dog to tire him out, or at least to calm him down.

The Poodle Pundit

If you are going to be gone for any length of time, pack a little suitcase for your Poodle (you can actually buy a special one) that includes water bowls, grooming tools, leashes, toys, health records, and medicine. 🐾

Keep your car at a comfortably cool temperature—for the Poodle. Dogs tend to get very excited or anxious in a car, and what seems comfy to you may be unbearably hot for them. Open the window a crack and get some fresh air circulating. This will help you both avoid the dreaded car trip vomiting.

The Poodle Pundit

If you are a tense or aggressive driver, you will communicate this attitude to your dog. Then you'll both be on edge. 🐾

We all should know enough in this day and age to keep car windows open a few inches when we have to leave our pets in the car—even briefly—on warm days. It may be a pleasant 80 degrees outside, but the temperature inside your vehicle can hit a lethal 140 degrees really quickly. Puppies are especially vulnerable to heat stress.

If it is not unbearably hot and you absolutely must leave your dog in the car for a few minutes, do as many of the following as possible:

▼ Park in the shade.

▼ Leave the car running with air conditioning on and the dog in a crate. Get extra keys if you lock the doors.

▼ Open the windows as wide as you safely can.

▼ Put a cold wet towel over the crate.

▼ Check your pet as often a possible.

▼ Leave a note on the windshield stating where you are in case of an emergency.

▼ Make sure the dog has access to fresh water.

The Poodle Pundit

Never leave your dog in a closed car if the temperature outside is over 60 degrees and you are parked in the sun. A white vehicle reflects sunlight and keeps cool slightly longer than a dark one. 🐾

You can buy a folding plastic barrier (it looks like a miniature baby gate) for your car windows. This allows air circulation if you absolutely must leave your Poodle in the car. Still, be sure to park in the shade. And don't be gone long.

Seat Belts

As a rule, your dog should ride safely in the back seat wearing proper doggy seatbelts. Some countries, like Germany, actually require dogs to have seatbelts. Several varieties are available, all of which safely restrain your dog, keeping both you and him safe. Having a Poodle leap into your lap while you're trying to negotiate a difficult turn is not as much fun as it sounds. Unanticipated sharp stops can hurl a dog into the windshield.

You can purchase barriers to insert between the front and back seat, which are adjustable both vertically and horizontally, and pressure-mounted for quick installation. Some versions are netlike, which is fine if don't think your dog will chew them to pieces.

Pickups

Although Poodles are much too sophisticated to want to ride in a truck, some unenlightened owners just don't get it. In fact, they even put their dogs in the back of the truck. This is dangerous. Dogs can jump out of trucks, or be thrown out, which will result in severe injuries or even death. If your Poodle must ride in the back of a truck, place him in a heavy-duty plastic crate that protects his eyes from dirt and pebbles, then secure the crate in the cargo area. If your Poodle is allergic to pollen, a ride in the back of the truck will make his allergies much worse.

Poodle Peril

I do not recommend that your dog ride in the back of a truck without being crated. Even the special dog harnesses used to keep them from bouncing out of the truck do nothing to protect your Poodle's eyes from flying debris. 🐾

Water

Dogs pant and drool a lot, especially when excited, and so are in danger of becoming dehydrated—and quickly, too. To reduce this risk, bring along a canteen and a plastic dish. Many companies make special traveling water and food containers, some of which are soft-sided for easy handling and storage. There's a product called Pet Galley that holds about a gallon of water and 7 cups of food. Freeze the water to keep it extra cool for your pet. I own a scrunchable-foldable food-and-water dish that attaches to my purse.

The Poodle Pundit

Bringing your own water is especially important for puppies. Young animals are very sensitive to water changes and can suffer a bad case of diarrhea from drinking strange water. Believe me, puppy diarrhea is the last thing you want to deal with while on vacation. 🐾

Car Sickness

One good way to help your Poodle avoid carsickness is to begin travel training early; between 7 and 9 weeks of age is ideal.

If your dog has a tendency to become carsick, it's usually best not to feed him for 4 to 6 hours before the trip. (Even if he does throw up, it won't be quite so bad.) In a few cases, however, feeding the dog actually helps stop carsickness. Check the vomit the next time your pet is carsick (you have to anyway when you clean it up). If it seems very liquid, try giving him a little snack before the next trip; if he's thrown up chunks of food, let him fast before the next ride, or at least reduce his food intake to one-third the normal amount. Remember to keep the car cool.

The Poodle Pundit

Older dogs often have more of a problem with carsickness than younger ones. 🐾

Dramamine can help stop canine carsickness. The dosage needs to be adjusted for the size of your Poodle; check with your veterinarian. Dramamine should not be given to dogs who have had seizures, glaucoma, or a bladder problem.

Some dogs do not get carsick if kept in a well-ventilated crate that discourages them from looking backward. Uncrated in the back seat, some dogs start gazing out the back window, which tends to make them rather woozy. Even most Poodles aren't smart enough to know that if they just turned around, they'd feel better.

Some folks use holistic remedies for carsickness; chief among these is ginger, which can be bought in capsules or as an extract at the health food store. Make sure you ask a qualified animal herbalist or a nutritionally-expert vet for the proper dosage. If you don't happen to know a qualified animal herbalist, a ginger snap or two will be fine. Then you can both munch down.

Sometimes riding in the back seat will make your Poodle a bit woozy (it certainly has that effect on me). Let him ride in the front seat with you, and put the kids in the back. That's where they belong anyway. Don't forget the seatbelts!

Often the reason your pet gets sick in the car is psychological. He knows the only time you take him anywhere is to the vet, which is exactly where he doesn't want to go. Make trips a joy for him by taking him to fun places—and see if his carsickness doesn't improve.

Stop frequently to give your dog a breather and a bit of exercise. When parking, turn off the motor. Gas fumes from the engine make pets and people sick.

The Poodle Pundit

It's a good idea to bring paper towels with you, just in case of—well, anything, almost. I also keep a little brush or lint remover handy to remove pet hair from my suit before going to an appointment. Or at least I would if I had any appointments. 🐾

Public Ground Transport

Some municipalities allow you to bring your Poodle on a bus, even if he's not a certified guide or service dog. Some places require the dog be restrained on a leash or confined in a crate. A few cities just stipulate that the dog should be "well-behaved" while using public transport, while others add size requirements. Some cities want dogs to be muzzled. Sometimes pets must pay a fare. Some cities employ a "one dog per bus or car" rule, or limit dogs to non-rush hour traffic. The regulations are too varied to make generalizations.

Most commonly, however, dogs are forbidden to use public transport. Always check before you go.

By Air

Many airlines and state health officials require health certificates issued by a licensed veterinarian within 10 days of a scheduled flight, so have your pet checked out within that time period. The United States Department of Agriculture produces an excellent booklet that details federal regulations called *Traveling by Air with Your Pet*. Call 301-734-7833 for a copy. The ASPCA has a similar pamphlet as well.

Poodle Precautions

U.S. territories and many foreign countries have quarantines or special health regulations. Hawaii, which is rabies-free, has a quarantine. Check with your travel agent, the airline, or appropriate consulate for specific information about your destination. 🐾

Call several airlines and compare pet policies; the same rules are not used by all. In general, however, dogs must be at least 8 weeks old and weaned at the time of flight, and airlines will not transport pets in temperatures below freezing or above 85 degrees. So if you're traveling in the summer, plan the trip for the morning; in winter, choose the afternoon.

If possible, schedule a direct, non-stop flight. It's less stressful for your pet and will reduce his chances of being lost. (This can indeed happen; some airlines treat pets more like luggage than passengers!) Try to schedule flights during less busy times—but beware of weekends; if something happens, the people in charge are never around.

It's not a good idea to have your pet sedated before a flight, because tranquilizers can play havoc with a dog's heat regulatory systems. Be sure to check with your veterinarian. Crate your dog in an approved container and attach all necessary instructions to it. Approved containers must allow the dog to sit, lie down, stand, and turn around; the floor of the container must be solid and covered with absorbent lining or litter. Pegboard flooring is not allowed.

Most airlines require that wheels on such a container be removed or made immobile prior to the flight. Kennels must be ventilated, and the rules are quite specific about it. At least 14 percent of the total wall space must be ventilated, with at least one-third of the opening located in the top half of the kennel.

Put a favorite toy or an old sock of yours in the kennel. Things with your scent will keep your Poodle comfortable and happy. Your old underwear provides an amusing plaything—especially for the airline personnel, who could use a good laugh.

Make sure your pet is wearing a flat buckle collar with two identification tags firmly attached. Never use a choke chain. Include your name and a phone number where you can be reached during the pet's flight time. Provide food, water, and any necessary medical information. Food and water dishes must be securely attached. If your dog needs medication, attach it to the side of the crate in case of emergency, along with complete directions for its use.

Puppies between 8 and 16 weeks of age must be fed every 24 hours and given water every 12 hours. This is sufficient to sustain life, but not much more, so it's vitally important to do your part in not letting your pet get lost. You are required to feed your pet within 4 hours prior to flight, and document the time and date of feeding on the crate. (Don't overfeed, however. In fact, feed your pet a little less than usual. This will help prevent airsickness.)

The words "LIVE ANIMAL" must be written clearly on the crate. Include arrows or "THIS END UP" to make sure your pet doesn't get transported upside down! You should also print directions reading, "KEEP AWAY FROM HOT SUN AND EXTREME

COLD," and hope somebody pays attention. Secure the crate firmly, but do not lock it. It's more likely that someone will need to reach your pet to help him than it is your pet will be stolen from the crate.

Poodle Peril

Bitches in heat and elderly animals should not be shipped by air. 🐾

Remember, airlines are not required to carry pets at all, and may refuse to do so for any reason. For some reason, animals have not yet benefited from antidiscrimination laws.

As for yourself, be sure to bring along a current photo of your pet in case he gets mislaid. This will be immensely helpful in relocating him. Believe me, saying "He's a Poodle" will not create an instant mental image in the mind of most people, unless your pet happens to be in a recognizable Poodle trim—and maybe not even then. I once had a basset hound mistaken for a pit bull.

"I Want My Poodle to Ride in the Passenger Area with Me. Is That Allowed?"

Maybe. He must be in a crate, and you'll need to buy a separate ticket for him. Most airlines charge about $50 for a pet ticket. In nearly all cases, his crate must be able to fit under the seat, which excludes a Standard Poodle. A few airlines do not accept pets in passenger areas at all; check in advance. Other requirements may include a limit to the number of pets per cabin (book early) and so on. The rules differ from airline to airline, so check several.

By Ship

Forget it. Ships don't allow you to bring pets. Your cruise to Bermuda will have to be sans Poodle.

"Are There Any Countries I Can't Take My Pet?"

Many countries require a quarantine period. Until recently, Hawaii (and that's part of the United States, in case you've forgotten) demanded a 3-month quarantine. In most cases, you can get away with a 30-day quarantine in Hawaii now, but there are restrictions. Pets are welcome in Canada, Mexico, and most of continental Europe. Europe, in fact, is much more pet friendly than the United States; dogs can frequently be seen in stores and restaurants. Specific requirements for each country differ, however, so investigate the rules thoroughly and far in advance.

On Arrival

Your life will be easier if you have an exercise pen for your dog. These are terrific for camping, shows, and vacation trips. A Standard Poodle will not get a tremendous amount of exercise in them, despite the name; however, they're a lot better than nothing. There are portable ones available that set up in seconds, and some are collapsible and fold up into suitcase size. Some portable exercise pens can be expanded by adding interlocking panels.

Motels and Hotels

According to a survey taken by the American Animal Hospital Association, 41 percent of pet owners take their pets along on vacations—at least sometimes. Some hotels allow pets, but you need to inquire first. Expect to put down a deposit or even an extra fee, since motels take a dim view of having their carpets and furniture eaten or urinated upon by pets. (It's bad enough when humans do it.)

The Poodle Pundit

Ask for a first floor room, if one is available; it's easier on you and the dog when it comes to those late night strolls. 🐾

It's disturbing, but the number of motels and hotels that do accept dogs has dropped by 25 percent in recent years. If your dog is not well-behaved in every way, it's best to leave him at home.

It is an odd thing that a dog who never chews anything at home may suddenly develop a tremendous taste for curtains when away. Most motels will not allow you to leave your pet alone in the room; some require that the animal be kept crated at all times, even when you are there. This is another excellent reason to crate train your pet. If you must go out and leave the dog inside, put a "Do Not Disturb" sign on the door so the maid won't decide to wander in, make the bed, and play with your Poodle while you're gone.

It's very important for dogs to make a good impression on hotel management and staff. People make decisions about welcoming dogs based on the behavior of those who have gone before. Ask the management where you should walk your dog, and remember to pick up after your dog every time. (It's not a bad idea to be ostentatious about this, so that everyone can see just how responsible you are.) Wipe off your dog's feet before re-entering the room.

"I Have to Leave My Poodle Home. Any Ideas?"

In many cases, leaving your pet home is the only feasible option when you go on a trip. However, you have some good options.

Pet Sitters

For many people, pet sitters are the ideal solution. If your Poodle can't go with you, he would probably prefer a pet sitter to a kennel. Most animals resent being hauled off to a pet motel, even the luxury kind with heated pools and exercise classes.

A good pet sitter should have references and be knowledgeable about animals. Make sure you discuss fees in advance and have your Poodle and the sitter meet beforehand. If there is a negative response from your pet (especially if he's usually friendly with new people), try a different sitter.

Before you leave, make sure your pet sitter has all the information she needs about food and medication, as well as your itinerary and phone numbers. She should also have your vet's emergency number. Depending on the arrangements you make with the sitter, you may need to sign a release for emergency treatment of your dog. Be sure to ask your sitter if it's necessary—he or she should know.

Finding a Good Boarding Kennel

Ask for recommendations from your vet, groomer, and friends. Many vets and groomers operate boarding facilities themselves. No matter what option you choose, your pet will board much more successfully if he has been crate-trained at home. Animals unused to being confined can really suffer at a kennel where it's usually necessary for at least part of the day.

Inspect the facilities beforehand, and ask questions. Provide the kennel management with all the information they need, including your itinerary, where you can be reached, your veterinarian's number, and a complete health record for your dog. A release for emergency treatment of your dog is usually included in the contract you sign with the kennel, but be sure to ask about this. Leave the name of a local person who can pick up the dog in case you cannot. Be sure to give them a big clear photo of your dog in case he should get mislaid somehow while you're gone.

Boarding Kennel Checklist

▼ Is it clean?

▼ Is the kennel heated and cooled according to the season?

▼ Is there a vet on call?

▼ Does the kennel employ veterinary technicians on its staff?

▼ Are there both indoor and outdoor runs?

▼ Is the kennel secure? If your Poodle is an escape artist, let the kennel manager know in advance.

▼ Is the indoor area well ventilated?

▼ What kind of bedding is provided? (Most kennels will allow you to bring your dog's own bed for him, if you like.)

▼ How are the animals separated? Good kennels do not allow nose-to-nose contact between animals, both for fear of spreading disease and to prevent barrier fighting.

▼ Does the kennel have adequate quarantine facilities? This is an important consideration if a boarded dog should develop symptoms of a contagious disease.

▼ Can you pick up your pet on Sunday? Many boarding kennels are closed on Sundays—the very day when most people want to pick up their pets.

▼ Is the kennel accredited by the American Boarding Kennel Association (ABKA)?

Clancy, enjoying the beauty of the desert   *Courtesy of Lou Murphy*

Chapter 17
The Poodle as Partner

Poodles have been performers, playmates, and partners for human beings almost since the beginning of recorded history.

Poodle Performers

As entertainers, Poodles have had no equal in the dog world. One of the most famous was the French Standard Poodle Munito (or Mirito), who was apparently skilled in mathematics and card tricks. Munito and his partner, a learned goat, were the talk of Paris back in 1818. Apparently there wasn't much else going on.

Poodle Potpourri

A pair of Poodles with the names of Philax and Brac, owned by one Monsieur Leonard, was credited with playing a tolerably good game of dominoes. 🐾

Another Parisian Poodle was trained by his owner, a boot-black, to dirty up the boots of passers-by in the Pont Neuf region of the city. (It's not clear how the dog was encouraged to do this, and it's something that doesn't bear much thinking about.) After the fact, the innocent citizens were eager to have their boots cleaned by the enterprising Poodle owner.

Cassis, the dancing Poodle

Courtesy of Suzanne Daltom
Photo by Clyde Foles

Poodle Potpourri

Queen Anne of England (r. 1702-14) had Poodles as entertainers at her court—and this alone says something about Poodles. It wasn't everyone who could entertain Queen Anne. It was hard to get her to laugh, or even to pay attention. She had 17 children, for one thing, and none of them made it past the age of 11. She was in constant agony with the gout and other maladies (undoubtedly relating to her interminable pregnancies), so one really can't blame her for finding a little innocent enjoyment in performing Poodles. King George III also enjoyed dancing Poodles from France, but he was insane.

Poodles joined the circus, of course. The most popular ones were the French Poodles who toured England with great regularity. They did all the usual things: dancing, walking tightrope on their hind legs, and racing. The jockeys were small monkeys. The English found this sort of thing endlessly amusing; the opinion of the Poodles is, fortunately, not recorded.

Poodle circus performers did it all—pushed wheelbarrows, jumped rope, performed acrobatics and even operated a spinning wheel. Whether or not they actually were able to spin Poodle hair into yarn for a sweater in another matter. If they did, no one mentioned it.

Other famous Poodles made their mark as vocalists. M. Habeneck, director of the Paris Opera, taught his Poodles to sing Mozart in a Poodle chorus.

The problem with all these fancy tricks is that, over time, people associated Poodles with being tricksters, unable to perform their original duties. This sad situation prevails today, with the AKC placing Standard and Miniature Poodles into the Non-Sporting Group, rather than in the Sporting or Working Group, where they really belong. Toy Poodles are, of course, correctly placed in the Toy group.

Although Poodles still act in circuses, their performances today are more likely to be found in the conformation and obedience rings and on the agility field.

Poodle Prestige: The Conformation Poodle

The Poodle is perhaps the world's ultimate show dog. He has everything: glamour, style, and sheer pizazz. Almost inevitably, a Poodle is in strong contention for Best in Show at Westminster.

The Poodle Pundit

Handlers often do not like to have spectators pet or even touch their Poodles, especially just before entering the ring. Always ask first, and don't be offended if your request is refused. If you are given permission, it's best to just stroke the dog lightly under the chin—leave that spectacular topknot alone, no matter how tempting it is. (Handlers do enjoy having their Poodles looked at, however, whether they admit it or not.) 🐾

Am/Can Ch My Deer Whisperwind Music Man at the Westminster Dog Show
Courtesy of Marlene Ann Heacock

Is conformation showing for you? Even if you have a Poodle whose body conforms perfectly to the breed standard, that doesn't necessarily mean you have a show Poodle. Before everything else, a show Poodle is a showman. He is not only beautiful, but he also wants everyone else to appreciate that fact. He prances. He gleams. He dazzles. And because it seems as if even the lowliest Poodle has at least some of these characteristics, the show Poodle is truly a dog to behold. It is no accident that Poodles walk off with Best of Group and Best in Show time after time. Their performing heritage makes the conformation ring just another act.

So, does your Poodle have it? You are too biased in his favor to be objective; ask his breeder or another knowledgeable person to evaluate him for you. The breeder is a good choice, because he'll be the first one to tell you if, in his opinion, he can't quite cut it. Breeders want only the best of their line on parade as examples of their finest endeavors.

Poodle Potpourri

Only intact and unspayed dogs may compete in con-formation. This is because the original purpose of such classes was to select those dogs that would be most likely to produce the best offspring. The only reason to keep your dog unneutered or unspayed is for showing purposes. 🐾

For most people, the goal of conformation showing is to win a championship. To do this, a dog needs to accumulate 15 points at AKC-sanctioned dog shows. Dogs can win as many as 5 points at a given show, although this is very rare. More commonly, a dog will win 1, 2, or 3 points—or none, which is the most likely outcome.

The number of points depends on how many dogs are entered in your dog's breed and sex. It's all rather complicated, so your best bet is to contact the AKC and request a copy of their free pamphlet, "A Beginner's Guide to Dog Shows." You can call them at (919) 233-9767.

If you decide to show your Poodle, consider it a learning experience. If you handle him yourself, you'll gain a lot of knowledge; if you're a novice, however, you're probably not giving your Poodle his best shot at winning. Experienced handlers not only understand how to make the most of their charge's best points, but also know which judges are likely to appreciate your Poodle's finer qualities.

Choosing the right handler is as important as choosing the right vet or groomer; sometimes a handler who is perfect for one dog just doesn't get on with another. Go to some shows and watch various handlers in and out of the ring; when you find one you like, get his business card, and ask around about him. If you like what you hear, make an appointment to meet and discuss your dog's future.

Poodle Precautions

There is no financial reward in showing dogs. Except in puppy sweepstakes classes, no money is handed out, only ribbons. People show dogs as a hobby, although it's true that some people's lives seem to revolve around it. 🐾

Show Time!

Line 'em Up!

You may decide to handle your own dog, of course. Before you step into the ring, however, take some handling classes at your local kennel club and go to a few dog shows. Handling classes can be invaluable. You'll learn dog show protocol, dress, terminology, how to gait your dog, and how to show smaller Poodles on a table.

There will be several dog shows near you every spring and summer weekend. At the show you can get a feel for how the classes are conducted. Don't bring your own dog to the show, however, unless he is entered. Most shows have a rule against this practice because space is limited.

The Poodle Pundit

The different classes into which dog shows are organized are confusing for the beginner. There are puppy classes, junior classes, open classes, veterans classes, winners classes, winners dog, best of winners, best of variety, best of group, and a host of others. All this is explained in the aforementioned AKC pamphlet. 🐾

If you and your dog are still learning, it's fun to enter a "match" rather than a show. Matches are informal affairs that you can enter the very day of the event. They are specifically designed for novice handlers and their dogs, so it's a great way to learn the ropes. You won't receive any points for winning, however, even if your dog turns out to be Best in Match.

If you decide to show your Poodle, ask your breeder or another knowledgeable person to get you started. You'll need to enter the show a couple of weeks before it is scheduled; this is the "closing date." You'll receive a "premium," which contains the requisite forms you need to fill out. You'll be confronted with a multitude of choices for classes to enter; ask your breeder for help in deciding which one is best for your Poodle: puppy, novice, bred by exhibitor, American-bred, or open. There's some strategy involved here; your handler or breeder will know what's best for your dog. Part of the premium will ask you to write down your dog's breed and variety. That's Poodle, of course, then Standard, Miniature, or Toy.

Standard and Miniature Poodles are judged as separate breeds within the non-Sporting Group. Toy Poodles are judged in the Toy Group. For example, if your dog is judged as the best Miniature Poodle, he will then compete in the group competition against other Best of Breed winners from a variety of breeds.

When you and your dog are at the show together, make sure your Poodle leaves other dogs strictly alone. It's possible that an untoward disagreement might occur. I have seen large dogs urinating on smaller ones—a very unfortunate event for a show dog.

Get your Poodle used to having his teeth looked at, and in the case of males, their testicles handled—by strangers, yet!

Poodle Potpourri

There's currently a motion to move the Standard Poodle into the Sporting Dog class. If this change occurs, each variety of Poodle will be considered in a different group; Sporting for the Standards, Non-Sporting for the Miniatures, and Toy for the Toys. 🐾

Obedience

Formal obedience is a key part of the showing circuit in United States today. The credit for this goes largely to Helene Whitehouse Walker, a Standard Poodle fancier. She imported three Standard Poodles from England and began to show them under her kennel name, Carrillon. She not only showed her dogs in conformation classes, but also began to develop obedience tests similar to those already in place in England. In 1933, she sponsored the nation's first all-breed obedience tests. The AKC assumed responsibility for obedience events in 1935, but Walker continued to promote education and awareness of the discipline.

The Poodle Pundit

The Poodle Club of America held its first obedience competition in 1948. 🐾

Poodles do extremely well in obedience trials. (A white miniature Poodle won the AKC Obedience Invitational in October 2001.) Their intelligence and willingness to work puts them among the winners consistently. And since obedience is a game where every dog can win, it's great sport for those who like to show their dogs off but are not keen on formal competitive events. Competitive or not, however, obedience is a highly structured activity with its own culture. To become proficient in obedience, join your local kennel club and take classes.

Poodle Potpourri

In one sense, obedience can be considered competitive. At every event, one dog is awarded "High in Trial"; if your dog is one of the top 4 finishers in his class, you'll get a ribbon stating that. Obedience has something for everyone 🐾

To receive a "leg" toward an obedience title, all your dog needs to do is to pass the required events for his level. Currently, there are 3 levels: Novice, Open, and Utility. The Novice and Open levels are further divided into two classes, A and B; the A classes are for dogs who have not yet competed successfully at that level. Every competition is worth 200 points; to qualify, your Poodle must earn 170 of those points. He has to do this 3 times under 3 different judges. If he does, he wins his CD (Companion Dog) title. Higher level competitions result in the CDX (Companion Dog Excellent) and UD (Utility Dog) titles. Dogs who have earned the UD are eligible to win the coveted OTCh Obedience Trial Champion, a title earned by outscoring other dogs at several events.

The Poodle Pundit

At all-breed shows, Poodles compete on an even footing with other breeds; the tests are not separated. 🐾

Obedience trials are now held in conjunction with most all-breed dog shows. To attain the first of these "degrees," the CD, a dog must heel on leash, heel free, stand for examination, recall, and complete a long sit (60 seconds) and a long down (3 minutes). When heeling, he'll have to execute left and right turns, stops, and move at various speeds. On the "stand" he'll need to stand still, off lead, while a judge examines him, with the handler at least 6 feet away. The recall requires the dog to sit 30 feet from the handler, come quickly, and sit. On command, the dog must move to the heel position, then sit once more.

Earning a CDX title requires your dog to work entirely off lead. He will have to heel off lead in a figure 8 pattern, drop on recall (going "down" rather than just sitting on recall), retrieve a dumbbell from 20 feet over level ground, retrieve a dumbbell over the high jump, and execute the broad jump. They must also do longer sits (3 minutes) and downs (5 minutes) with the handler completely out of sight.

Utility dogs must follow hand signals for heeling, moving, and standing for examination. The handler cannot use voice signal in this section. Dogs also do directed jumping, directed retrieving, and scent discrimination. Dogs can work for their Utility and CDX degrees at the same time.

Tracking

Another noncompetitive sport is tracking, which is, formally, a part of obedience. The 2 events are held separately, however, and separate titles are awarded. Your Poodle can earn a Tracking Dog title (TD) at a tracking test.

In tracking, a dog is required to follow a trail by ground scent—not air scent. He must track an article, such as a leather glove, that has been dragged through grass and along the ground. You will follow your dog—he leads you, not vice versa. Your Poodle will wear a special tracking harness for this purpose.

Poodle Parlance

Three tracking titles are possible; TD (Tracking Dog), TDX (Tracking Dog Excellent), and VST (Variable Surface Tracker). 🐾

Cassis Tracking

Courtesy of Suzanne Dalton
Photo by Clyde Foles

Agility

Dog agility is modeled on the equestrian version—the dogs jump obstacles in a stadium-like setting. Your Poodle will practice scrambling over A-frames, balancing on a dog walk, crossing a teeter-totter, charging through tunnels, and jumping though hoops (the last, of course, is an almost genetic skill with Poodles!). As in obedience, Poodles compete against other breeds unless the event is held at a Poodle specialty show.

Agility trials were first held at the famous Crufts Dog Show in 1979; it has since become the fastest growing dog sport in this country.

Dogs don't have to be Mr. (or Ms.) Universe to compete well in agility trials. However, the agility dog will need to be able to run full speed for several minutes, turn, twist, climb, jump, and dart through tunnels.

Agility Class in session   *Courtesy of Suzanne Dalton*
                                                        Photo by Clyde Foles

In the United States, several organizations hold sanctioned agility events. These include the AKC, the United States Dog Agility Association (USDAA), and the North American Dog Agility Council, Inc. (NADAC).

The Poodle Pundit

Obstacles used in agility trials include the A-frame, dog walk, chute or closed tunnel, pause table, seesaw, weave poles, tire jump, open tunnel, and other kinds of jumps. Handlers may not touch the dogs or the equipment during trials. 🐾

The Poodle's extreme intelligence, athleticism, and willingness to please make him a natural for agility training. There's more than that, however; many breeds of dog fly around the agility ring just for the joy of it, while a Poodle wants to make sure you're watching! You can never take the performer out of the Poodle.

Agility Course

Poodle Precautions

Do not begin agility training until your Poodle is physically mature. Agility puts a lot of stress on muscles and joints, and starting too early can induce an injury that will plague the dog for a lifetime. 🐾

The SeeSaw

Cassis masters the A-frame   *Courtesy of Suzanne Dalton*
                                                Photo by Clyde Foles

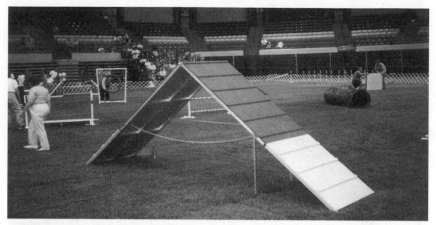

Activities on the agility course include the A-frame, weave poles, tire jump, open tunnel, and other kinds of jumps

Mastering the jumps, Cassis and Suzanne

Courtesy of Suzanne Dalton Photo by Clyde Foles

Flyball

The new sport of flyball is sweeping the country, probably because it's fun to watch and cheap to participate. Flyball is a relay race in which dogs run down a 51-foot lane (leaping 4 hurdles along the way), retrieve a tennis ball at the end, then hurtle back to the starting point. The dogs compete in 2 teams of 4 dogs each. The sport has no breed or size classes, and all dogs compete together in order to earn points for a title

Service Dogs

Poodles have helped blind people see, lame people walk, and deaf people hear. And some people say they're not miracle dogs!

Seizure assistance dogs can learn to push a button or bark to alert medical personnel in case of an emergency. Some dogs are even able to predict a seizure as long as 45 minutes in advance, which allows their owners to take medication or get to a safe place. So far, trainers have not been able to teach dogs to sense an oncoming episode; it seems to be a special gift of certain dogs who are well-bonded with their owners.

Mobility assistance dogs learn to open doors and drawers, and push wheelchairs up ramps. They are also trained to bark if their owner needs assistance. They can pick up phone receivers, retrieve dropped objects, and carry packages home from the store. They can even help with the laundry, although they are not very good at folding.

Guide and Service Dogs

"Poodles can learn to be seeing-eye dogs in
half the time it takes the member of any other breed,
but they are rarely used for this purpose because their
independent spirit rebels against the repetition of a
pattern, because they hate muzzles and leashes, and
because they insist on inventing rules of their own."
—James Thurber, *Christabel, Part One*

Thurber is wrong, at least in part. Poodles have been guiding the visually impaired for at least 300 years; there exists a 17th century engraving which shows a Poodle leading a blind man. Early

Seeing-Eye Poodles helped their owners in other ways, too. They were trained to look pathetic and forlorn so their owners would gather in alms. Although Labradors, Golden Retrievers, and German Shepherds are most noted for this work today, several Poodles are showing the world how well-suited they are to this task. James Thurber notwithstanding, today's leader dogs are not muzzled and adjust perfectly well to their working harnesses.

Poodle Potpourri

In England, Standard Poodles have been crossed with Labrador retrievers to produce the Labradoodle, an animal particularly useful as a guide dog for the blind. They combine the calm and steady nature of the Labrador with the Poodle's greater height and innate intelligence. Both breeds, of course, are highly trainable. These crossbreeds tend to inherit a poodle-type, shed-free coat, which is beneficial if the owner is allergic to most dog hair. 🐾

Search and Rescue (SAR) Dogs

Jo-Jo, Level C SAR with the Central Arkansas SAR K-9s
Courtesy of Michelle Mace

Although we are accustomed to thinking of German Shepherds or Labradors in this role, it's pleasing to note that a white Standard Poodle named Cassidy is among the most accomplished of this rare type. Cassidy, handled by Carla Tomaszczyk of Aspen, Colorado, is an avalanche-certified search and rescue dog. She is trained to find victims of avalanches. In one demonstration, Cassidy found two "victims" buried under 5 feet of snow in a 10,000 square foot snowfield. It took her less than a minute. Experts estimate it would have taken 30 people 30 hours to get the same result.

Therapy Dogs

Poodles are the ultimate pet therapy dog. They are cute, calm, friendly, and come in a variety of sizes. Pet therapy dogs visit hospitals, nursing homes, and even prisons. They can make a tremendous difference in the lives of many—including your own. They help people to socialize, improve motor skills, and relieve boredom and loneliness. Contact a local nursing home to see if there is a pet therapy program in your area.

Truffle Hunters

One of the earliest uses to which keen-nosed Poodles were put was truffle hunting. Truffles are delicious fungi that grow about a foot beneath the earth. Truffles cannot be domesticated, so it's up to truffle hunters to go out and find the things. They are usually found near the roots of oak, beech, or pine trees, but that doesn't narrow the search all that much. A truffle can weigh more than 8 pounds, so it is nothing to be sneezed at. Pigs are actually better than any dog at locating these savory treats, but they have an unfortunate habit of gobbling them up when they've rooted them out.

Poodles have proved more amenable to this task. Although not capable of actually digging up the truffles (in fact, small Poodles were used just so this would not occur), they were able to sniff out where they were, then stand waiting for their slow-witted owners to catch up.

In Barbara Cherry's excellent book, *Pet Owner's Guide to Poodles*, she asserts that the truffle-hunting Poodle was an "inferior type," but fails to explain what was inferior about it—after all, it's not easy finding truffles. Ms. Cherry may have been referring to the fact that these early Poodles were apparently black-and-white parti-colored dogs. Black-and-white Poodles may be *canis non gratis* in the show ring, but their coloring obviously didn't hamper their truffle-finding ability. At any rate, Poodle historians credit these Poodles as ancestors to today's Toy Poodle.

Truffle training began when the pup was about 4 months old. The first part of the training consisted of the master throwing a truffle and having the Poodle retrieve it—which they do practically instinctively. Soon the master began hiding truffles behind trees and under leaves, and eventually the truffle was buried a couple of inches in the earth.

Sad to say, American Poodles are no good at finding truffles, but perhaps this is because there are none in this country; truffles are a European species.

Poodle Potpourri

At one point in their history, some Franciscan friars who were living about 30 miles from Paris taught their Poodle to catch crayfish. The animal would wade into the water and stand stock-still while the deceived crayfish crawled eagerly around to eat him. Instead, they became tangled in his fur, and the dog then waded back to shore, laden with crayfish for the good friars' supper. As one might expect, the dog eventually drowned. The friars erected a very handsome monument with a Latin inscription in his honor, and I suppose that's all that matters after all this time. 🐾

Hunting Dogs

There are old engravings and colored prints that show Poodles participating in both fowling and rabbit hunting. Poodles are excellent swimmers and hunters. They are natural retrievers, too. Even though they are seldom used as hunting dogs today, there is no reason why they can't revert to their ancestral calling. Some experts, like Dr. Grace Blair, believe that the Poodle is the oldest retrieving breed presently in existence.

Since 1997, Standard Poodles have been eligible to compete in AKC Junior Hunting Tests for Retrievers. In 1999, they began to

Cosmic Romance ("Gable) retrieves a training bumper from the water during a training workshop. Owner, Dr. Grace Blair, was the founder of Versatility in Poodles and a major proponent in the movement to "rediscover" retriever instincts in Poodles.

Photo by Kristi Murdock

compete at the Senior and Master levels. Dr Blair, who is president of Versatility in Poodles (VIP), has been working hard with the Poodle Club of America to convince the AKC that it should acknowledge the suitability of the Poodle as a retrieving breed.

The Poodle Club of America offers a Working Certificate (WC) and a Working Certificate Excellent (WCE). To achieve these titles, a Poodle must retrieve birds from both land and water and show no fear of guns.

Since 1994, VIP has offered a "Versatility Certificate." This is a 2-level award—the VC (Versatility Certificate) and VCX (Versatility Excellent). To earn these certificates, Poodles must accumulate "points" from various activities including conformation, obedience, tracking, agility, retriever fieldwork, and herding. (Yes, Poodles can herd. They can do anything.) They can also get points for passing temperament and health tests. To learn more about qualifying, check out the VIP website at www.pageweb.com/vipoodle.

Bev Duerst and Lemerle Crystal Lite CGC, WC, NA, NAJ, OA, OAJ, NAC, NJC

Ready to mark the fall of the bird that Crystal will retrieve from the water. Crystal has a Poodle Club of America Working Certificate (WC), a test of retrieving instinct and basic retriever training.
Courtesy of Bev Duerst
Photo by Kristi Murdock

Ch. Silverado Howard huge, CGC with a drake green-winged teal, 1998 duck season.

Courtesy of Steven Chin

Poodles on Patrol

> *"They have courage, too, and they fight well and fairly*
> *when they have to fight. The poodle, moving into battle,*
> *lowers its head, attacks swiftly, and finishes the*
> *business without idle rhetoric or false innuendo."*
> —James Thurber, *Christabel: Part One*

All three varieties of Poodles are alert watchdogs, and a large Standard Poodle makes a surprisingly effective guard dog. Despite their playful, friendly nature, they are instinctively protective animals. The main drawback in this regard is that would-be intruders do not take them seriously, so Poodles are less likely to ward off attackers than say, a wolf-like Siberian Husky (which is, ironically, much less protective than a Poodle).

Poodle Parlance

A watchdog is one who will alert his owners to the presence of welcome or unwelcome visitors. Most dogs do this instinctively. A guard dog is one who is trained to protect his family in case of attack. The operative word here is trained. Dogs who attack visitors without regard to their status are public menaces, not guard dogs. 🐾

Poodle Pullers?

No discussion of Poodles would be complete without a mention of John Suter's famous Poodles. Suter has mushed his team of Standard Poodles and Alaskan Huskies in nearly every big sledding competition on the North American continent including the Iditarod, a grueling 1,049-mile race. His first attempt using a mixed team, in 1988, landed him in 38th place (out of 52 starters). He ran and finished the race again with an all-Poodle team in 1989, 1990, and 1991. Although Poodles are not ideal sled dogs physically (their fur freezes to the snow), their heart and courage in the face of enormous odds is very moving.

Chapter 18
Your Poodle Past Prime

*"My poodle was fourteen years old last May and she is
still immensely above ground. She slips more easily that
she used to on linoleum, makes strange sounds in her
sleep, and sighs a great deal, but more as if she had figured
something out than given it up."*
—James Thurber, *Christabel: Part Two*

Like fine art, a Poodle's value only increases with time. According to the AVMA, 14 percent of dogs in this country are aged 11 years or older—that's 7.3 million senior canines. In the 1930s, the average dog lived only 7 years; today it's up to 11. We can thank better medical care, fenced yards, and better-informed owners for this encouraging statistic. Your dog will be an old dog for a lot longer than he will be a puppy. Senior dogs definitely deserve their own chapter!

When is Your Poodle a Senior Poodle?

Aging in dogs depends upon a number of factors, the single most important of which is weight. A 50-pound dog is older at age 11 than a 40-pound dog of the same age. This, however, is a very general rule. Some breeds seem to age faster than others of the same size. The most significant difference, of course, is between individual animals. Even littermates of the same weight can seem to be of different ages. There are so many individual differences that it seems the most one can say is that, unless an accident or unforeseen illness intervenes, you can expect to have your Poodle for between 10 and 17 years.

One important factor to take into consideration is bloodline. Longevity runs in certain dog families, as it does in human ones. If you are getting your Poodle from a breeder, ask how long your puppy's ancestors lived. This then gives you an indication of what you can expect with your own Poodle.

What you feed your dog, how often you exercise him, and environmental stresses also play a part in the aging process. Aging is inexorable, however. As your dog grows older, you can expect problems to develop in organs that are particularly age-sensitive, like the lungs, heart, liver, and kidneys. The efficiency of the immune system declines as well.

In general, I would say that a Standard Poodle reaches seniority at about age 8, and Miniatures and Toys at about 9 years. This doesn't mean get out the rocking chair; it means pay more attention to diet and exercise, and begin keeping track of changing behavior so you know the difference between normal aging and signs of illness.

For instance, older dogs hear less well, see less well, and need more rest than younger ones. This is normal. Unfortunately, many illnesses mimic normal signs of aging. Be observant; monitor your dog's food and water intake, bowel movements, and urination patterns. Unexplained weight changes, foul smells, coughing and sneezing, unusual bumps, and so on should be checked by your veterinarian.

Old people and old dogs suffer from similar ailments: cancer, obesity, arthritis, dental problems, eye disorders, thyroid problems, kidney problems, and senility. Luckily, we can combat all of these, and, to some extent at least, turn back the clock.

General Care

Older dogs are especially sensitive to both heat and cold. Keep your older Poodle, especially a small one, in a jacket when you go outdoors on bitter mornings.

Poodle Precautions

Older dogs don't fare very well at boarding kennels. The unhappiness every dog endures when being left in a strange place can place stress on the immune system, which can, in turn, trigger an illness that an older dog may have difficulty fighting off. Consider getting a pet sitter for your senior dog instead. 🐾

Rest

Give your older dog a comfortable place to rest—put a soft dog bed in his favorite spot. Special orthopedic ones are available. Dogs resting on hard or rough surfaces can develop sores and ulcerations on their elbows. A young Poodle is agile and shifts around to get comfortable, but your older dog may be feeling too creaky to move even when he's obviously in pain. You'll have to look out for him.

Check on your dog frequently when he's outside for the same reason; sometimes older dogs tend to lie in the hot sun too long.

Exercise

Take your dog for a walk before eating to improve his appetite, and afterward to help his digestive system. The exercise help stimulate the weakening muscles of his intestines.

Short, frequent walks are better for your senior pet than occasional longer ones. If the walk will be a brisk one (assuming your dog is up to it), include a warm up and cool down period. If not, go slowly and let your old dog enjoy the pleasures of sniffing around. Don't let him wander away, however. He could become disoriented and fail to return. His hearing and sight aren't all that they used to be.

The Poodle Pundit

If your senior dog still enjoys swimming, it's very important that you towel him dry thoroughly afterward; his heat control isn't what it used to be. For the same reason, I don't advise using a blow dryer on an older dog. 🐾

If your dog's head and tail begin to droop, take the hint and go home. Be sure to offer your dog plenty of fresh water before and after a walk, too.

Grooming

Even if your elderly dog doesn't leave the house much anymore, good grooming is just as important as ever. Not only will it make him feel better (touch is one sense that dogs don't lose), but it will also enable you to check for lumps and bumps. Combine your grooming with a medical examination.

Older dogs have problems standing for extended periods of time. Give your dog a break and let him lie down; the grooming process will be easier for both of you. Make sure he is relaxed and comfortable on the grooming table. Like a small puppy, an older dog can easily fall off—not because he's puppy-wiggly, but because his dulled senses don't allow him to see and react as quickly.

You may find that the shampoo that worked perfectly well up until now isn't doing the trick anymore. Perhaps his fur feels dry, or the skin feels oily afterward. The shampoo probably isn't at fault; it's more likely that your dog's hair and/or skin has changed over time. Experiment with shampoos designed for aging dogs.

Include a massage with your grooming. This feels good and is therapeutic at the same time. You can develop a special bond with your older dog through grooming.

Nails need to be clipped more frequently in the older dog, usually because he is not getting the amount of exercise he did before. Because older dogs often have imperfect balance and leg strength, it is critical to keep the nails at the correct length. Be sure to keep the hair trimmed between your dog's pads. You can also buy slipper socks for your dog (if he'll wear them) or a tacky foot spray to improve your older dog's traction on slippery floors.

Teeth

Dogs over the age of 6 are likely to have tartar buildup or gingivitis. Some of this is due to the natural aging process, and some is due to diet. If people could agree on the type of diet most likely to produce healthy teeth, we'd be well off, but such is not the case. Most practitioners advise a diet of dry kibble and hard biscuits to keep teeth at their best; others, however, feel a diet of raw, tough meat works best because it acts as a natural dental floss. It's what wild dogs eat. However, wild dogs don't generally live to be 12 or 14, so it's hard to tell what their teeth would be like if they did.

Poodle Precautions

Although older dogs exhibit a gradually reduced interest in chewing things, sudden loss of interest may indicate dental problems. Inspect your Poodle's mouth and gums. 🐾

In any case, poor dentition can make it hard for your dog to eat properly. It can also cause a serious case of bad breath. Get your dog's teeth checked and cleaned regularly, and don't stop brushing them!

Diet and Feeding

If your older dog has gone off his feed, try warming it slightly to make it more appetizing. If you must hand-feed your dog to encourage him to eat, that's all right. It's not spoiling him; it's letting him know you care. A raised food bowl may be easier on the joints than one placed directly on the floor. If your home is large or your older dog has trouble getting around, place several bowls of water in convenient places so he won't need to walk up and down the stairs so much.

Energy Requirements

An aging dog has a slower basal metabolic rate than a young dog. Even though his weight may remain constant, the percentage of water and lean muscle decreases as the percentage of fat increases. As a rule, dogs who are 8 to 10 years of age need about 80 percent of the energy intake of a 1 year old. Most commercial senior dog foods are adequate in this regard.

Protein

Make sure your geriatric Poodle is getting enough protein. Unless your dog is suffering from kidney disease, the protein level of older dogs should be increased by as much as 50 percent. This is contrary to what was believed for many years; new research, however, shows that a decreased protein intake slows wound healing and lessens immune function. It also demonstrates that high protein levels in the diet do not damage renal function in healthy dogs. Although older dogs can extract the same amount of protein from their food as a younger dog, they are unable to use it as efficiently. Therefore, 30 percent of all calories your healthy older dog consumes should come from protein. Since the dog food industry is slow to recognize the results of this research, however, many senior foods do not have sufficient protein. Check the label.

Kidney impaired dogs, however, need to be on a low protein, low phosphorus, low potassium, and low sodium diet. Several companies make prescription foods for renal-impaired dogs, including Purina, Waltham, Hill's, and Nature's Recipe.

It's also a good idea to increase B-complex, E, and ester-C vitamins for older dogs. Supplements of zinc, selenium, omega fatty acids, and co-enzyme Q10 are advisable as well. The B vitamins are helpful in fighting allergies, stress, and infection; vitamin E, ester-C, zinc, and selenium all help the immune system. Ester-C (calcium ascorbate) is a form of vitamin C. It has a neutral pH value and so is easy on the gut. Most important, it's been shown to be beneficial in treating arthritis. Vitamin C also helps the body absorb other supplements.

Poodle Precautions

Although healthy young adult dogs can do well on a surprisingly wide variety of foods, the optimal range for elderly, ill, and stressed dogs is much narrower. 🐾

Monitor your Poodle's food and water intake carefully. Increased drinking can be a symptom of diabetes, which is common in older dogs. The water should be as pure as possible. Although healthy young dogs can usually filter contaminants from their systems easily, older dogs need your help. If the water is not pure enough for you, don't let your dog drink it either.

Obesity

It is estimated that over a quarter of the cats and dogs in this country are obese, and the older the dog, the more common the problem. As dogs age, they need less exercise and, consequently, fewer calories. Unfortunately, many owners fail to take this into consideration and continue to fill up the old food bowl. Obesity not only makes your dog uncomfortable, it is hard on the joints, which can aggravate arthritis. Too much weight can also contribute to diabetes, another disease of old age.

Since older dogs generally get less exercise, you'll need to keep a careful check on your older Poodle's weight. If possible, several small feedings a day are psychologically more satisfying to an older dog—especially one on a reducing diet.

If your Poodle needs to lose some poundage, replace a small part of his food with fiber, which is best served in the form of raw or steamed veggies. Many "light" commercial diets are too low in fat and may cause skin problems in your dog. Dogs need fat in their diets, and a normal geriatric diet should be high in fat. Have your dog lose weight by reducing the total amount of his food.

Keeping Your Older Dog Healthy

Even though you may not be vaccinating your old dog as frequently as your puppy (many new protocols suggest once every 3 years, except where the law dictates otherwise), it's important to make regular veterinary appointments for general maintenance and checkups, including dental work.

Arthritis

Arthritis occurs when joints are damaged or inflamed. There are several types. Larger Poodles in particular are apt to suffer from degenerative osteoarthritis, which occurs when the cartilage that protects the ends of the bones where they meet at a joint is destroyed. Small Poodles can suffer patellar luxation (loose kneecaps). Sadly, arthritis often begins long before there are any symptoms. Cartilage has no nerves, so the dog can't feel pain (and express it to you) until the joint is compromised. Characteristically, arthritic dogs have a hard time getting up and walking.

However, don't simply assume that a dog who walks stiffly has arthritis; other conditions can cause the same symptoms. Get to a veterinarian for a definitive diagnosis.

The Poodle Pundit

Try using a towel as a sling to help your dog get up, or as an aid in walking up the stairs. You might also want to consider installing ramps. 🐾

Therapy for Arthritis

Keep your Poodle's weight down—it will ease stress on the joints. You can use traditional painkillers like buffered aspirin (there is one, Palprin, made specifically for dogs) to ease aching joints. Newer prescription drugs like Rimadyl and Eto-Gesic are available as well.

You can also add dietary supplements to your Poodle's diet. Glycosaminoglycan (GAG), a polysaccharide important to the structure of the joint, is often used. Look for "nutraceutical" supplements containing glucosamine, chondroitin sulfate, manganese, and vitamin C. An injectable form of glycosamine glycan, Adequan, can be given twice a week for a month. It works not only to relieve pain, but also to help repair the cartilage, destroy the harmful enzymes that cause inflammation, and stimulate the production of joint fluid. While undergoing treatment, be sure your dog gets plenty of rest.

Diet also has a role in treating arthritis. Keep excess weight off your dog by watching his calories, and be sure he's getting enough omega-3 fatty acids in his diet to help reduce the production of inflammatory prostaglandins.

Poodle Parlance

"Nutraceuticals" are a separate class of natural substances that fall somewhere between food and drugs. Nutraceutical products do not have to meet the U.S. Food and Drug Administration's (FDA) drug requirements, so their efficacy is not proved. Although research with glucosamine and chondroitin sulfate is promising, existing studies have been done with high-quality, very expensive forms of these substances. Nearly all glucosamine and chondroitin products available in the United States—except Cosequin—are of much lower purity than those tested in Europe. 🐾

Cancer

This illness usually affects older animals. You can use diet to help manage the wasting effects of cancer. Cancerous tissue processes food inefficiently and produces excess lactic acid. Converting the lactic acid into a usable form requires an increased energy output that can cause severe fat and muscle wasting. Even dogs who have recovered from cancer continue to have high lactate levels. Hill's manufactures a special cancer recovery diet.

Seizure Disorders

Even if your Poodle has had epilepsy for years, you may notice that it takes him longer and longer to come around (the postictal) after a seizure as he gets older. This is normal.

Aging Eyes

Most older dogs develop nuclear sclerosis. In this condition, which develops at around age 7, the lens begins to harden and looks like it's taken on a bluish haze. It's very common and not serious, although your Poodle's near vision may be affected.

Canine Cognitive Dysfunction/Cognitive Dysfunction Syndrome

One condition often seen in otherwise healthy older dogs is Cognitive Dysfunction Syndrome (CDS). Although it may look like senility, CDS is apparently an aging-associated brain disorder. No one is sure what causes it, although researchers have found suspicious plaques in the brains of affected animals.

Maybe your Poodle doesn't seem to recognize you anymore, and seems dazed and disoriented. Perhaps his house-training skills have vanished, his sleeping patterns have changed, and he seems old and slow. About two-thirds of dogs aged 11 or more years show at least one of these symptoms; the older the dog, the higher the likelihood that he will display more symptoms.

Anipryl, developed by Pfizer, was approved by the FDA in December 1998 to treat this common condition. Anipryl (the trade name for L-deprenyl or selegiline) can turn back the clock. Although it was originally developed to treat humans with Parkinson's disease, it has turned out to be amazingly effective for dogs with CDS—over 70 percent of dogs treated with this medication show improvement. The Tufts University Veterinary Newsletter states that no one knows exactly why it works.

Depending on the size of your Poodle, Anipryl can cost between $1 and $5 per day. So far, no side effects have been noted.

Surgery and Anesthesia

If your older dog requires surgery, the choice of anesthetic agent can be important. If possible, ask your vet about the possibility of using isoflurane. Although more expensive than other anesthetics, it is quickly eliminated from the dog's system once administration stops. Even newer is propofol (brand name Rapinovet), which is a very safe injectable anesthetic drug.

Flea Control

Parasite control becomes increasingly important as your dog grows older and is less able to groom himself. Also, fleas can seriously affect the compromised immune system of an older dog. It seems that such pests can just sense that your older dog is more vulnerable. His drier skin is also more easily inflamed by insect bites.

Company for Your Older Dog

Many people, sensing that their older dog will pass away before long, seek to soften the blow for themselves by acquiring a new dog as company for the old one. Sometimes this works and sometimes it doesn't. It depends largely on the temperament of your older dog. If he is a healthy, friendly, outgoing sort who seems to welcome friends, then a new family member may be just the ticket. But if he is not feeling well or is solitary by nature, a new dog will just irritate him. Some people get a puppy in the hopes that the youngster will rejuvenate the older dog, but that only works occasionally.

It's likely that your older dog will be tired and irritated by a puppy. Test your older dog first to see how he responds to other dogs. Take him visiting, or ask some friends to come by with their dogs. In most cases, it's better if the second dog is a more sedate adult who won't pester your senior.

The End

After a long and joyful life, the time will come when your beloved Poodle reaches the end. If you are lucky, your pet will die peacefully, asleep in your arms, but it is more likely that you will require the help of a compassionate veterinarian to help your dog reach the end of his sufferings. One of the hardest decisions to make in dog ownership is choosing that day. Your dog will help you. When you see that he no longer finds joy in food or petting, or when he seeks to be alone most of the time, take the hint. Consult your vet. In any case, it is your responsibility as a dog owner to be with your pet during his final hour. It's a painful experience, but one you absolutely owe your dog.

The Poodle Pundit

Many veterinarians will make house calls to euthanize your pet. This is a less stressful option for both you and your dog. 🐾

You also have many choices about the way in which you want to remember your Poodle. You can bury him at home or in a pet cemetery; you can opt for cremation and scatter his ashes over her favorite field or river—or you may decide to keep them. I have no proof, of course, but I somehow know that whatever choice you make, your Poodle will approve. If he doesn't, he'll let you know when you meet again.

The Poodle Pundit

Consider memorializing your pet by making a contribution in his name to Poodle Rescue. 🐾

Perhaps James Thurber, great writer, great cartoonist, and great lover of Poodles said it best:

> *"When my poodle dies, I will bury her sorrowfully*
> *under the apple tree, and remember her bright spirit*
> *and her gentle gaiety all the years of my life."*
> —*Christabel: Part One*

"Casey"   *Courtesy of Marsha Lorette MacDonald*

Sources and Resources

Organizations: Poodles

Poodle Club of America, Inc.
Charles Thomasson, Corresponding Secretary
503 Martineau Drive
Chester, VA 23831-5753

The Poodle History Project: Visit www.poodlehistory.org for complete information about the history of Poodles and their role in art and literature.

Versatility in Poodles (VIP) is a non-profit organization devoted to Poodles. Its primary purpose is "to improve the health and promote the many talents of this remarkable breed." VIP produces a wide range of educational materials ranging from general information for the new poodle owner to detailed health bulletins for breeders. It also produces a newsletter, offers versatility certificates, maintains a health database, gives support to first-time owners, sponsors seminars related to health, performance, and provides support for Poodle rescue. To learn more, see their website at www.pageweb.com/vipoodle

Organizations: General

ASPCA National Animal Poison Control Center—an excellent site with a vast amount of information, it can be accessed at: http://www.aspca.org/site/PageServer?pagename=apcc

The American Kennel Club (AKC)

Headquarters:

American Kennel Club
260 Madison Avenue
New York, NY 10016
Phone: 212-696-8200

Operations Center:

American Kennel Club
5580 Centerview Drive
Raleigh, NC 27606

Customer Service: 919-233-9767
Or access online: www.akc.org/index.cfm

Organizations: Performance

United States Dog Agility Association (USDAA)
P.O. Box 850955
Richardson, TX 75085

North American Dog Agility Council, Inc. (NADAC)
HCR 2, Box, 277
St. Maries, ID 83861

Organizations: Rescue

Poodle Club of America Rescue Contact:
Helen Taylor
(713)-668-1021

Books

Brown, Robert M., DVM *The Poodle Owners' Medical Manual.* Breed Manual Pub. 3370-M Jackson Dr, Jackson WI 53037 414/677-3122: $17.00.

Cherry, Barbara. *The Pet Owner's Guide to the Poodle.* New York: Howell Book House, 1994.

Dahl, Del. *The Complete Poodle.* New York: Howell Book House, 1994. 269p. Illus. $25.00.

Elliott, Rachael Page. *Dogsteps.* New York: Doral Publishing, 2002. 95p. Illus. $14.95.

Irick, Mackey J. *The New Poodle.* New York: Howell Book House, 1986. 384 pages. Illus. (Out of print, but can be found at used bookstores or used book websites.)

Kahlstone, Shirlee. *The Complete Poodle Clipping & Grooming Book.* New York: Howell Book House, 1986. (Out of print, but can be found at used bookstores or used book websites.)

The Merck Veterinary Manual. 8th ed. Whitehouse Station, N.J.: Merck and Company, 1998.

Nicholas, Anna Katherine. *The Book of the Poodle.* Neptine, N.J.: TFH Publications, 1985. (Out of print, but can be found at used bookstores or used book websites.)

Sabella, Frank T. *Your Poodle, Standard, Miniature, and Toy.* Middleburg, Va.: William W. Denlinger, 1969. (Out of print, but can be found at used bookstores or used book websites.)

Tilley, Lawrence and Smith, Francis. *The 5-Minute Veterinary Consult: Canine and Feline.* 2nd ed. Philadelphia: Lippincott, Williams, and Wilkins, 2000.

Ullman, H.J. and E. Ullman. *Poodles.* Hauppauge, N.Y.: *Barron's Educational Series*, 1987. $9.95.

Magazines and Journals

AKC Gazette

Poodle Review. Hoflin Publishing, Inc. 4401 Zephyr Street, Wheat Ridge, CO 80033-3299

Poodle Variety. P.O. Box 30430, Santa Barbara, CA 93130. (805) 966-7270.

Videos

Poodles. The American Kennel Club.

Preparing the Poodle for the Show Ring, Tapes 1, 2, and 3. Sue Henly, 6320 Gregory St West, Tacoma, WA 98466. (206) 564-4567

Index